Friends for
Two Hundred Years

Friends for Two Hundred Years

A History of Baltimore's Oldest School

Dean R. Esslinger

Baltimore: Friends School
in cooperation with
Museum and Library of Maryland History
The Maryland Historical Society
1983

All correspondence and inquiries should be directed to:
Public Relations Office, Friends School
5114 N. Charles Street, Baltimore, MD 21210

Library of Congress Cataloging in Publication Number: 83-80846
ISBN 0-9610826-0-7

Printed in the United States of America

Contents

Preface

Dean Esslinger's *Friends for Two Hundred Years* is the first history of Baltimore's oldest school. The author has placed the school in the context of the growth of Baltimore, linked it to the educational changes of the day, and has focused on both the religious and philosophic ties of the school. This is the story of both people and ideas. It traces the major events from Friends School's founding in 1784 to its bicentennial in 1984.

The history of Friends School in Baltimore mirrors the influence that Quaker schools have had on the educational scene as part of the growth of independent school education in the United States. The first Quaker schools were founded in Philadelphia in the late 1600s, and Baltimore Quakers were not far behind in seeking to provide a "guarded education" for members of the Religious Society of Friends.

From its earliest location in a meeting house at Fayette and Aisquith streets, to its current thirty-acre campus in north Baltimore, Friends School has been under the continual influence of Quaker thought, leadership, and religious practices of the Stony Run Friends Meeting and its forebears. Although the school's population has gradually shifted from a tiny Quaker community to a predominately non-Quaker enrollment of 850 students, the school's mission has not fundamentally changed from its inception. It remains today one of the most influential arms of the local Quaker Meeting, even though separately incorporated.

The history of Baltimore's oldest private school is a tribute to basic Quaker tenets—the dignity and worth of the individual, the significance of the educative influence of Meeting for Worship, the striving for the perfectibility of the individual, the reliance on consensus in the conduct of business (Quakers do not vote, but seek a consensus)—all framed in the fundamental belief that there is that of God in every person. Howard Brinton's description of Quaker education in the context of harmony, simplicity, equality, and community has been visible at all stages of Friends School's history.

Private schools in Baltimore have educated thousands. They represent the full spectrum of private schools—religious and nonsectarian independent, boarding and day, single sex and coeducational. Although each school has experienced its peaks and valleys (and indeed

v

many have closed), these institutions currently are thriving with record enrollments. Their reasons for existence basically are no different today than in earlier years. Often their significance stretches far beyond their limited numbers. They stand as an alternative to the public sector, providing primarily college-preparatory programs under separate boards of trustees, and are funded through tuition and gift dollars rather than public funds. Each private school has its own mission and is guided by its own philosophy to create programs and services which it deems appropriate for its students.

Friends School has provided unusual leadership in the local independent school setting. It is one of the few coeducational schools; it is one of the few to offer an educational program for students from pre-primary age through twelfth grade; and it has graduated thousands of students. Most significantly, Friends has had the capacity to adapt itself to the changing nature of the world around it. Although its form may have changed throughout its two-hundred-year history, its substance has remained constant.

The history book project was under the care of a sub-committee of the Board of Trustees comprised of Board members, administrators, faculty, parents, alumni, and members of the Stony Run Friends Meeting. The remarkable records of the Quaker Meeting and the prolific reports of the school's governing body provided excellent primary sources of information. An oral history project also yielded valuable recollections. Indeed, alumni may miss a favorite description of their day or mention of a memorable faculty member, but Dr. Esslinger has done a skillful job of chronicling the highlights of Friends' growth over two hundred years.

Those who have ties to Friends can be justly proud of its past. Its record today as one of the leading schools in the city testifies to its strength, and the school looks to its third century with confidence and optimism.

W. Byron Forbush II
Headmaster

Acknowledgments

Many people deserve thanks for helping to make this book. My former colleague at Towson State University and good friend, John Boles, who first suggested the idea, gave generously of his assistance and advice. Both he and his wife, Nancy Gaebler Boles, a graduate of Friends School, read the manuscript with care and made valuable suggestions. I was fortunate as well to have the encouragement and support of the History Committee of Friends School: Elizabeth P. Carpenter, Melinda B. Curtis, Nicholas B. Fessenden, Ann F. Forbush, W. Byron Forbush, Nancy T. Grant, Jack I. Matthews, John B. Maclay, Jr., Barbara C. Mallonee, Carol C. Maus, William F. Melton, Dorothy Michel Mardos, Peggy D. Molander, J. Frederick Motz, Doris M. Neumann, Mary Ellen Saterlie, Harry S. Scott, and Frank A. Windsor. Rarely does the historian have the benefit of such a talented group of readers who helped immensely through their knowledge of the school, their kind suggestions, and their many hours spent collecting oral interviews. Nick Fessenden organized the oral history project and offered many excellent insights as a historian. Harry Scott deserves a large measure of thanks for his wealth of detailed knowledge about the school's past and for his keen editor's eye which saved the book from many errors. Melinda Curtis made a significant contribution through her selection of the book's illustrations and her careful organization and planning of the publishing details. And of course the Forbush family was both an inspiration and a valuable source of information. Delightful conversations with Bliss and LaVerne Forbush, as well as with Bliss Forbush, Jr., provided insight into the school's development and helped me to understand the Quaker spirit of the institution. My special thanks and admiration go to Byron Forbush. If the book has avoided the pitfalls of being only an affectionate reminiscence of the school's triumphs, it is because Byron insisted upon full cooperation with and support of my research regardless of where it might lead. His enthusiasm for scholarship and his personal warmth made the project a delightful experience. The Friends School faculty and staff, including John Carnell of the Business Office, Rhoda Doughty in the Headmaster's Office, and the staff of the Development and Alumni offices, were always cheerful in their help. I am deeply grateful for the cooperation and most of all for the friendship that was given to me by the Friends School community. My life is much enriched by the friends I found here.

I am also indebted to my colleague at Towson State University, Mary Catherine Kahl, who read the manuscript and whose sharp eye helped to make many improvements. Fellow historians in the Baltimore History Research Group read the early chapters and made valuable criticism that put the book in proper perspective. Albert Fowler and the staff at the Friends Historical Library at Swarthmore College, as well as the librarians at the Maryland Historical Society, Maryland Department of the Enoch Pratt Free Library, and Towson State University all have my appreciation for their aid in the research. Mary Bowersox, typist, and Barbara Sandaal, who helped with the final draft, provided excellent services and have my gratitude for easing the process of publication. The Thomas H. and Mary Williams Shoemaker Fund of Philadelphia gave financial support for the project.

And finally I want to thank my wife, Sandy, whose advice added to the book's style and substance, and my children, Regina, Joel, and Carey.

DEAN R. ESSLINGER

Chronology

1781   Quaker Meeting House opened at Aisquith and Fayette streets.

1784   First mention of a school in Meeting records. A committee appointed to oversee the school.

1792   Baltimore Monthly Meeting established.

1800   School house constructed on Old Town property.

1805   Lombard Street Meeting House built.

1816   Girls' School opened; Susan Yarnall, teacher.

1829   Baltimore Public Schools established.

1840s   School moved to Lombard Street Meeting House.

1860   Baltimore Monthly Meeting took over collection of tuition and paid teachers' salaries.

1864   Eli M. Lamb appointed principal.

1865   Introduction of high-school classes.

1866   Name changed to "Friends Elementary and High School," Baltimore's first private high school.

1872   Introduction of "collegiate department" for students going to college.

1877   Introduction of English course of study for students not going to college.

1887   Lombard Street property sold.

1888   Baltimore Monthly Meeting relinquished control of Lamb's school at Preston and McCulloh streets.

1889   Park Avenue Meeting House built, and primary and kindergarten school opened. Louisa P. Blackburn, principal.

1892   Purchase of lot next to Park Avenue Meeting House.

1899   Merged with Lamb's school and renamed Park Avenue Friends Elementary and High School. John W. Gregg appointed principal.

1900   Name changed to Friends School.
First boys' basketball game—defeated Poly 8-0.

1901   First issue of *Friends School Quarterly*.

1903   Edward C. Wilson replaced John Gregg as principal of the school.

1908   Electric lighting installed in the school.

1909   Swimming pool constructed, and new gymnasium built on the third floor.
         Beginning of girls' basketball.

1911   Purchase of 1712 Park Avenue for kindergarten and primary grades.

1912   Purchase of 8½ acres in West Forest Park for athletic field.
         First football team.
         First sex education classes.

1913   First May Fete held.
         Student government organization begun.

1914   First girls' field hockey team.

1921   School uniforms adopted.

1924   Boys' lacrosse started.

1925   Purchase of Homeland campus property on Charles Street.

1927   William S. Pike replaced Edward C. Wilson as principal.
         Girls' lacrosse started.

1928   Cornerstone laid for Primary Department building at Homeland.

1929   Primary Department moved to Homeland campus.

1931   Intermediate Department building constructed at Homeland.

1935   Edwin C. Zavitz replaced William S. Pike as principal.

1936   High School moved to Homeland.
         School organization changed to create a Lower School (grades 1—6) and an Upper School (grades 7—12).
         Friends School Association formed.

1937   Clubhouse remodelled to house nursery and kindergarten classes.
         New gymnasium built at Homeland campus.

1943   Bliss Forbush replaced Edwin C. Zavitz as headmaster.

1944   Park Avenue property sold to Baltimore City.

1949   Tenure system established for faculty.

1952   Roman Steiner died after 53 years of teaching at Friends.

1954 Education Committee changed admissions policy to allow desegregation.

1955 First black students admitted to Friends.

1956 Construction of the Bliss Forbush Auditorium.

1960 W. Byron Forbush II replaced Bliss Forbush as headmaster.

1964 All classes desegregated.
First secondary school in the U.S. to be visited by teachers from the Soviet Union.

1965 Summer Writing Opportunity Program established.

1966 New science building and new addition to gymnasium.

1967 First full-time black faculty hired.

1970 Middle School established.

1971 Tenure system replaced by annual and multiyear contracts.

1973 Friends School incorporated and separated from the Monthly Meeting.

1974 Faculty Meeting for Business established.

1975 Auditorium extended to house Middle School.

1978 BOOST Program started for minority teaching interns.

1982 Addition to Upper School building.
Purchase of 2.1 acres from Cathedral property.

1984 Two Hundredth Anniversary of Friends School.

List of Illustrations

Illus. 1-1   Friends Meeting House, erected by the Society of Friends at Aisquith and Fayette streets in 1781.

Baltimore and Friends

The snow made Baltimore look more like a New England port than the liveliest new city of the Chesapeake. As Elisha Tyson and Samuel Matthews walked east along Pratt Street toward the Quaker Meeting House in Old Town early in the evening of January 29, 1784, they pitied the night watchman they passed. He was employed by the insurance companies to keep an eye out for vandals and fires, but the early darkness of the January day and the biting wind off the harbor made his job seem uninviting. The winter of 1783–84 was harsh. Since the beginning of the new year, temperatures had remained below freezing, filling the bay with ice and bringing shipping to a standstill. The freeze came so quickly that boatmen whose craft were caught in the ice had to walk to shore. Several crewmen caught too far out in the bay were later found frozen. A few young sports, however, turned the weather to their pleasure by skating from Baltimore to Annapolis for a holiday.[1]

But for the two Quaker men who faced the cold to reach the meeting house at Fayette and Aisquith streets, the weather brought little cause for amusement. Tyson, still a young man of 35, wondered if the harsh winter would mean a slowdown in business at a time already threatening depression. Only five months had passed since the Peace of Paris ended the War for Independence and the future for the new nation and Baltimore seemed more unpredictable than promising. As they walked the men talked quietly of new problems the conclusion of the war and separation from the British Empire might bring for business. Like many Americans they were divided over the wisdom of printing paper money. Under the Articles of Confederation the new country had no national coinage and the Congress had no control over the value of currency. To make matters worse, Americans after seven years of scarcity and self-sacrifice were buying European, especially English, goods at a greedy rate. Far more was being spent on foreign imports than was being collected on exports. Not only did the achievement of peace leave trade patterns disrupted, but American shippers now found themselves in strong competition with powerful British capitalists. They had won the war, but whether Americans could survive the peace was now the question. As the two Quaker merchants pushed through the snow-packed streets eastward toward the bridge across the Jones Falls, the masts of the new square-rigged sailing ships in dry dock or locked in the harbor's ice emphasized for them Baltimore's dependence on the sea. Could the city continue its prosperity of the previous decades in this post-war time?

Barely a half-century old in 1784, Baltimore was now the most rapidly developing port south of Philadelphia. From its founding in 1729 until the beginning of the French and Indian War in 1754, Baltimore Town showed few characteristics that would distinguish it from dozens of other small, tobacco-trading ports along the rivers and shores of the Chesapeake Bay. John Moale's drawing of 1752 shows twenty-five houses, one church, and two taverns for a population of only 200—hardly a booming metropolis. But the French and Indian War, like the American Revolution that followed it, brought growth and prosperity. Baltimore profited from other cities' woes. Annapolis, for example, as the capital had attracted the attention of the British army and navy during the Revolution, while Baltimore was ignored by the enemy forces. The tobacco-based economy of Annapolis stagnated when the English market was cut off, but Baltimore turned to the wheat trade and the lucrative practice of privateering. With Philadelphia in British hands during part of the war, Baltimore became the natural trading center for the northern Chesapeake-Susquehanna Valley farming region. Both Washington's Continental Army and the French allies looked to Baltimore for food supplies.[2] Politically and patriotically, Baltimore's wartime importance reached a high point late in 1776 when the Continental Congress briefly made its home in the city—though the sophisticated members of the Congress found this upstart town on the Patapsco too boring and expensive for their tastes.

By 1784 the streets travelled by Tyson, Matthews, and others like them on their way to the Friends Meeting, were the thoroughfares of a flourishing town. New York City lost more than half of its population after British forces occupied it during the Revolution, but Baltimore gained 2,000 during the war years. Newcomers from the Chesapeake region, and Germans and Scots-Irish from Pennsylvania, came, attracted by jobs and business opportunities. They joined older groups like the Acadians who settled in "Frenchtown," a neighborhood southwest of the harbor, after they had been driven from Nova Scotia in the 1750s. Baltimore had become a city of many languages, though English and German were spoken most often. Not as cosmopolitan yet as New York or Philadelphia, Baltimore at the end of the American Revolution was no longer a fledgling town.

But if Baltimore seemed to be changing in 1784, its greatest expansion and transformation was yet to come. From the late 1780s until New York began to assert its dominance in the 1820s, Baltimore was the fastest growing urban center in the nation. Whether or not Baltimore would continue to grow and what effect it would have is what worried these Friends in 1784. The opening of three new markets in that year was indicative of the change that had already occurred. The old market at the northwest corner of Baltimore and Gay streets was no longer enough. It was to be torn down and replaced by new markets at Hanover and Harrison streets, and at the waterfront in Fell's Point. From Maryland and Pennsylvania farms came a variety of foodstuffs: beef and bacon, hams and salt pork, fruits, flour, and a variety of fresh vegetables. The choicest items of course were the fresh fish, scallops, oysters, clams, and crabs from the Chesapeake. The Quaker women who walked to meeting with their husbands might have talked of the changes the new markets would bring. Since each market would be open only two days each week, careful planning and selection would be necessary to avoid lengthy trips to other parts of town. In the warmer summer months trips to the markets would be more frequent.

There were other places too where the women could shop for less perishable goods. In the *Maryland Journal and Baltimore Advertiser*, the local newspaper, William Stevenson praised the goods available in his grocery store on Baltimore Street. He had wines, cinnamon, cloves, oranges, syrups, pickles, pineapples and peaches in brandy, sugared almonds, ginger, barley sugar, a variety of teas, coffee and chocolate, rice, salt, oatmeal, Castile and Irish soap, figs, and snuff. Across the street from the market on Gay and Baltimore streets was Coale and Goodwin's Medicinal Store. There mothers could purchase sugar cakes for treating worms in children, or Turlington's Balsam of Life, Godfrey's Cordial, and Anderson's Pills. Dry goods just imported from Europe were on display at Crotchett's and Harris' store. Even if they were not interested in Stevenson's wines and snuff or Anderson's Pills, these Quaker women could appreciate the advantages of living in a port where the freshest and latest of imported and native products were abundant.[3]

Illus. 1-2   Friends Meeting House, Aisquith and Fayette Streets, ca. 1865
Maryland Historical Society

Whatever topics the conversations wandered over, by the time the Quakers reached their meeting house at the corner of Fayette and Aisquith streets (then called Pitt and Lloyd) their thoughts had turned to the warmth inside. Fortunately the members of the meeting who lived nearby, like David Wilson, a carpenter who resided at 43 Front Street in Old Town, and a few who came north on Broadway from Fell's Point, like John Brown, owner of the stoneware and pottery works, had arrived early and already had the stove fired. The last to arrive were usually the Friends who lived outside the city. At this time of year, some came by sleigh and others on horseback, travelling in on Harford or York roads, then making their way along the streets bent by the course of the Jones Falls. By the time they all arrived, the large room had lost its chill.

The meeting house in which they gathered was a plain but comfortable red brick building. George Matthews, owner of a nail factory and member of the meeting, was the architect. Built only three years earlier in 1781 when the Quakers moved the Patapsco Preparative Meeting into the city for the first time, the grounds around the house had an unfinished look. To the south of the structure the open land between Fayette and Baltimore streets at Aisquith Street served as a small pasture for the horses in the summer and contained a stable for shelter in the winter months. In time the building would be surrounded on three sides by a brick wall with a wrought iron and wooden gate.[4] Trees too would be added to the yard for shade and a natural attractiveness. But for the time being the simple Quaker building was not out of place. Baltimore had only begun to pave its main streets with cobblestones in 1781, so the unfinished look of the meeting grounds matched the rude appearance of the dirt roadway.

The building itself, constructed by members of the meeting, faced the interior of the block with two rows of small-paned windows, balanced by two simple entrances—one for men and one for women. The gabled ends repeated the balance of the design, while within simplicity was the guiding principle. The single large room was divided equally by a partition that could be raised. On one side of the divider the women held their meetings for business or worship and on the other sat the men. With the partition raised all could worship together. A large balcony with corner stairs leading up to each half was the dominant feature of the interior. Seated on the rows of broad wooden seats the Quakers of Baltimore would discuss the business of their meeting and worship in respectful silence.

On the evening of January 29, 1784, however, some of the members were expressing concern about the ways the urban community was changing. Only two days earlier Benjamin Dashiell had opened a new tavern at Fell's Point near the Market House.[5] The appearance of more and more taverns and grog shops was alarming. The Bull's Head, Maypole, Golden Horse, Three Tuns, and Rising Sun were all taverns where intemperance and late-night revelry disturbed the peace. Baltimore was becoming a city, but it was also losing its innocence by Quaker standards. If the word from Annapolis was correct, the State Assembly would be passing a bill within the next few months authorizing the first publicly-financed police for Baltimore—three night watchmen—and providing for the erection of street lamps.[6] The city night watch would relieve the town's merchants and insurance companies of the burden of providing their own guards and would create a more regular protection against fires and burglary, but the acknowledgment that Baltimore needed better police protection was disturbing. There was no doubt, however, that as the town's economy and trade expanded, the number of transients had increased. Sailors ashore after a voyage to the West

Indies for slaves and sugar had too little respect for either the property or the social order of what to them was just another port. Likewise the longshoremen who unloaded the cargoes at the docks and the teamsters who hauled them away broke the tranquillity of the town's life when they sought rowdy entertainment along the waterfront. At least the slave trade, to the relief of the Society of Friends, had been abolished by the State the previous year. But the problem of runaway slaves and indentured servants was still serious. Every issue of the newspaper had long lists of rewards and advertisements for information on runaways.[7] Men like Elisha Tyson and George Matthews, who became charter members of the Maryland Society for Promoting the Abolition of Slavery, realized that as long as slavery existed there would be a certain tension in the society between those who defended it and those who wished to see its demise.[8]

Of course the dangers of a youthful town like Baltimore could easily be exaggerated. Compared to the older cities of Europe or even to the metropolis Baltimore itself would later become, the streets of this pre-industrial port were safe enough. Nevertheless, each new problem that arose or each new sign that the local environment and society were undergoing change, no matter how small, was cause for concern. If this might have been true for the average Baltimorean in 1784, it was even more so for the Society of Friends. For the Quakers who met in the Old Town Meeting House were in many ways not average citizens. They looked upon themselves and were viewed by others as a people apart.

By 1784 the Quakers had been in Maryland 128 years—25 years longer than those who came to Penn's colony. Even at the beginning they were treated as a separate and distinct people. Arriving in the Chesapeake Bay area in 1656, only four years after George Fox founded the Society in England, they were met with mild opposition and persecution. Because of their refusal to participate in military training or to take oaths, they were fined and punished. Dozens suffered the loss to the courts of crops, livestock, house furnishings, cash, and other possessions because they held to the convictions of their faith. Still, conditions were better in Maryland than they were in New England where Quakers were whipped and driven out or in nearby Virginia where they were imprisoned and their lands sometimes confiscated by the Anglican-supported government. As the Maryland colonists and government came to understand the Quakers better, the persecution ceased and the Society of Friends flourished.[9]

The basis of difference between these early Quakers and their Protestant and Catholic neighbors was in their belief that the Spirit of God dwells in every man.[10] With roots in mystical Christianity and the English Protestant Reformation, Quakerism spread throughout England after 1652 when George Fox began to teach its doctrines—its "Truth." Fox believed in an Inner Light or Spirit of God that dwells in every person and is the true word of God. The Scriptures are to be studied and accepted as a statement of God's revelations, but they are not in themselves the only source of God's word.

As a mystical and inward religion, Quakerism is not dependent on priest or institution. There is no clergy because in fact all believers are clergy. Quakers were a part of the Puritan movement but they went beyond it by removing every priestly vestige. Quakers also went beyond other English Protestant reformers in their emphasis on perfectionism. By following the teachings of the Bible and by accepting the guidance of the Holy Spirit, they hoped to achieve the perfect life free from sin. This goal of perfection, however, was to be for all of society, not just for individual Quakers—for "there is that of God in every man." Quakerism was a religion and at the same time a movement for social reform. Unlike the contemplative monks who meditated in solitude, the Quakers remained in the world of men and worked to bring about its conversion to "the Truth."

If the Quakers of Maryland and Baltimore by the end of the eighteenth century hadn't yet brought society to a state of perfection, they had at least gained respect and a reputation for moral probity. In daily life as well as in their religious organization and practices, the Quakers followed three basic principles: equality, simplicity, and peace.[11] God gave the Spirit equally to all persons, men and women, black and white, rich and poor; to treat anyone as less than equal would be to contravene God's creation. All persons should be addressed equally using *thee* and *thou*, avoiding the pronoun, *you*, which at the time retained a hint of social superiority from earlier English usage. Within the Society of Friends, the women's meetings were equal to the men's, although the sexes were separated in worship and in business.

Simplicity too was required in all things: in houses, dress, commercial and social relationships, and entertainment. Simplicity was the purest expression of the truth and its strongest protection. Among Baltimore's merchants few were trusted more than the Quakers because of their direct, honest treatment of all customers. Regarding entertainment, the Quakers were in many respects more strict than the Puritans of New England. Theatrical performances, music, the reading of fiction, horse racing, and any other frivolous or nonproductive ways of passing time were to be avoided as activities that tempted persons away from the "simplicity of truth."

The Quaker principle that evoked the strongest reaction from non-Quakers in Maryland and in the other colonies was their dedication to peace. As pacifists they believed that *all* wars and violence were contrary to the will of God. It was in part the likelihood of having to make or share in policy decisions that would violate this principle that kept many Quakers out of public office in Maryland and Pennsylvania. Preferring negotiation and faith in the power of the Spirit in each man to the alternatives of war and force, the Quakers placed themselves in an unpopular position at a time when colonial wars for empire and attacks against American Indians were frequent. Only by holding firm to their values and by caring for the ill and wounded, in substitution for fighting roles, did they eventually win community respect for their pacifist position.

But Baltimore's Quaker community in 1784, though no longer as isolated as their ancestors' had been, still possessed a distinct identity and self-consciousness. After more than a century, the Quaker movement had modified its efforts to reform the social order and concentrated more on preserving its traditions and values. It was by then a time of "quietism" in which the unity of the membership was emphasized, rather than a time of evangelicalism.[12] In particular, as Baltimore left its uncomplicated past and rushed toward the expansive but disordered nineteenth century, the Quakers felt a need to tighten the boundaries of their spiritual and social community. Every meeting now included discussion of members whose behavior and lifestyle violated or challenged the traditional principles of the faith. At an alarming rate the number of persons who neglected their religious responsibilities or who succumbed to the temptations of the more cosmopolitan urban atmosphere increased. The ships that brought the woolens, wines, and immigrants from Liverpool, Dublin, Nantes, and Lisbon also brought the silks, laces, and new ideas of fashion. Too many, like Sarah Hopkins, had to be reprimanded for deviating "in Dress and address from the Principle" required of Friends. She was also rebuked for having attended a non-Quaker wedding. Although she claimed to be ignorant of the prohibition against being present at non-Quaker weddings, she promised at a later meeting, September 27, 1787, to reform her dress and manner.[13]

Like the increase in taverns, the popularity of musical and theatrical entertainment in Baltimore by 1784 was a visible sign that the moral definitions and high standards of the Quakers were not shared by the broader urban community. Newspaper advertisements for the two months of January and February alone, illustrate the problem. On January 3 *The Beggar's Opera* and *Cross Purposes,* a farce, were performed at the new brick theater recently decorated with an attractive "Frontispiece" of the figures Tragedy and Comedy painted by Charles Willson Peale.[14] *Macbeth, The Miser, School for Scandal,* and *The Virgin Unmasked* were all scheduled for the first two weeks of February.[15] Musical performances, too, tempted many away from more fruitful pursuits. Baltimore had already had its first concert, and George Frederick Handel's popularity in American cities suggested that the local public would demand more. The same week in January that the Quakers were meeting in Old Town, a Mr. Brown advertised an evening of entertainment on the German Flute in the "new assembly room." Tickets for musical and theatrical events were readily available at the Fountain Inn and other public places.[16]

More serious than the misbehavior of youths and Quaker attendance at the theater or concert hall, were the number of Friends marrying outside the Society. Several committees had to be created to deal with the cases of individuals who had married nonmembers or who had not followed the traditional forms for a Quaker marriage. Laxity of individual members in this regard may have been a reflection of the more liberal attitude besetting all religions in the post-Revolution era. Certainly the act of destroying one system of government and of creating a new one had weakened American commitments to past traditions and strengthened confidence in the ability to construct new laws for society.

The Revolutionary years also witnessed a mushrooming of new religious denominations. Between 1770 when the German Reformed Church appeared in Baltimore and 1784 when Francis Asbury and Thomas Coke were chosen bishops of the newly organized Methodist Church in America, the number of churches and denominations increased notably. Coupled with the town's population explosion in the final quarter of the eighteenth century, the opportunities for marriage outside the Quaker membership were abundant. Even if the multiplication of churches didn't directly tempt the youth away from the Society of Friends, it was still a subtle statement that the urban, Christian community contained several alternative and competing institutions.

More insidious than the multiplication of denominations, however, was the trend toward deism and the argument that man needed no church at all. In this age of Jefferson, Paine, Barlow, and Freneau the deism produced by the American Enlightenment rested on the presumed superiority of reason over faith. By the application of reason to nature man could discover those universal laws that govern the world. The Quaker religion which emphasized the power of the Inner Light over the natural faculties of the rational mind could hardly have faced a more threatening philosophy.

And finally, as if the social, religious, and philosophical challenges were not enough, the very prosperity of the Quaker community was itself a danger. The devotion to hard work and middle-class values, as well as the willingness to support one another in time of need, had made Baltimore's Quakers among the city's most prosperous merchants and craftsmen. The names of Hopkins, Ellicott, Tyson, McKim, and Thomas were already associated with Baltimore's business elite. The dilemma of these Quaker fathers, however, was to carry on successful enterprise without instilling in youth a love for the comforts and refinements of wealth. To walk that narrow line between fulfillment of one's duties in business and devotion to spiritual simplicity, free from the love of riches, was never more difficult.

While the men and women who sat in the meeting house on January 29, 1784, did not identify or directly articulate all of these anxieties about the changes occurring in their town and society, they were conscious of their responsibility to protect the Quaker way of life and to prepare the younger generation to continue in the faith. What better way to shield the children from unwelcome influences and ideas and to prepare them to carry on the businesses and trades of their fathers than to support a Friends school. In fact the meeting need only acknowledge a school recently begun by one of its members. Twenty-eight-year-old Joseph Townsend had come to Baltimore only a short time before from Little Falls on the Gunpowder River where he had kept his own school. "But a more favorable situation presenting itself, in the Town. . . of Baltimore," his son wrote years later, "he removed to it; and established himself there, in the fall of 1783: —and continued in the occupation of Teacher, for a number of years. . . ."[17] Present at the meeting himself as a new member, Joseph Townsend assured the men who questioned him that his school would provide the "guarded education" they required for their children. Satisfied that the Meeting should give its moral and financial support to the school, the members were united in agreeing that a committee be established to oversee its operation. After discussion as to who should serve, the Clerk recorded in the minutes:

> There being a school opened for some time past at this place for the instruction of youth in useful learning, The following Friends are appointed to have the care and oversight thereof agreeable to the directions of our Yearly Meeting, to wit, Isaac Williams, John Malsby, Elisha Tyson, David Brown, and David Wilson who are desired to attend there from time to time as way may open and report of their care to this Meeting as they may see occasion therefor.[18]

As they retraced their snowy steps home, these Baltimore Quakers might have felt an especial peace from their evening's devotion. The shared silence of their worship coupled with the decision supporting the school no doubt lessened some of their worries about the future of their bustling community. Their own quiet values would not be drowned out by the noisy commercial world. Confident in the Spirit they now looked forward to the warmth of home.

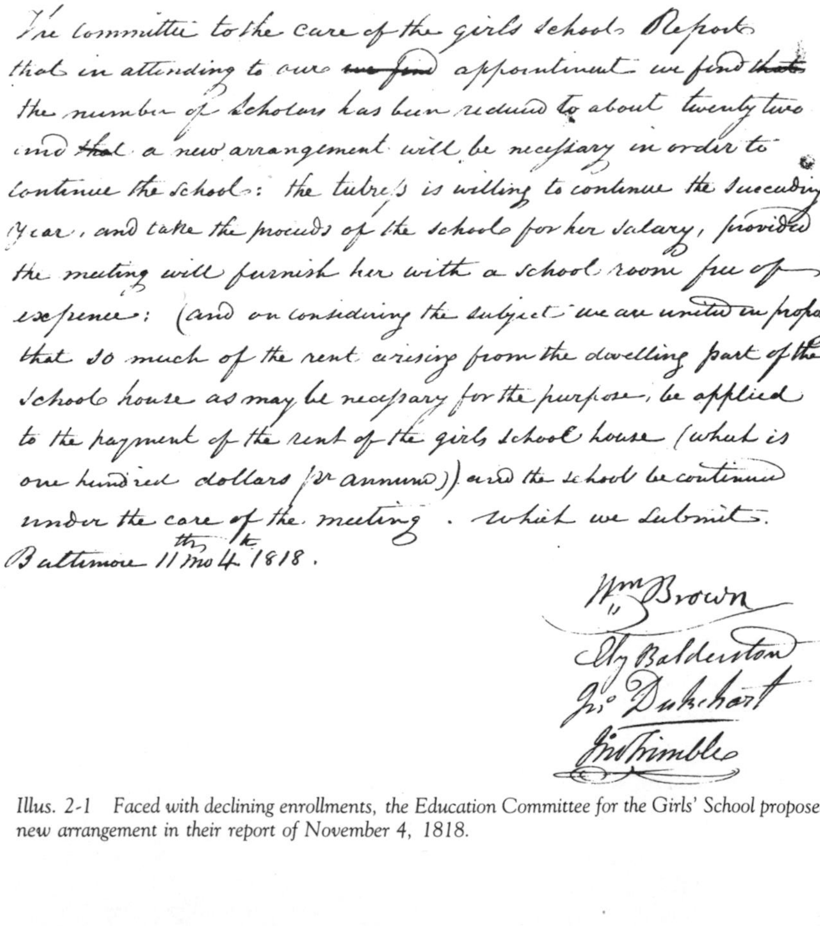

The committee to the care of the girls schools Report that in attending to our ~~we find~~ appointment we find ~~that~~ the number of scholars has been reduced to about twenty two and ~~that~~ a new arrangement will be necessary, in order to continue the school: the tutre's is willing to continue the succeeding year, and take the proceeds of the schools for her salary, provided the meeting will furnish her with a school room free of expence; (and on considering the subject we are united in proposing, that so much of the rent arising from the dwelling part of the school house as may be necessary for the purpose, be applied to the payment of the rent of the girls school house (which is one hundred dollars per annum)) and the school be continued under the care of the meeting. Which we submit.

Baltimore 11 mo 4th 1818.

Wm Brown
Ely Balderston
Jno Dukehart
Jno Trimble

Illus. 2-1 Faced with declining enrollments, the Education Committee for the Girls' School proposed a new arrangement in their report of November 4, 1818.

CHAPTER 2

A Guarded Education

When the children gathered for Joseph Townsend's new school in 1784 they were fulfilling an ambition their parents had held for some time. Since the days of the Revolution when Friends of Patapsco Meeting bought land between Baltimore and Fayette streets, it had been their intention to establish a school. The property where the meeting house now stood was to include a "yard and stabling, burying ground and School house, and a small piece of said lot to accommodate a School master. . . ."[1] The school house was not built yet but classes could be held in the meeting house. In fact, making the place of worship also the place of education illustrated Quaker belief that schools should teach morality as well as mathematics.

The new schoolmaster who met the children each day was well qualified to teach both the academic subjects and the religious values the Quaker parents cherished. At age twenty-eight Joseph Townsend was more mature than the teenagers who could often be found teaching in small rural schools. At the same time he was not one of those persons who had turned to teaching for bed and board after failing at other pursuits. His chosen profession so far in his life was that of teacher; equally important he was a Friend who tried to live according to the values and manners preached by George Fox. From the time Townsend arrived in Baltimore he was actively involved with the Meeting and the school. Years later after he had left teaching, married, and become a successful businessman, he was still a leader in the Quaker community and a person of importance in Baltimore. In 1794, at the end of a decade in the city, he was appointed to the committee of health that was entrusted with the responsibility of preventing an epidemic of yellow fever such as ravaged Philadelphia a few years earlier. When a number of Quakers joined together to form the Maryland Society for Promoting the Abolition of Slavery and the Relief of Free Negroes and Others, Joseph Townsend was chosen secretary. At another time he was a member of an association to relieve the suffering of the poor through the manufacture and sale of cotton goods. Through all of this time during the late eighteenth and early nineteenth centuries, he continued to participate as an active member of the school committee and of the Monthly Meeting of Friends.

Indeed Townsend may have been too talented and active to remain for long as teacher in the small Quaker school. Keeping school was a modest profession in the late eighteenth century that offered few appealing financial rewards—especially to a young man with a family to support. Male teachers in the older established Quaker schools of Philadelphia earned about four dollars per quarter of the school term for each older student and half that amount for small children; it was unlikely that the Baltimore Friends paid as much.[2] Since there were probably not more than ten or fifteen pupils in the school when it first opened, Joseph Townsend might have earned only $40 to $60 for each quarter he taught—in other words about half the wage a shoemaker or carpenter earned in the same number of weeks. Moreover, there is evidence that at first the school was in session for only one three-month term. Little wonder then that by 1796 Joseph Townsend listed his occupation in the first city directory as a dry goods merchant. He later founded the Baltimore Equitable Society—one of the city's first insurance companies.[3]

Although no record of the curriculum remains, Townsend's school would probably have been called an English School where the practical subjects of grammar, reading, penmanship, and spelling were emphasized. Since he later demonstrated his abilities as a merchant in the commercial world, it is also likely that he was capable of teaching arithmetic and perhaps some algebra and geometry. It is unlikely that he taught Latin, Greek, and the classics; not that he wasn't capable of it, but rather that the English School pattern would have been more appropriate to the needs of the Quaker community at that particular time. As Baltimore grew and the society changed in the nineteenth century, the expectations of a classical and college preparatory school would increase. But for the time being the basic 3 Rs were common fare for this type of school.

If parents were not satisfied with the academic offerings of the small school at Fayette and Aisquith streets, however, they had others to choose from. William Dick, a "Professor of Languages," added elementary subjects to the school he had taught since 1771.[4] Christopher Hill announced in the September 17, 1784, *Maryland Journal and Baltimore Advertiser* that he was opening an evening school "at the School-House a few Rods Westward of Mr. DeWitt's Coffee-House— where will be taught Reading, Writing, English Grammar, and Arithmetic in all its Branches, both vulgar and Decimal." The school would "begin at Candle-lighting, and continue till Nine o'Clock, P.M.," apparently as an attempt to attract Baltimore's young apprentices and journeyman workers. Both of these men faced competition from teachers like the one who advertised himself as "A Single Man, qualified to teach grammatically the English, French, Latin and Greek Languages; also Arithmetick, Accounts, Geography, with the Use of Globes, History, Rhetorick, etc."[5] Indeed, as Baltimore grew at a quickening pace in the decades after the Revolution it probably had more than an adequate supply of teachers offering day and evening classes or private tutors of reading and writing, surveying, "keeping accounts," translating the classics, or even dancing.

Most schools were for boys, but the education of girls was not neglected. Frances Poillievre opened a French school in January 1784; and in May, M. Smith promised to open a school "for the Instruction of the young Ladies in Baltimore" in which the basics of French and English would be taught along with "Music, Tambour, Dresden, Embroidery, plain and coloured Needle Work, Mantua-Making, Millinery, and clear starching."[6] Such elegant subjects would have been inappropriate to the standards of plainness and simplicity of most Quaker parents, but perhaps Sarah Moffitt's Reading and Sewing School that she had just moved "to an agreeable Situation near the Quaker Meeting House" would have been more acceptable and convenient.[7]

For a brief time Baltimoreans could send their children—or themselves for that matter—to the school and lectures presented by the new nation's leading lexicographer and advocate of a national language. Noah Webster was impressed enough by Baltimore when he passed through in 1784 that he returned the next year as teacher and lecturer. In May, 1785, he announced the opening of his private school "for the instruction of young gentlemen and ladies in reading, speaking, and writing the English language with propriety and correctness." Besides language he also offered to teach "vocal music." In the fall Webster took a larger public platform to expound his views on the English language by presenting five lectures at the First Presbyterian Church on the history of the language, rules and exceptions for pronunciation, common errors, and general remarks on the value and effects of education. For one dollar the listener could buy the whole series or pay twenty-five cents for a single evening.[8] The fame of Webster's *Speller*, which he published in 1782, made his name familiar to Baltimoreans and established his credibility as an able teacher; nevertheless he moved on the next year either finding Baltimore less responsive than he expected or because he wished to continue his campaign for a national language elsewhere.

In some ways, although he was by far the most famous of the teachers who opened private schools in Baltimore, Noah Webster was typical—typical in that his school was short-lived. Between 1784 and 1829, when the first public schools were established in the city, dozens of schools and hundreds of teachers furnished to Baltimore's residents an assortment of ephemeral educational alternatives. Besides the single efforts of individual schoolmasters and tutors, the organized efforts of community leaders and societies were hardly more successful in establishing permanent institutions. A good example was the Baltimore Academy that was established on North Charles Street after a public meeting of several religious denominations (not including the Quakers) called attention to the need for better schools. The Academy's purpose was to teach the classics, mathematics, natural philosophy, and other college or professional preparatory courses for which students had previously been sent to Pennsylvania. But it, too, had failed by December of 1787.[9]

Of all the schools created in the fifty years after the Revolution, most were either those of individual teachers and tutors, or they were supported by a religious denomination. After 1800 the number of free or charity schools for the poor also increased. St. Peter's Protestant Episcopal School, established in 1806 by a $10,000 bequest from Captain Jeremiah Yellott, and the Male Free School, incorporated in 1808 by the Methodist Episcopal Church, were testimony to the growing belief that all economic classes and social groups should have access to some type of formal education.[10]

What Baltimore was struggling with during these years—and that included the Quakers as well—was a changing concept of the purpose and process of education. In the colonial period most American schools were simple institutions. Except for the academies that prepared a small elite for college and the professions, school was where boys and girls from ages six to twenty-six went for a few weeks or months each year—for as little as two or three years—to learn the barest rudiments of reading, writing, and perhaps arithmetic. Few children in the decades before the Revolution went beyond that meager beginning. In the preindustrial, rural society of the eighteenth century, the school occupied a relatively minor place. The simple fact of earning a living from farm or trade took up too much of a person's life to leave much time for formal schooling. Much of what a child learned was acquired from within the secure walls of the home. Boys learned occupational skills from their fathers, although in cities the son might be apprenticed to another craftsman or shopkeeper. Even so, apprenticeship in the eighteenth century still performed a nurturing function, for the master was legally bound to care for young apprentices, including a responsibility for teaching them to read and write. Daughters learned household skills from their mothers, and all children were taught the manners, morals, and social values of their community.

The upheaval of the Revolution gave voice, however, to new demands for education that went beyond the capabilities of the middle-class family. Benjamin Rush, Philadelphia physician and signer of the Declaration of Independence, argued in 1786 that the values and responsibilities of citizens in the new nation could best be advanced and reinforced through a plan for universal national education.[11] Thomas Jefferson carried the argument farther in his proposal for a unified system of education extending from local counties to state universities and perhaps even a national university (George Washington left money in his will for such a university). All citizens would then be guaranteed basic literacy—essential to a democratically based government—and the nation would be assured of a locally educated leadership. Although Jefferson's lofty plan was never realized, Congress took a step toward universal education in the Land Ordinance of 1785 by setting aside land for the support of education in each township of the newly opened Northwest Territories. By the end of the eighteenth century the belief that education was a natural right of every citizen was being voiced in press, pulpit, and political platform. Education would supposedly make the people more productive, reduce crime and poverty, and promote national growth. The gap, however, between recognizing the importance of education in the new republic and providing the schools to carry on that education, was a wide one. Only in the later decades between 1830 and 1860 would the nation begin to create schools adequate to its needs. The residents of Baltimore, including the Society of Friends, were in the broad current of America's educational development as they struggled to establish their schools after 1784. Although they were not in the forefront, as were the educators of New England, they were traveling in the same direction.

From the 1780s on, then, Quaker parents had a gradually expanding number of choices as to where they could send their children to school. If Quaker parents could overcome their reluctance to send their children to Protestant or Catholic schools, they could find a variety of educational opportunities in Baltimore. Some undoubtedly placed children in the school nearest to their home, while others were limited by what they could afford to pay. But a significant proportion of the Quakers—if the minutes of their meetings are an accurate reflection of their feelings—preferred to have a truly Quaker education and environment for their young. In many ways the Friends thought of themselves as a "people apart" whose religious practices, which included manner of speech, style of living and dress, as well as doctrine, should remain unaffected by contact with the rest of the world. If parents were to pass the Quaker way of life on to their children in undiluted form, then a distinct education was essential.

The desire of Baltimore's Friends to establish their own schools reflected a long tradition among the Society of Friends. Contrary to the misconception that Quakers were opposed to schools, they had encouraged the education of the youth since the early days of George Fox. The confusion about the Quaker attitude toward education arose from their dependence on the Inner Light for direction and their insistence that university training was not a prerequisite for the ministry.[12] Unlike the Protestant denominations that founded all of America's colonial colleges in order to supply themselves with educated leaders, the Friends had set up no institutions of higher learning by the end of the eighteenth century. This impression of opposition to schools was compounded by the preference of Quaker parents for the tutorial system in order to avoid the worldly influence that non-Quaker schools might have on their children.[13] Nevertheless, despite their hesitations about the negative aspects of schools, the early Quakers clearly recognized the values of a practical education. George Fox advised the members to:

> See that schoolmasters and mistresses who are faithful Friends and well qualified be placed and encouraged in all cities and great towns and where they may be needed: the masters to be diligent to forward their scholars in learning and in the frequent reading of the Holy Scriptures and other good books, that being thus *seasoned with the truth,* sanctified to God and taught our holy,

self-denying way, they may be instrumental to the glory of God and the generation.[14]

Fox went on in other correspondence to encourage what amounted to vocational training. Since the student was expected to take his place as a useful member of society, it was natural that he should not take any subject that would interfere with that goal.[15] This same utilitarian emphasis in education was argued more than once by William Penn. In writing to his wife in England about his own children he advised:

> For their learning, be liberal. Spare no cost, for by such parsimony all is lost that is saved; but let it be useful knowledge such as is consistent with godliness, not cherishing a vain conversation or idle mind; but integrity mixed with industry is good for the body and the mind too. I recommend the useful parts of mathematics, as building houses, or ships, measuring, surveying, dialing, navigation; but agriculture especially is in my eye. Let my children be husbandmen and housewives; it is industrious, healthy, honest and of good example....[16]

The study of foreign languages Penn thought to be of little use, but Latin was acceptable since so many important books were written in it.

By 1700 it had become common practice for Quaker meetings in England to establish schools for the education of youth. Education was slower to develop in the colonies, but London Yearly Meeting urged the local monthly meetings to set up their own schools. The small groups of Quakers scattered throughout the Chesapeake region were not successful in maintaining schools on a continuing basis before the Revolution, but their more populous brethren in Philadelphia had established five schools—most of them elementary—by 1779. Friends Public School, which later became William Penn Charter School, was established as early as 1689, as was Friends Select School.[17]

By the time the Baltimore Quakers were ready to set up their school in the 1780s, several common characteristics had appeared. Quaker schools were usually held in the meeting houses where both boys and girls—though taught separately—received training in the fundamentals of grammar, reading, and writing. Enrollment was open to non-Quakers as well as members, but until the schools developed strong academic reputations, the pupils were most frequently the children of Quakers.[18] The teachers were always Friends and education was free to those too poor to pay.

The Baltimore school of Joseph Townsend and his successors was typical too in its emphasis on a "guarded education." Since Quakers saw themselves as set apart, they must be more virtuous, loving, modest, pure, and humble than those who followed other faiths. For the Quaker way of life to be passed on to the next generation it "meant, first, an indoctrination in the history and beliefs of the Society of Friends, and, second, a protection from the corrupting influence of the world. . . ."[19] In a "guarded education" students would be exposed only to those conditions that promoted the principles of the Society of Friends while at the same time taught useful knowledge. The leaders of South River Monthly Meeting who set up a school in Virginia in 1788 carefully prescribed the teacher's responsibilities:

> Teaching each scholar to read, write and arithmetic as far as his and their capacity admit, having due regard for children's morals, and in keeping them to plainness as the principles of Truth require. Discouraging all tale bearing, restraining them from vice and vain customs of the world. Enjoining them to keep strictly to the truth, not to use artful evasion to defraud nor provoke one another, nor mock their school-fellows, but behave in an obliging manner one toward another, and with due respect to their Master.[20]

The "religiously guarded education" was based on the historic Quaker belief that the child was neither naturally good nor naturally evil. During the period of immaturity the child was merely innocent; he was free to choose right or wrong. The proper goal of education was to insure that the environment in which the child learned encouraged and strengthened the will toward good, and helped him create a firm conscience that would lead him to the highest moral values. The "guarded education" did not mean simply the teaching of religion in school, but rather it meant preparing the child for a way of life in which the spiritual and temporal goals were unified.[21]

As Baltimore developed into the third largest city in the United States by 1810, it was little wonder that the Quakers felt a strong need to shield their children from the corrupting and unsettling changes of the urban environment. Whether it was the increase in taverns or theaters, the proliferation of competing religious organizations and intellectual principles, or the growth of materialistic values in a prospering city, the "guarded education" was an important barrier against the turbulence of the urban and industrial revolutions.

But maintaining a sound and effective school required more than piety and a belief in traditional values. It also demanded proper facilities, trained teachers, adequate funding, and a certain amount of persistence, along with the commitment of Quaker parents and the leaders of the local meeting. The history of the Friends School between 1784 and the Civil War suggests that some of these factors were not always present in equal measure. When the first school committee was appointed in January, 1784, its instructions were simply to visit the school and periodically report to the Preparative Meeting. Although Joseph Townsend "continued in the occupation of Teacher, for a number of years," this committee made no regular reports until 1792.[22] The lack of comment suggests that while a "guarded education" was a concern of these early Quakers, school was viewed in a much more casual way and held a less important place in eighteenth-century society than it does in the twentieth century. Most education still took place at home.

The delay in providing a proper schoolhouse illustrates the attitude of Baltimore's Quakers toward formal education in the post-Revolutionary decades. Although a committee appointed in 1792 recommended the construction of "a suitable house, for the education of males and females separate," years passed before any action was taken.[23] Finally around 1800 a school was built in Old Town,

> near the east corner of our burying ground lot, fronting on York Street [now Baltimore], about the distance of twenty five feet from the same, and Harford Street [now Central Avenue] of the following dimensions, about forty eight feet in length, and twenty four in width, one story high. This we conclude may be divided into two convenient rooms, one for the accommodation of the Boys, and the other for the Girls, ...[24]

By 1806 this first building had been used enough that the Meeting spent over $500 altering and repairing the schoolhouse on Aisquith Street. (See the bill for work submitted by Thomas Matthews in illustration 2.2.)

Some of the delay in constructing a school may have come from uncertainty about where the majority of the Quaker community would live. When Baltimore's economy boomed and its population expanded, the city grew in a westerly direction. The best deep water docks were still at Fell's Point, but the commercial center of the city shifted west

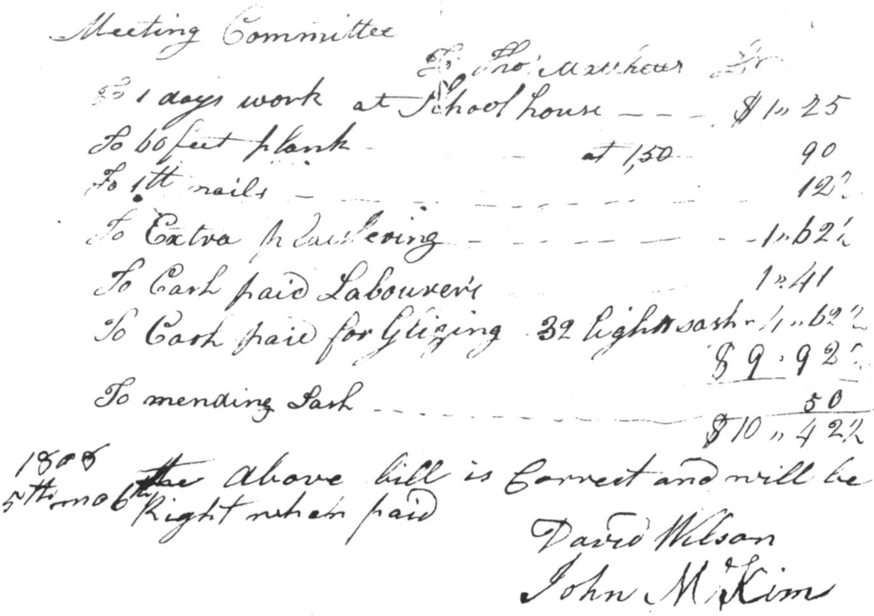

Meeting Committee

To 1 days work at School house — — — $1,,25
To 60 feet plank at 1,50 90
To 1 lb nails 12½
To Extra [illegible] 1,,62½
To Cash paid Labourers 1,,41
To Cash paid for Glazing 32 lights sash 1,,62½
$9:92½
To mending Sash 50
$10,,42½

1806 5th mo 6th the above bill is Correct and will be Right when paid

David Wilson
John McKim

Illus. 2-2 Bill for work on the school house, 1806.

along Baltimore, Pratt, Charles, and Light streets where merchants like Tyson and others built new wharves and filled in the marshy land to make the harbor more attractive and convenient to shipping. Indeed, by 1805 there were enough Quakers living west of the Jones Falls to justify spending $16,000 on a new meeting house on Lombard Street, between Eutaw and Howard.[25] For the next two decades these members of the Lombard Meeting attempted to rent or build their own separate school, but with little result. Most pupils, if they went to a Quaker school at all, attended the one in Old Town or were sent off to one of the boarding schools in Pennsylvania, New York, or rural Maryland.[26]

A good example of a student from the Western District of Baltimore Monthly Meeting attending the Old Town school was Richard Townsend—son of Joseph Townsend, the first teacher. In 1810, when Richard was only six years old, he was taught at home by Betsy Husband in the nursery over the dining room. Along with Griffith and William Jones, who were also pupils of Miss Husband, they read *No Cross, No Crown* by William Penn, the sermons of Samuel Fathergill, and the journal of Catherine Phillips. The next year Richard, who lived with his parents at 18 Baltimore Street, attended the Old Town Meeting school where Robert Cornthwait was teacher. The quality of education may not have satisfied the elder Townsend, for he sent his son to other schools in 1812 and 1813. Richard first went to school with John Cox "in Gay above Market in Baltimore...," then to Ennion Cook, who taught a school at Birmingham Meeting House in Chester, Pennsylvania. The quality of education at the Old Town Meeting school under Robert Cornthwait is suspect, although possibly the historical records are misleading. In 1805 when he married Alisana Wilson, Cornthwait was referred to as a merchant.[27] In 1808, three years before he became Richard Townsend's teacher, a notice of his insolvency appeared in the local newspapers.[28] It is possible that his brief career as a teacher in the Friends School may have been only a temporary occupation to help restore some of his finances. Certainly the period from 1807 to the War of 1812 was one of economic stagnation for Baltimore. Even large merchants like Elisha Tyson suffered under President Jefferson's embargo and later from the British interference with American shipping.[29] If prominent merchants found the times difficult, then Robert Cornthwait's personal economic misfortune is understandable and his solution of turning to teaching was a reasonable one. Nevertheless, it suggests that well-trained professional teachers were not always in charge of the pupils. Too often in these early years being a Quaker and willing to teach were considered qualification enough.

Richard Townsend continued to move from school to school for much of his education. He returned to Baltimore to the classroom of his cousin Sarah, located "on the south side of Lombard Street, adjoining Friends Meeting." Whether this was a school under the direct care of the Monthly Meeting is not clear—probably not, since it is mentioned in none of the Meeting's records. In the following year, 1814, when the British marched on Baltimore and bombarded Fort McHenry, Richard was back at the Old Town school, this time with George F. Janney, who taught there until May, 1815. Whether Janney was any more of a professional teacher than Cornthwait is hard to say, but at least he later ran a book, stationery, and hardware store at 20 Baltimore Street, which suggests he may have had a sustained interest in distributing knowledge as well as nails. His store was next to Joseph Townsend's Baltimore Equitable Society, so he may have had a continuing influence on young Richard.[30]

The school experiences of Richard Townsend illustrate again the erratic nature of private education in the early nineteenth century. Certainly there was little continuity to his education as he moved from school to school and back again. His reason for attending his cousin Sarah's school near the Lombard Street Meeting House may have been convenience or cost—even familial duty for that matter—rather than quality of teaching. In an age of wandering students, at the beginning of each year the teacher either started all pupils together in the same books or simply guessed at the level of education a student had achieved at his or her last school. There were no uniform standards or regulations for either schools or teachers. Obtaining a good education in the post-Revolutionary era was no easy task.

For the Quakers the existence of an education or school committee was not always a solution to the problem of maintaining uniform quality. In the years up to the Civil War the committee too often made only a token effort at support and supervision. Before the middle of the nineteenth century the relationship between the Meeting and the school was never clearly defined. Although the school committee was expected to visit and "oversee" the classroom, it was often the case that the teachers were expected to collect the tuition from their pupils rather than receive payment from the Meeting. The Monthly Meeting provided the space, either in the meeting house or in a separate school building, as in Old Town, but the teacher retained considerable autonomy as long as he collected the fees. At those times when the Monthly Meeting appropriated funds for altering the building or buying supplies, the interest of the committee and perhaps its control seems to have increased. At other times the teacher was apparently free to run the school as he saw fit, providing that the basic criteria were met. These criteria, common to Quaker schools in the early nineteenth century, were that the teacher be morally sound, a member of the Society of Friends, and "competent to teach the subjects for which employed."[31] The first two—morality and membership as a Friend—were easiest to judge and for many parents were more important than the teacher's academic qualifications. The child's education was considered incomplete if the instructor were not a devout Quaker.[32] Moreover, at a time when there were few standards and little uniformity in American education, the evaluation of a teacher's credentials was difficult.

On occasion the school was fortunate in being able to hire an instructor with experience and an established reputation. Such was the case in 1816 with Amos Bullock, an experienced teacher from the Quaker school at Westtown, Pennsylvania. Taking over what was now called the "Male Select School" from George F. Janney, the previous teacher, Bullock earned his salary of $800 by improving the quality of teaching and by increasing the enrollment to thirty-three.[33] As enrollment increased Bullock apparently took on an assistant teacher,

John Creery, who helped to give personal attention to each student. After signing the receipt for the payment of a portion of William Lee's tuition, Creery added a note of encouragement to the boy's mother: "Wm. improves and conducts himself well. He better be continued at School as he appears to have a desire to learn—it is for his good I mention it." (See illustration 2.3.) When the school committee visited classes on October 4, 1816, and again in January, 1817, they were impressed by what they observed. Flushed with enthusiasm and optimistic about the school's future, the committee raised Bullock's salary to the handsome sum of $1,100. Enrollment for the year reached fifty boys and larger numbers seemed likely. But the expansion they envisioned never materialized. By the spring of 1818 the school committee anticipated that only twenty-five or thirty students would return in the fall—barely enough to generate half of Bullock's large salary. The enthusiasm of the committee waned when he announced his refusal to return to the school for less than $1,200. When the committee's treasurer, Thomas Ellicott, learned through a discreet enquiry that the superintendent of the Westtown School, which enrolled 170 pupils, received only $600 in addition to room and board, they made no further efforts to rehire Amos Bullock.[34]

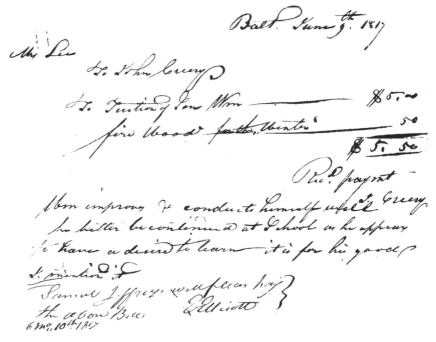

Illus. 2-3 Tuition bill (for $5.00, plus $.50 for firewood for the winter), 1817.

When Joseph G. Hopkins took over the school as teacher in the fall of 1818 the committee was far more circumspect in its financial agreements. In a written memorandum the school committee of the Old Town Meeting promised to provide the room, school yard, "Desks and benches—Globes and chairs and stove, free of expense...." Hopkins was to receive a half-day vacation each monthly meeting day, four days to attend quarterly meetings, and one week for yearly meeting. In turn he agreed to teach spelling, reading, writing, arithmetic, bookkeeping, grammar, and mathematics. It was the teacher's responsibility to collect fees from the family of each student. For spelling, reading, and writing he received four dollars per quarter; for arithmetic, bookkeeping, and grammar, five dollars; and for teaching mathematics, eight dollars for each quarter. He was also permitted to charge a reasonable amount for supplying the students with stationery and could teach a night school in winter without paying rent for the school room. Students of the day school were expected to supply fuel for the stove in cold weather.[35] This arrangement for the 1818-19 school year was the most complete and detailed that the Friends have ever made for the education of their children. For the first time they had established a few simple guidelines that would allow them to control and evaluate the progress of the school.

The interest and attention given to the Male Select School, however, did not carry over equally for the support of a separate girls'

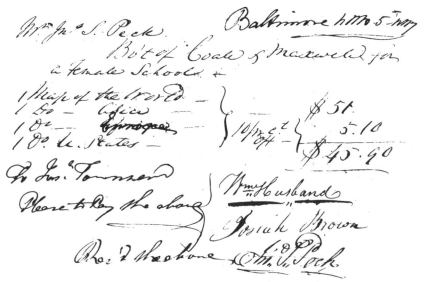

Illus. 2-4   Bill for maps purchased from Coale & Maxwell for the Girls' School, 1817.

school in the Old Town district. In the earlier years of the school, before 1816, apparently boys and girls attended the same school, although they were taught separately. With the remodeling of the building and the hiring of Bullock, however, the female pupils were to be taught elsewhere. A member of the committee for educating females, which was made up of men and women, complained of "the backwardness manifested in a number of friends (*sic*) to promote [a school] for the girls." Nevertheless they advertised for a teacher whom they promised to pay $400 for instructing thirty pupils.[36] By November they had found a teacher and the Girls' School was in session, although it apparently was not in the schoolhouse on the Aisquith Street meeting house grounds. Instead it was a few blocks to the west on Front Street near Jones Falls. It was there that Richard Townsend's three sisters, Phebe, Hannah, and Mary, attended the school of Susan Yarnall, a member of Friends Meeting.[37] The curriculum might have been different from the boys' school but at least we know they studied such practical subjects as geography. In 1817 the school spent $45.90 (they received a 10 percent discount) on four maps of the world, Africa, Europe, and the United States. (See illustration 2.4.)

This new Girls' School had a more precarious existence than the boys' school. However many started at Miss Yarnall's in November, 1816, the number had "declined" to twenty-two students by the same month two years later and the school committee reduced its commitment. Joseph Townsend, treasurer, paid her $300 in January for the "last three Quarters Sallary (*sic*) Teaching School Ending 12th Mo. 24th 1818." (See illustrations 2.1 and 2.5.) For the following year she agreed to accept the students' tuition as her salary. The rent money ($100) from the dwelling part of the school house, which had been

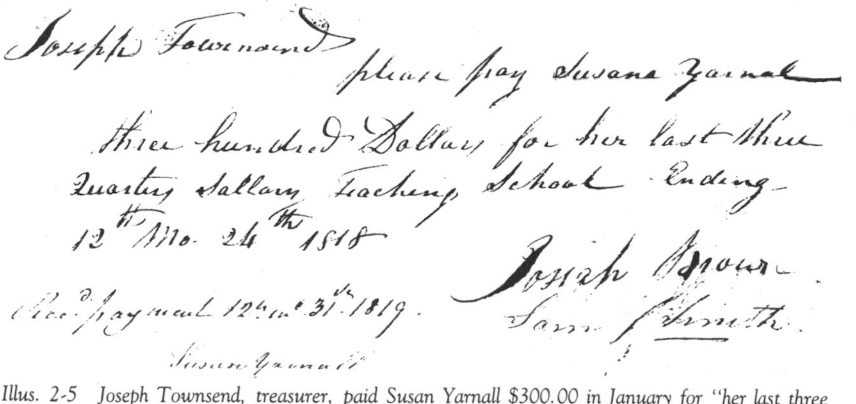
Joseph Townsend
please pay Susana Yarnal
three hundred Dollars for her last three
Quarters Sallary Teaching School Ending
12th Mo. 24th 1818

Joseph Brown
Sam. Smith

Rec. payment 12th mo 31st 1819.
Susan Yarnall

Illus. 2-5 Joseph Townsend, treasurer, paid Susan Yarnall $300.00 in January for "her last three Quarters sallary [sic] Teaching School Ending 12th Mo. 24th 1818."

remodeled in 1807, was to be used to pay for a school room for the girls.[38] After 1819 the Girls' School faded out of the records and was not mentioned again. Probably it continued for a while in an informal capacity still under the "care of the Meeting," but with the teacher collecting the fees.

Eighteen nineteen marked the end of the first thirty-five years of the Old Town school. Its origin and growth had been peaceful and quiet in typical Quaker fashion. It had yet achieved no noticeable reputation outside the Quaker community and few would have suspected that this small school would survive to eventually become Baltimore's oldest educational institution.

Illus. 3-1   Interior of Lombard Street Meeting House, built in 1805.

CHAPTER 3

Modest Beginnings

For the next four decades, from 1820 to 1860, the small Quaker school struggled to survive in a rapidly changing environment. These were the years of urban and industrial revolution, of economic panic and prosperity, of new party politics and the "rise of the common man," and of social reform and the great debate to end slavery. Baltimore, the nation's third largest city, felt the impact of all these changes. In 1819 and again in 1821, a yellow fever epidemic struck the city, leaving death in its wake. While the wealthier inhabitants escaped to the fresh air of their country estates, the majority of city dwellers—school child and adult alike—stayed in their homes and faced the dread disease. These were the years too when Baltimore earned the nickname of "Mobtown." The mass violence caused by political and group rivalry was a direct contradiction to the principles of peace advocated by the Society of Friends. More than once the daily lives of Baltimore's school children must have been interrupted by the noise and news of conflict and tragedy.

Nevertheless these were also years of excitement and prosperity for Baltimore's citizens. Parades and celebrations marked the return of General Lafayette in 1824, and in 1832 most of the city turned out to celebrate the 100th anniversary of George Washington's birth. In the 1850s Baltimoreans enjoyed the privilege of visits from international personalities like Jenny Lind and Louis Kossuth, and felt the excitement of national party politics when the Democrats and Whigs chose Baltimore as the site for their presidential nominating conventions.

Urban expansion, despite its disruptive consequence, also brought prosperity to Baltimore. New banks, retail stores, mills, factories, and shipping companies appeared regularly in the growing city. A new business elite based more on manufacturing and commerce than on the land and agricultural activities of the past was emerging.[1] And scattered among these new city leaders were a rising number of Quaker merchants and manufacturers. John McKim's Union Manufacturing Company that used steam-driven machinery to produce cotton cloth was already worth one million dollars. Philip E. Thomas became president of the nation's first railroad—the Baltimore and Ohio—and of course Johns Hopkins acquired his fortune and reputation as a leading merchant during these years.[2]

Whether or not this prosperity and rising social status was an advantage to the Friends' school, however, is difficult to determine. It may in fact have been a disadvantage. Some of the more successful Quaker merchants, like Johns Hopkins, either ceased or never became active in the Meeting or the school. Others, like Joseph Townsend, who continued to be a strong force in the Meeting, sent their children to reputable boarding schools outside the city. Richard Townsend attended Nine Partners School in New York State where he found fellow-students from Baltimore. A number went to Benjamin Hallowell's school in Alexandria, Virginia, or to Fair Hill Boarding School near Sandy Spring.[3] Even John McKim's final act of charity may have had a negative effect on the original school in Old Town. At his death in 1817, McKim left a fund that produced $600 per year for the support of a free school. Intended for the education of Baltimore's poor children, regardless of religious denomination, it opened with 94 pupils in March, 1821. Although middle-class Quakers probably would have avoided the stigma of sending their children to a free school for the poor, the existence of the McKim School undoubtedly weakened the support for the older school. Without more specific records, however, it is impossible to tell who enrolled in the McKim School.[4]

Less directly threatening to the school, but certainly disruptive to the Quaker community, was the Hicksite separation of 1828. While most Baltimoreans that year were debating the prospects of the new Baltimore and Ohio Railroad or were marveling at the newly-completed shot tower, the Society of Friends was preoccupied with a serious division over religious beliefs. At Baltimore Yearly Meeting in the early fall, four-fifths of the membership chose to follow the more liberal views of Elias Hicks, while the rest withdrew to form a separate Orthodox meeting. Since this Orthodox group later built its own meeting house and for a short time supported its own school, the strength of the original Friends school was further weakened.[5]

The greatest challenge to the survival of the school, however, came from outside the Quaker community. On September 21, 1829, Baltimore opened its first public school in the basement of a Presbyterian church on Eutaw Street. A year later the first public schoolhouse was built on Aisquith Street near Fayette, only a short way from the old Friends Meeting House. By the beginning of the Civil War, thirty years later, the public school system enrolled nearly 15,000 students each year.[6] With such strong competition from tax-supported institutions, many private schools could be expected to fail; and indeed, many Quaker schools disappeared from the American scene before the end of the nineteenth century.[7] A few gave up the effort at elementary education and concentrated on secondary or college preparatory education.

But the Friends school in Baltimore survived—although its records for the period between 1820 and 1846 are incomplete. The fact that there were about 5,000 Quakers in the Baltimore vicinity—more than in most cities, except Philadelphia—might account for its survival. More likely, however, it was the desire to provide a "guarded education" and the Quakers' dissatisfaction with the quality of education available in the early public schools. On several occasions in the decades before the Civil War the committee on education of Baltimore Yearly Meeting expressed the view that an "education in literature and science was felt to be of secondary importance, if, with it, those great testamonies (sic) we uphold are not ingrafted upon the tender and plastic mind—if the frequent reading of the Holy Scriptures, and the withdrawal from outward pursuits to wait for Divine counsel and guidance, be neglected."[8] This sentiment, when combined with the complaints about the early public schools, may have been enough to keep the Quaker school alive.

Even though Baltimore was more progressive than most southern or border cities in regard to public education, its schools suffered from several problems. Because demand was high and space was limited, overcrowding was a common complaint in the first decades of the school system. To resolve the difficulty and to take advantage of one of the popular and inexpensive educational reforms of the day, the school board adopted the monitorial method in which the older and better students were given responsibilities for teaching the other pupils. By using such a method, each teacher in the city schools was able to "teach" over one hundred students in a single class. The objections of parents became so strong and the quality of education produced by children teaching children was so low that the school board finally abandoned the practice in 1839. The hiring of assistant teachers reduced class sizes, but other problems remained. Buildings used for schools were often in poor condition, sanitation was frequently lacking, excessive noise near classrooms was disruptive, and the supply of properly trained teachers was always low because of inadequate salaries (assistant teachers received only $150).[9]

Although the public schools improved through a broadening of the curriculum, reduction of class size, and the addition of evening classes to accommodate working children, the Quakers apparently were not ready to abandon their independent school for the public institutions. By the 1840s Baltimore Monthly Meeting had moved its school from the original site in Old Town to the Lombard Street Meeting House where it was loosely supervised by the Women's Committee. Between 1847 and 1849 they repaired the old classrooms, which were on the second floor, and added a new room on the rear of the meeting house. A new joint committee of men and women was set up to oversee the school's operation. When school opened in the fall of 1849 Jane S. Jewett and her two teaching assistants had fifty pupils, half of whom were the children of Friends.[10]

Although this revival of support at the mid-century carried with it a spirit of optimism and confidence, the school again failed to grow in the decade before the Civil War and, in fact, was close to disappearing altogether from time to time. The weakness of the school lay in the fact that the teachers were responsible for collecting the tuition from the students' families and for paying rent for the use of the rooms. In order to make the school competitive with the public schools, however, and in order to accommodate those Friends who could not afford high fees, the tuition was kept so low by the school committee that few teachers could survive for very long. Seldom did any of the teachers—all of whom were women by this time—stay for more than two years (Table 3–1). If the teacher had a good reputation, like that of Jane P. Graham who was hired in 1853, the enrollment crept up to forty or fifty students; when teachers with less well-established reputations took over, it declined (enrollment dropped to fourteen when Jane L. Hibbard replaced Jane Graham after 1854). The committee themselves recognized the problem when they reported that the prosperity of the school "depends upon the efficiency literiry (sic) attainments of the teachers, coupled with the rare facility for governing and instructing the pupils...;" but there was little they were able to do to change the situation, given the shortage of qualified teachers who were willing to work for low compensation.[11]

Attendance in the ante–bellum period reached a peak of 67 pupils in the 1858-1859 school year when Jane Graham returned as teacher.

Table 3–1

FRIENDS SCHOOL 1850-64

Year	Teacher	No. of Pupils
1850	Jane S. Jewett	52
1851	Susan Shaw	27
1852	Sarah & Anne Griscom	50
1853	Jane P. Graham	41
1854	Jane P. Graham	NA
1855	Jane L. Hibbard	NA
1856	Jane L. Hibbard	14
1857	*Jane L. Hibbard/ Jane P. Graham	NA
1858	Jane P. Graham	NA
1859	Jane P. Graham	67
1860	Mary J. Turner	40
1861	(Mary J. Turner?)	52
1862	Elizabeth Smith	NA
1863	Elizabeth Smith	40
1864	Lydia C. Stabler	40

* Jane P. Graham apparently took over the school sometime during the 1856-57 school year. Source: Reports of the School Committee to Baltimore Monthly Meeting, 1850-64 in Friends School Archives.

Shortly thereafter, the Monthly Meeting, in an attempt to create more stability for the teachers and the school, agreed to accept financial responsibility for the school and to collect tuition from the parents. Teachers received a modest salary and were not required to pay rent for the use of the classrooms. But whatever chance the school had for growth was cut short by the coming of the Civil War—a war particularly disruptive to Baltimore, which was torn by conflicting Union and Confederate sympathies. Not until the war's end did a newer and brighter era begin for the struggling Friends' school.[12]

For the children who attended the school at Old Town or later on Lombard Street, the problems of enrollments, tuition, or administration mattered little. What did interest them were the day-to-day experiences of meeting and playing with classmates, preparing for or worrying about the day's lessons, staying on good terms with the teacher, and knowing the excitement and frustration that learning brought. In some ways education in the half-century before the Civil War possessed characteristics common to any era. But in so many other ways the school and the city of that past time seem far away from the present.

Whether they went to the first Friends' school in Old Town, or the later one on Lombard Street, students arrived on foot. Despite its size as the nation's third largest city, Baltimore was still a "walking city" no part of which was more than half an hour's walk from the center. By 1844 horse-drawn omnibuses, a kind of urban stagecoach that ran over a set route, appeared on Baltimore's streets. Few children would have ridden these rumbling "buses" to school, however, for even at twelve cents per round trip, it was still too expensive for most families. Besides, children were expected to walk. Not until the development of the automobile and the city bus in the twentieth century would children develop the habit of riding to school.

The streets the children walked were not the concrete walks and paved avenues of a later Baltimore, but were the cobblestone, gravel, and mostly dirt roads of a city just entering the industrial era. The sights, sounds, and smells that were a part of the streets' atmosphere were those of the carriage, pedestrian, and horse. Even as late as the 1840s hogs still wandered freely through some of the thoroughfares, feeding on household garbage and frightening smaller children. The streets were worst when choked with dust or deep with mud, and best in snowy winters when the children could pull or ride their sleds to school.

That these were the streets of an older time was evident too from the presence of slaves, who passed on their way to work at the wharves along the harbor or at the mills beside the Jones Falls. Young Frederick Douglass, a slave to Hugh Auld, found the streets of Baltimore to be his only school. As Douglass remembered it, "I used to carry, almost constantly, a copy of Webster's spelling book in my pocket, and when sent on errands, or when playtime was allowed me, I would step, with my young friends, aside, and take a lesson in spelling." Perhaps some of these "young friends" who helped Douglass to spell were on their way to the Quaker school.

By whatever route they came, the schoolroom at which they arrived was probably a plain but comfortable place. With the help of a few old bills for equipment and work submitted to Baltimore Monthly Meeting by a member, Ely Balderston, and with a little imagination, we can guess what the Quaker school was like, since nineteenth-century

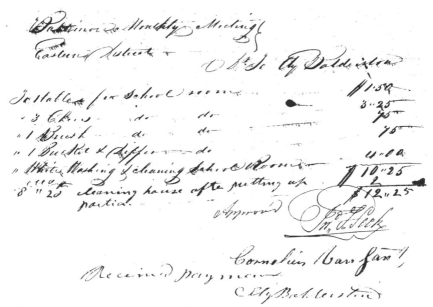

Illus. 3-2 Bill for classroom furniture and equipment, ca. 1818.

classrooms were often much the same. Unpainted pine or oak benches and desks were probably arranged around a stove in the center of the room. At the front was usually the teacher's desk with at least one drawer for penknives, balls, rocks, marbles, and other treasures confiscated from unlucky pupils. Large sash windows let in fresh air in summer and were the main source of light on most days. From at least one white-washed wall would have hung a blackboard, which had become common in schools after 1820. Next to the door was a small table with a pail of water and a tin cup or dipper, and nearby, either in an outside hallway or just inside the entrance, were pegs for boys' hats and children's coats in cold weather. Over all would have hung the pleasant odor of the wood-burning stove in the winter and the distant sounds of street traffic when the windows were open in the spring and fall.

The teacher who presided over this scene was likely to be a recent graduate of the same school or one like it. After 1820 it was usually a woman rather than a man who was in charge of the classroom; for as the American economy expanded, the majority of males were encouraged to engage in some form of business or production. An unspoken prejudice developed that men who became teachers were misfits unable to succeed in business. The low social status of teaching, coupled with meager salaries, meant that teaching was left to young single women, or to women who were not the sole support of families. Anne and Sarah Griscom, for example, who conducted the school in 1851, collected the tuition from twenty-seven students, but were required to pay $40 per month rent for the school rooms in the meeting house. Since tuition was about five dollars per quarter, they were earning approximately four dollars each week, which was near the average wage for female teachers in urban areas at that time, but was less than enough to support a family.[13] The school committee finally convinced the Monthly Meeting in 1863 that good teachers could be hired only if they were guaranteed

Illus. 3-3 Classroom, Lombard Street.

adequate salaries. Five hundred dollars for teachers and three hundred dollars for assistants were agreed upon as appropriate rates. It was no coincidence that the quality of education and the school's reputation improved after this decision was made.[14]

Because society had paid such little attention to the professional training of its teachers (Maryland did not establish its first normal school until after the war), the teacher had to rely on her ingenuity and past experience as she faced the class each day. School usually began at about eight o'clock with the children being called in from their outdoor play. A few minutes of silent worship at their desks helped the pupils settle down physically and prepared them mentally for their lessons. The first activity was probably reading, with the students divided into small groups according to age and level of learning. While the teacher or assistant worked with one group, the others were expected to study quietly. The advantage of these methods was that each pupil received personal attention and progressed at his or her own pace. The disadvantage was that memorization and repetition were emphasized at the expense of understanding. Modern critics of the technique in which students replied to questions by repeating statements directly from a textbook labeled it "parrot-training." Grammar was learned by memorizing and reciting rules over and over, but little effort was made to actually put the lessons to use. Richard Townsend, for example, recalled the pride he felt when he memorized "the thirty Rules of Comly's Syntax."[15] Conformity to traditional values and rules were considered more important than creativity and originality of thought.

No doubt the teachers of the Friends' school resorted to the Lancastrian method when there were too many pupils for the teacher to handle. Developed in 1805 by Joseph Lancaster, himself a Quaker, the monitorial system used a few students to drill the others. With six or eight pupils standing in a circle—toes touching—the monitor called on each one to read aloud or to repeat answers that had been memorized the day before. But just as the public schools gave up this method by 1839, the Quakers too seem to have become quickly disillusioned with it.[16]

The best example of nineteenth-century teaching methods and the degree to which they encouraged standardization of thought is in the emphasis on spelling. Americans developed a passion for spelling and the Quaker schools were no exception. Often when the children returned indoors from a short recess at about 10 o'clock they prepared for a spelling drill or sometimes a contest in which individuals competed for the honor of champion speller. The teacher asked spelling words from a standard text, like that of Webster's *Blue-Backed Speller*, and each child recited aloud. In much the same way the teacher might review the students on abbreviations, weights and measures, or counting money.

After the spelling lesson, which sometimes stirred passions and created excitement as each student spelled the words triumphantly or sank back embarrassed into his seat, the teacher might turn the students' attention to the quieter activity of handwriting or penmanship. By this time in the school day the central stove had warmed the room and thawed the ink at the students' desks. The teacher sharpened the quill pens and prepared a copy of letters or sentences for each student to practice writing in his or her copybook. The younger children worked on the basic letters of the alphabet, and the older ones practiced the elements of the cursive style. Those who were particularly good might produce an exhibition piece with decorated borders and several styles of letters. The best would be displayed for parents at the end of the year.

The writing lesson might be followed with reading from the Scriptures or from the works of George Fox and William Penn. After a break of at least an hour for lunch, which most children ate at home, the afternoon session would begin with perhaps another round of spelling or reading. Arithmetic, more grammar, geography, and perhaps some history filled the rest of the school day. Richard Townsend remembered that at Amos Bullock's school in 1817 he studied arithmetic, algebra, and surveying, in addition to reading, writing, and spelling. Joseph G. Hopkins added bookkeeping to the curriculum the next year.[17]

If there was any change in the curriculum of the Friends' school in Baltimore in the years before the Civil War, it was to increase the number of practical subjects that were taught. The Quakers had always emphasized practical education, but this tendency was strengthened even more as the public school reformers of the 1830s and 1840s such as Horace Mann turned their advice in the same direction. English literature had gradually become predominant in most schools although Latin language and literature still continued to be taught. Certainly Baltimore's growth as a commercial and industrial center influenced the choice of subjects that parents and children expected in the curriculum. They saw education as a vehicle for upward mobility and the key to achieving a higher standard of living. The school still retained its function as promoter and protector of moral values, but as the modernization of Baltimore's society occurred, both private and public institutions attempted to meet the practical needs and demands of their students. The school filled the gap in education that was created when apprenticeship disappeared and the family ceased to be adequately equipped for vocational training.

The books from which the students learned their lessons also conveyed this combined purpose of moral and practical education. There were a number of schoolbooks written by Quaker authors, but even the non-Quaker texts had the same strong mixture of moral and useful lessons. *Murray's Grammar* for example was written by Lindley Murray in 1795 specifically for a Quaker school in New York. Revised by Enoch Pond in 1835, it remained in wide use among Friends' schools, not only because of its sound moral teachings, but because it was one of the first texts to bring system to the study of grammar.[18] Unfortunately much of it was written in a form that made for easy drilling on rules by the teacher but with little consideration for the student's understanding. Only the attractive engravings in the 1835 edition, which illustrated the meaning of some of the sentences, kept the rules from being a complete mystery to pupils.

Several primers for reading were well known for their moral lessons. The famous *New England Primer*, from which many generations of American students were taught, advised that

Good children must

Fear God all day,	Love Christ alway,
Parents obey,	In secret pray,
No false thing say,	Mind little play,
By no sin stray,	Make no delay,

In doing good.[19]

The Quaker school at some time probably used George Fox's *Plain Directions for Reading and Writing True English and Instruction for Right Spelling*. And many schools encouraged teachers to teach from William Penn's *Reflections, Maxims* or *Advice to His Children*. Anthony Benezet's *Pennsylvania Spelling Book* was older, but was also used for many years in Quaker schools.[20]

Both Noah Webster's famous *Blue-Backed Speller* and McGuffey's *Readers* found their way into most classrooms. For the beginning reader the hornbook was still in use in the early nineteenth century. It was of course not really a book at all, but a single piece of paper nailed to a board and covered with a thin sheet of horn. At the top was the alphabet, followed by combinations of vowels and consonants, and concluded with The Lord's Prayer.

The only specific record of books used in the Baltimore school indicates that geography was a regular part of the curriculum. Richard Townsend remembered using *Gummere's Geography and Surveying* at Amos Bullock's school in 1817, and thirty years later the Women's Committee on Education of Baltimore Yearly Meeting provided one dozen copies of *Mitchel's School Atlas* for the school on Lombard Street.[21] A year later the same group spent nearly $100 on books for the school and the Meeting library.[22]

It was not the use of particular books, however, that made the Quaker school distinct from the public schools of Baltimore or from the other independent schools. It was rather the Quaker commitment to the belief in human worth and equality, and the insistence "that man is a being of infinite value and of divine possibilities...." Nowhere was the contrast between Quaker and non-Quaker beliefs regarding human nature more evident than in regard to classroom discipline. For much of the nineteenth century a strong debate occurred among teachers, parents, and administrators over the use of corporal punishment. Traditionally in American and English schools, whipping had been used for a variety of offenses: tardiness, not doing homework, inattentiveness, poor manners, or failing to do lessons correctly. A teacher, writing in the *Southern Literary Messenger* in 1841 defended flogging as a proper punishment because it "saves time" and is "refreshing— composes the wandering thoughts, brightens the wits, quickens the animal spirits and braces the nerves. It is a sort of Animal Magnetism, a galvanic battery—a thunderstorm to purify the moral atmosphere." A Baltimore schoolmaster agreed and went on to argue that God and nature approved the use of force: "swishing [has] 'the highest authority,' from which Christians should not dissent—the twenty-odd allusions to the rod in the Scriptures." He concluded that, "Experience is the best teacher, and young buttocks had been pinked since time immemorial."[23]

In the 1780s, when the Friends' school in Baltimore began, teachers and parents might have agreed with these harsh sentiments. Quaker families in colonial society were urged to control their children with persuasion and good counseling, but when that failed, to resort to corporal punishment.[24] But by the beginning of the nineteenth century—and certainly by the 1820s and 1830s—physical punishment was discouraged in most Quaker schools. At Sandy Spring Boarding School, for example, students were required "when in school [not to] run, jump or scuffle, but walk with as little noise as possible." For those who broke the rules, "a place of seclusion will be provided. . ., where they could have not much light, but plenty of air, and where they could be kept comfortably warm in pretty cold weather."[25] This use of solitary confinement was a common method of punishment used in English as well as American Quaker schools.

The other accepted punishment for restlessness or disobedience was humiliation. The ways of humiliating students were only limited by the teachers' imaginations. Joseph Lancaster, the Quaker educational reformer, recommended suspending pupils in a cage from the ceiling, putting a sign on their backs listing their sins, and making them walk backwards around the room. Other popular methods were "sitting on the wall," in which the student sat with his back against the wall without the support of a chair, and "holding nails into the floor," which kept the violator in a stooped position. Sometimes the student who had not learned his lesson for the day was humiliated simply by the names the teachers used to reprimand him—"laggard," "slow learner," "re-tarded," "reluctant," or "hand-minded" were commonly used.[26]

The Baltimore public schools relied primarily on corporal punishment when persuasion and humiliation failed. The Board of Commissioners gave in to the reformers briefly by abolishing corporal punishment in the Male High School in 1848, but they apparently felt that the reform did not work—or perhaps the teachers demanded the right to whip unruly students—because the prohibition was removed eight months later and it was never applied to the elementary schools.[27]

In the Quaker school in Baltimore, however, the reform for more humane treatment of students was accepted more readily. By the second decade of the nineteenth century, corporal punishment was disapproved of by the Friends in the Baltimore area. Although the records are not specific, the Quaker school was probably the first in Baltimore to prohibit corporal punishment.

It also seems to have been the first school in the city to accept co-education as its normal policy. Although the education of girls may have been neglected or kept separate from time to time—as it was at the end of the War of 1812 when most attention was given to the Male Select School—the Quakers of Baltimore were educating boys and girls in the same school on Lombard Street by the 1840s. This acceptance of co-education was typical of Quaker schools in the nineteenth century.

In both the supervision of the schools and in the enrollment of pupils, the equality of the sexes was not questioned. There was, however, a careful separation of older boys from female students. A correspondent from the Westtown School in Pennsylvania reported that there were few boys in the classes above the age of fifteen, while girls were sometimes as old as twenty. "I should not be willing," he stated, "to admit of boys advancing to manhood and girls or young women being educated at the same establishment."[28] The problem of older boys in school was of little concern in Baltimore, however, since the emphasis was on elementary education and boys could go on to attend the public Male Central High School (Baltimore City College), which opened on October 20, 1839. By the middle of the nineteenth century the education of young boys and girls in the same classroom caused no controversy or debate among the Quakers who sent their children to the Lombard Street school and, in fact, served as a good example for other private and public institutions to follow.

The children who studied together also played together. Despite the emphasis on practical subjects and the utilitarian purpose of schooling, there was always time for games and play. American Quakers of the colonial period oftentimes discouraged children from "over indulging" in play, believing that many sports were sinful. But by 1800 Quaker parents had softened their attitudes toward childhood, and play was encouraged.[29]

Before class began in the morning, at recess and the lunch hour, or even after school, children enjoyed a variety of games and sports. Richard Townsend remembered playing "rattle-snake" at the school in Old Town. In this game children set up rows of bricks like dominoes, then tipped the first one over.[30] "Skying a copper, pitch-penny, chuckers—all games involving pitching a coin at a mark or into the air"—were popular at other Quaker schools.[31] Games that required exercise were especially encouraged in most nineteenth-century schools. Kite flying, ice skating and sledding in winter, jumping rope—with sometimes as many as twenty children—leap frog, prisoner's base, croquet, and bean bag were common games and sports. Beginning in the 1850s and spreading rapidly after the Civil War, baseball became the favorite game of both adults and children. Since the Quaker properties at Aisquith and Lombard streets had large areas for pasturing horses, it can be assumed that children soon learned how to mark off a baseball diamond.

By the time the Civil War disrupted life in Baltimore by dividing the population and bringing violence to the streets, the Friends' school was already three-quarters of a century old. Because it had the support of Baltimore Monthly Meeting—a morally and economically stable group—it was able to survive where other institutions had failed. To be sure, its achievements at this point were modest at best. It had accepted co–education and abolished corporal punishment, but there is no evidence to suggest that it was academically superior to numerous other private institutions in the city or even to the fledgling public schools. Much depended upon the quality of the teacher who ran the school; and with the rapid turnover of instructors that occurred, the school's academic reputation fluctuated unevenly. The greatest strength of the school in the period between the Revolution and the Civil War was the quality of its moral education. By the nineteenth century, Baltimore had accepted its Quaker inhabitants and appreciated the sincerity of their beliefs. As the Society of Friends became more like the rest of the urban community in dress and outward behavior, their school became more appealing to non-Quakers. The schoolbooks of the early nineteenth century are a clear indication that what parents sought for their children was a good moral education. Emphasis upon academic excellence would not become the dominant concern until after the Civil War—and by then the Friends' school would have as its principal one of the most respected teachers in the city.

Illus. 4-1   Eli M. Lamb on the porch of the Lombard Street Meeting House.

CHAPTER 4

Eli Lamb,
Quaker Schoolmaster

Whien Eli M. Lamb—"Cousin Eli" as he would come to be known by generations of Friends' students—stood on the front porch of the Lombard Street meeting house on the first day of school in September, 1864, he must have felt excitement and enthusiasm. This was the opportunity he had carefully prepared for and sought, a chance to take charge of a school. As he quietly greeted each student who passed through the brick courtyard and around the right side of the meeting house to the rear where the school rooms were, Cousin Eli might have thought back over his preparation for this moment. The son of John Emerson Lamb, headmaster of the Milton Boarding School several miles north of Baltimore at Gunpowder, Eli was following his father's lead. After completing a degree at Haverford College, the younger Lamb returned to the Milton School to serve a short apprenticeship as associate principal. But the boarding school in the wooded hills of Baltimore County offered too few opportunities to try out the educational ideas he had learned at Haverford. At the age of 27 he was ready for the challenge of the city. Specifically he hoped to open his own high school.

But if Eli Lamb recalled his eagerness to set up his own school, he could also recall that when he arrived in Baltimore in 1861 he found an angry and confused city. The elections of the previous fall and the events of the next year revealed a sharp division of Marylanders between Union and Confederate sympathizers. Although Maryland never seceded from the Union, it never wholeheartedly embraced the Northern cause either. Baltimoreans, like their fellow residents of the state, were caught between the power of the government in Washington and their Southern sympathies. In February of 1861, for example, the city was the site of a mass meeting calling for a constitutional amendment to support slavery. Respect for the national government further diminished when later that same month the new president-elect, Abraham Lincoln, slipped through the city unexpectedly at night on his way to the inauguration in the capital. Lincoln had been warned by his guard, Alan Pinkerton, of a plot against his life; and the secret passage through Baltimore was intended to foil the would-be assassins. Baltimoreans, however, who were expecting Lincoln the next day, saw this action as cowardly and unnecessary. Four years later these same city residents felt embarrassment and shame when Marylander John Wilkes Booth assassinated Lincoln.

By April of 1861 the discontent and anger turned to rioting and bloodshed when the Sixth Massachusetts and Seventh Pennsylvania regiments marched through the city on their way to Washington. After a dozen civilians and three or four soldiers were killed in the streets, the Union Army moved in with force to stabilize the atmosphere in Baltimore. For the rest of the war the army's presence dominated the landscape and life of the city. Temporary forts and hospitals sprang up in Patterson Park, Lafayette Square, and other public areas. To the south, across the inner harbor, Baltimoreans could see the artillery set up by General Benjamin F. Butler on Federal Hill. The guns pointed at the city, threatening to flatten it at the first sign of trouble. Not until the war was over would life in Baltimore again seem normal.

As Lamb remembered, it was in the midst of the war-time turmoil that he arrived in Baltimore.[1] His intention was to open a private high school, which at that time would have been among the first south of the Mason-Dixon Line. It was obvious, of course, that this was no time to attempt such an enterprise. Rumors of impending attack by Robert E. Lee's Confederate troops often disrupted daily routines, and actual raids by Rebel cavalry into Baltimore County created an unnatural tension. Many parents sent children out of the city to northern boarding schools or on extended visits to relatives in safer communities. Faced with such conditions Cousin Eli, with his wife Anna and son F. Emerson Lamb, returned to Gunpowder in 1863.[2] As a Quaker and a pacifist he would not take up arms in the Civil War, but he evidently served for a short time with the United States Sanitary Commission. In later years he held students spellbound by giving an eyewitness account of the scene at the foot of the platform when Lincoln gave his famous Gettysburg Address.[3] Ever the teacher, he made sure his young listeners memorized the speech and learned a lesson in history and rhetoric.

Although the war disrupted life for Lamb and his family, his dream of opening a high school in Baltimore was soon to be fulfilled. Even while he was serving at Gettysburg, the Education Committee of Baltimore Monthly Meeting was making plans for a better school at the Lombard Street meeting house. Frustrated with the rapid turnover of teachers and concerned that too many parents were neglecting their responsibility to provide a guarded education for their children, the committee resolved to improve the Meeting school. To increase the quality of education and to discourage parents from sending children to the free public schools, Baltimore Monthly Meeting decided to raise teachers' salaries and to "take entire control of the school; and put the price of tuition so low, as to be within the reach of all our members."[4] The teacher and assistants were required to be Quakers, and the Education Committee would exercise greater control by visiting the classrooms and evaluating the instruction every three months. Furthermore, they now requested the head teacher to submit an annual report every July on "the progress and standing of the school."[5]

As Lamb might have recalled it later, standing in front of the meeting house, the decision of Baltimore Monthly Meeting to improve its school seemed like the opportunity he had been waiting for. Armed with a strong letter of recommendation from a friend in the Naval Office at the Custom House, he applied for the position of principal and was quickly accepted for the 1864–65 school year. For both Lamb and the committee it might have seemed like the right man at the right time. Cousin Eli was eager to put to use his education and experience, and the committee had never before had anyone with such academically sound credentials. Their enthusiasm shone through when they reported to the Monthly Meeting in July, 1864, that they "sincerely desire, and earnestly hope, that time is not far distant when the standard of our school shall be elevated and at the same time conducted on such liberal principals [sic], as to induce all our members, those of small means, as well as large to send their children to it."[6]

When Cousin Eli completed his first year as principal and submitted his report in July of 1865, the expectations of the Education Committee were fulfilled. Enrollment had reached as many as eighty pupils at one point during the year, and Lamb was enthusiastic about the possibilities of an even larger school. "We think it would prove," he wrote, "not a very difficult matter, to build up here, a large school, not only of those laying the foundation of an education, but of those finishing a scholarly course, if their needs could be supplied in the way of Lecture rooms, study and recitation rooms, Philosophical apparatus, etc." Lamb had apparently not given up his desire to open a high school in Baltimore, because he gently inquired of the Education Committee: "might it not be possible to arrange for a school of 125 or 130 pupils, that might provide itself, with at least four teachers, above the Introductory classes?"[7]

The success of Lamb's first year started the Monthly Meeting school on a path that would lead it away from the small enterprise it had been before the Civil War, designed primarily to serve the needs of the Society of Friends, and toward the more comprehensive institution it would become in the twentieth century. Many individuals influenced the growth of Friends School during its two-hundred-year history, but only a few had the impact of Eli M. Lamb. From the beginning of his tenure at the school, his annual reports and written records reveal the character and personality of a man confident in his own beliefs and firm in his expectations of others. More than a century later a pupil, Felix Morley, who remembered Lamb at the end of his career, described him as

> Thin spare and upright he invariably dressed in sober black on which, for all his neatness, professional chalk marks were toward the end of the morning obtrusively apparent. Like his costume, Cousin Eli's voice, even when irritated, was a quiet monotone, clearly and evenly articulated. Neither brilliant nor conspicuously inspirational, he was nonetheless a link with the simple, well-grounded education of the past and I know that he was loved, as well as respected, by all his exasperating little wards.[8]

This image of Lamb as a quiet but steady and firm man seems to describe him throughout the forty-seven years he was associated with Friends School. From that first photo as he stood in front of the meeting house on Lombard Street, until his death in 1911 from ptomaine poisoning, his dress and appearance seem to have changed little, except for natural aging. Likewise his ideas on education remained essentially the same, although he introduced many innovations into the school.

His first two achievements were to open a high school and to improve the physical facilities. Although the records are not clear, apparently Lamb began the high school classes during the 1865–66 year. In his annual report for that year he used for the first time the name, Friends Elementary and High School.[9] This was Baltimore's first

Illus. 4-2 The Lombard Street Meeting House became the school's second location in the 1840s. The school's name was changed to Friends Elementary and High School in 1866.

Maryland Historical Society

private high school. There were already three public high schools, all founded before the Civil War—City College for boys, and Eastern and Western high schools for girls—which was rare for a southern city. Lamb's school, of course, was initially intended for the children of Quakers, but in a city of over a quarter-of-a-million people it attracted non-Quakers as well.

Cousin Eli also increased the appeal of the school by persuading the Education Committee and the Monthly Meeting to improve the physical facilities. When he took over, the Lombard Street meeting house was already sixty years old. The rooms used for classes, above and behind the large meeting room, were poorly ventilated and had low ceilings. The roof and spouting were in need of repair. And to accommodate the increased enrollment some of the classes had to be held in the large meeting room.[10] But the persuasive powers of Eli Lamb and the determination of the Education Committee to make the school more attractive to Quakers were enough to convince the Monthly Meeting to spend $3,500 on an addition to the meeting house.[11]

In these new classrooms, which students entered by passing through the enclosed brick courtyard on Lombard Street and around the right side of the meeting house, the pupils sat in long rows of double desks. These were the standard hardwood desks that generations of American school children became familiar with: inkwells at the top, a shelf underneath for storing books, paper, and pencils, and a seat that folded upward when students stood. No doubt the Quaker children, like others, occasionally gave in to the temptation to carve their initials in the desk tops.

From time to time Lamb requested, and the committee allocated, funds to buy maps, globes, dictionaries, and bookcases. The Monthly Meeting quickly discovered, however, that Cousin Eli's expectations of financial support were racing ahead of the pace the Meeting was willing to accept. The first sign of trouble came when a special committee of Baltimore Monthly Meeting met with the Education Committee and rejected a request for more money to pay the tuition for the children of poor Quakers.[12] The controversy over increased funding intensified and continued through the summer of 1867. A rare statement in the minutes of Baltimore Monthly Meeting, which usually tended to be discreetly vague and seldom refer to arguments or disagreements among the Quakers, shows the passions that were aroused: "some of the sentiments and opinions therein contained [in the Education Committee's annual report], and the spirit that seemed to have dictated them, are in our view altogether inadmissible. At the same time, the [special] committee feel bound to say that the apparently angry comments, made in the monthly meeting, on that report, are highly censurable; and deserve the reprobation of every right feeling mind."[13] A new Education Committee was created in September, but the dispute over funds continued.[14] The controversy peaked in early 1868 when Eli Lamb submitted a bill for $402.48 which Baltimore Monthly Meeting again refused to pay. A hint of the emotion Lamb's bill stirred showed once more when a special committee reported that

> . . . we deem it due however to the Teacher, to state, that the enormous charges appear to have been made by him, in not taking a correct view of the rules, that govern Lombard and tenant, he being led into this error partly by his misunderstanding of an agreement had with the school committee, when he first took charge of the school in the old building, as being afterwards applicable to the furnishing of the new one.[15]

Lamb agreed to revise his bill and to pay part of the charges himself. By July of 1868 the committee reported that communication "with the Principal has been of the most pleasant character, and we hope that all past difficulties appear to be ended, that a career of usefulness, and prosperity awaits the institution . . . . "[16] That ended the controversy over funding, but twenty years later a more serious dispute arose and led to the severing of the relationship between Eli Lamb and Baltimore Monthly Meeting.

With the air cleared regarding financial arrangements (Lamb collected tuition and fees from the pupils and paid rent to the Monthly Meeting) the way was open for Cousin Eli to concentrate on what he knew best: teaching mathematics and directing the daily operations of the school. As Baltimore and the nation recovered from the Civil War during the next decade, Lamb steadily built Friends Elementary and High School into a solid institution of over 250 pupils.[17] For many within the Society of Friends, the success of the school was "due to the fact that it is known as a *Friends* school." Non-Quaker parents were believed to send their sons and daughters to the school because "we are accredited with being a substantial people, worthy of confidence, and [they know] that with us their children are safe."[18] No doubt this assessment of the school's reputation was partly true, for the Quakers had won respect for their sense of peace and order, and their commitment to basic Christian values. The irony was that at the same time the school's reputation was growing, it was becoming less uniquely Quaker. Before the Civil War the avowed purpose of the school in Old Town and later on Lombard Street was to provide a guarded education for children of members of the Society of Friends. Only Quaker teachers were hired and a majority of the students came from Quaker families. The involvement of the Education Committee in the affairs of the school and the fact that the school was held in or adjacent to the meeting house all added to the impression that the school's purpose was to develop the students' sense that they were part of the Quaker community. The use of non-violent methods of discipline, the emphasis on scholastic integrity, and the importance of practical subjects in the curriculum were also part of the Quaker policies of education.[19] But in the post-Civil War period the unique religious character of the school diminished, though it did not disappear.

The causes of this secularization were both internal and external. According to the most respected of twentieth-century Quaker historians, Rufus M. Jones, there was a new openness that appeared between 1860 and 1880 in the Society of Friends. The exclusiveness of the past was replaced with greater involvement by the Quakers in their local communities. Meeting houses were modernized and music was incorporated into the worship in some meetings.[20] The same openness appeared in education. In the last half of the nineteenth century, Quaker schools ceased "exercising their main function of preparing for a special community and . . . tended, like other schools, to prepare for the great community of this world."[21] This generalization certainly describes the development of Friends Elementary and High School between the Civil War and the end of the century. Although classes usually began with silent worship, followed by a brief reading from the Bible, and although students were expected to attend mid-week meeting, religion received less and less emphasis.[22] By 1901 Eli Lamb's son, F. Emerson Lamb, testified in a court case that there was no religious education in the school and that children were not required to attend religious exercises.[23]

The changed nature of the school was also reflected in its enrollment. As the total number of pupils increased after 1864, the proportion of children whose parents were members of the Society of Friends declined. Average enrollment grew from 80 students in 1864 to 225 by 1885 but the number of Quaker children increased only from 37 to 42.[24] Neither pleas to parents from Baltimore Monthly and Yearly Meetings, nor substantial tuition discounts of from forty to more than seventy percent were enough to significantly increase the number of Quaker children at the school.[25] A large majority of the teachers continued to be Quakers, but fewer than one out of five students were children of Friends—a condition that weakened the reinforcement of traditional values and behavior.[26] Friends Elementary and High School would continue to be known as a Quaker school, but the ideal of a guarded education had been left behind with pre-Civil War America.

The changing character of Friends School was not only the result of a greater openness within the Society of Friends, but also of the growth of Baltimore. Modernization—or that complexity of revolutions in industry, communications, urbanization, and organization—was changing life for all Americans in the nineteenth century. When the nation celebrated its one hundredth anniversary in 1876 its attention was more on the future than the past. The main attraction at the Philadelphia Centennial Exhibition was Machinery Hall with its giant Corliss steam engine—a symbol of the power and promise that modern technology could bring. And in Baltimore the anticipation of the future was just as great. The crowds that paraded through the streets on the Fourth of July in that centennial year saw a city they were proud of. Its population was over one-quarter of a million, its economy was prospering, and it had just constructed a new city hall—all signals for opti-mism. Along the wharves of Light Street stood the lumberyards, corn exchange, and tobacco warehouses that reflected Baltimore's past as a commercial center. The many banks, business houses, and retail stores along Baltimore and other streets in the central business district suggested that business would continue to be the principal economic activity. But industry too had made its influence known in Baltimore by the second half of the nineteenth century. Besides the older flour milling and sugar refining industries, the clothing, hat, fertilizer, canning and other new industries gave the city a new manufacturing diversity. Moreover, technology was changing daily life in the years after the Civil War. Horsecars carried passengers along city streets until they were replaced by electric trolleys in the 1880s. Canned and packaged goods made life easier for the Baltimore housewife who could reduce the number of trips she made to the Lexington, Hanover, or Northeast markets.

Along with the growth in population and the modernization of the economy went a new sophistication in culture and social life. The Peabody Institute joined the older Maryland Institute and Maryland Historical Society as a cultural center for the city, and the opening of The Johns Hopkins University nearby at Howard and Monument streets in 1876 brought new respect for Baltimore's intellectual life. Lectures, musical concerts, and theater joined the excursions on the bay, picnics in city parks, and baseball among the choices Baltimoreans had for using their leisure time.

As middle-class parents observed the changes in Baltimore they became more conscious of the need for more and better education for their children—especially their sons. To be successful in this modern society as a businessman, accountant, engineer, chemist, teacher, or supervisor required more and better education than in the past. The knowledge and skills needed to compete for jobs and profits could often be acquired only through formal education. While modernization threatened to weaken some social institutions such as the family and church, it actually strengthened the school and increased education's importance. "No longer casual adjuncts to the home or apprenticeship, schools were highly formal institutions designed to play a critical role in the socialization of the young, the maintenance of social order and the promotion of economic development."[27] For those schools that re-sponded to the needs of this modern society the rewards were larger enrollments and a higher reputation in the community. Those that clung to older models of education too often found themselves unable to compete, especially with the rapidly expanding public schools.

Herein lies a large part of the explanation of why Friends School in Baltimore was able to survive while so many other Quaker schools disappeared. Few of the fifteen schools supported by Quakers within the Baltimore Yearly Meeting in 1884 lasted into the twentieth century despite the moral and financial encouragement that this larger body provided.[28] Survival required more than support from a distance, it required strong local commitment and leadership on the part of teachers and interested parents.

In Baltimore it was the leadership of Eli Lamb and the men and women who made up the Education Committee who encouraged expansion of the school beyond its narrow ante-bellum limits. Besides dividing the elementary school into primary and intermediate departments, they added the high school in the 1860s, a kindergarten in the late 1880s, raised academic standards, broadened the curriculum, improved the quality of teaching, and provided better equipment and facilities. Without these changes Friends School would have disappeared along with the gray bonnets and plain dress of past Quaker generations. Each month the Education Committee met with Cousin Eli to discuss the school's progress, evaluate and hire teachers, and generally review school policies and budgets.[29] The men and women who shouldered this burden were members of the middle-class business community, active members of the Society of Friends, and often parents of school-age children. In 1877 for example Cyrus Blackburn served on the committee with Michael Offley, a bookkeeper, and Joseph Matthews, Daniel Pope, and T. Burling Hull—all merchants.[30] These were men who were acquainted with the changing economic opportunities in Baltimore and supported the efforts to expand the school. They were not willing to give up the traditional Quaker values and manner but they accepted a broader purpose for the school. They knew that their sons and daughters would need to become competitive in the new urban environment.

Despite the concern and attention of the Education Committee, however, Eli Lamb, in his own quiet way, was still the dominant influence of Friends Elementary and High School until 1899. His first goal, as mentioned before, upon taking over as head teacher in 1864 was to add a high school to the elementary classes in order to give children a unified program of education. In the school catalogue of 1872, Lamb proudly claimed that

The design of this Institution is to afford to all who may become connected with it, facilities for acquiring *thoroughly* the groundwork of *solid, practical* scholarship, and to enable pupils to *commence* and *finish* a scholastic course, thus avoiding the disadvantages attending changes from one course of instruction to another, and from the separation of parents and children at a period when the latter so much need counsel and sympathy.[31]

The students who chose to attend Friends Elementary and High School in the building attached to the back of the meeting house on Lombard Street were soon given a choice in courses of study when they reached the highest or last four years. In 1872 Lamb added a "collegiate department" which was really an extension of the old high school classes. A few new subjects, such as differential and integral calculus, English literature, and "Modern History of Continental Nations," were introduced, but most of the classes were a continuation of the reading, mathematics, science, and language courses that the school already offered.[32] Lamb called this a "post graduate" program but it was apparently intended for students who planned to go to college, rather than as a terminal degree. Whatever the purpose of this "collegiate depart-

Illus. 4-3   Friends Elementary School students, Lombard Street, ca. 1883.

ment," Lamb and the Education Committee clarified and expanded the school's programs in 1877 by setting up an English course of study for those pupils not planning to pursue any more formal education, and a college preparatory course for those who intended to continue. For the first time Lamb acknowledged in the 1877 catalogue that Friends now had a twofold purpose: "first, to prepare students for the literary or scientific departments of any of the leading colleges; second, to give a practical yet liberal education to all who intended to finish their scholastic course at this Institution."[33] This increased emphasis on preparation for college was a direct response to the founding of Swarthmore in 1864 and more particularly of The Johns Hopkins University in 1876. The improvement was made, Lamb said, "in order that our graduates may go out ready to matriculate in our home university or any New England college, or may join the junior classes at Swarthmore."[34] The expansion was also encouraged by the Quakers of Baltimore Yearly Meeting. After surveying the existing schools in the larger region under the care of the Yearly Meeting, a special committee on education, of which Lamb was the clerk, proposed a system of schools, each offering the same subjects and using the same books. Swarthmore College would be at the top of the system.[35] With this encouragement more than half a dozen schools were formed by the monthly meetings near Baltimore and Washington, D.C. None of them, however, approached the size of Friends' Elementary and High School of Baltimore.[36] (Table 4–1.)

The reason for the success of Friends Elementary and High School was that it had expanded its purpose and its curriculum at the right time. The reorganization of 1877 that created a five-year "introductory" department and a four-year high school with a college preparatory option made the school an attractive alternative to the public school system. The public system included twenty-one grammar and thirty-two primary schools, all segregated by sex. There were also five English-German schools to serve the needs of the newly arrived immigrants and nine elementary-level schools for black pupils. Baltimore City College high school for boys, located at the corner of Howard and Centre streets, the Eastern and the Western Female high schools, made up the city's secondary schools.[37]

Although Friends was unique by being coeducational, its curriculum was not unusual for nineteenth-century schools. Students in the primary department were drilled daily in arithmetic, reading, writing, spelling, and geography. They learned manners and morals from "Gow's and Cowdrey's text-books" and practiced drawing geo-

Table 4–1

Schools in Baltimore Yearly Meeting, 1883

Monthly Meeting		When Organized	No. Mos. Taught	Number Friends Enrolled	No. of 1 Parent Family	Non-Quaker	Total Attend.	Average Age	Teachers
Baltimore	Friends Elem. & High School	1864	10	50	14	320	384	15	17
Sandy Spring	Friends School at Sandy Spring	1883		30		14	44	13½	1
Little Falls	Friends Central	1850	10	1	3	6	10	11	1
Gunpowder	Gunpowder	1876	10	14	2	2	18	12	1
Nottingham	Friends Normal Inst. at Rising Sun	1874	10½	9	6	40	55	13	2
	B. M. House Friends School	1876	10	6	4	38	48	14	2
	Friends Select School, Oxford, Pa.	1881	9	36	7	43	86	14⅔	3
Pipe Creek	Pipe Creek	1883	10	12	15	13		14	1
West Branch	Friends School at West Branch	1870	3	16	7	11	34	16	1
Alexandria	Friends Select School, Washington, D.C.	1881		2		26	28		4
Hopewell	Branson's School	1875	6	7		2	9	14	1
	Ridge School	1883	2	6		12	18		1
				189	58	527	734		35

Source: Extracts from the Proceedings, Baltimore Yearly Meeting, 1883, p. 32.

metrical figures. In the intermediate department teachers continued the same subjects, adding United States and ancient history, natural science taught from *Hookers' Book of Nature,* and algebra. Students also had the option of taking Latin, French, German, or drawing. When students passed the required entrance exams they could enroll in the high school.[38] The English course there consisted of four years of mathematics, four of English, three of history and natural sciences, and an option to take languages and drawing. The collegiate course was similar, with the additional requirement of Latin and Greek. Likewise the history courses covered Greece and Rome, rather than the United States.[39]

In other words the subject matter taught at Friends was not very much different from what had been taught in many schools in the mid-nineteenth century. Nevertheless there was an indication that at least the methods of instruction had begun to change. Cousin Eli and his fellow teachers replaced the old pattern of requiring mechanical memorization and recitation with greater variety in their approach. After 1871 the catalogue proclaimed:

> As our object is to teach *subjects*, rather than books, we are careful to urge upon each pupil the necessity of self-dependence, rather than reliance upon text-books. To test the students' knowledge, and to accustom them to original research, questions and problems, not contained in the text-books, are frequently suggested. As a further aid, we introduce lectures, and experiments with whatever apparatus may be applicable, and thus render it almost impossible, by presenting the subjects in various lights, for the pupil to fail to comprehend thoroughly, whatever may be under consideration.[40]

Teachers gave written examinations frequently and sent home report cards monthly, rating the pupil on each subject as either perfect, good, poor, very poor, or failing.[41] Teachers urged parents to take an interest in their children's education and to set aside study time for pupils at home. The classrooms opened at least one hour before school started in the morning for those who chose to study then.[42] No student was allowed to fall behind in his assignments: those "who fail in the preparation assigned for the regular sessions of the week, will be required to attend a special session for delinquents . . . in order that such failures may not result in disadvantage to the pupil, or to his class."[43]

Some of the teaching methods used at Friends suggest that the teachers tried to introduce new techniques for students of different ages. Following the new ideas of Pestalozzi that the child develops different learning capabilities at different times, the primary teachers at Friends introduced "object teaching" for nature study. The school catalogue described the method to parents in this way:

> Object lessons are the easy lessons, which nature gives to the child from its infancy. The closer we follow nature in her teaching, the more likely will we be to succeed; therefore, we should teach as she does, through the medium of the senses. The first instruction should be calculated to awaken, and stimulate the mental faculties of the child, and the attention should be directed to simple, surrounding objects. That instruction must begin with real perception of things. Present the object to the eye, and the lesson, readily comprehended, will be clear and stable. Proceeding upon this basis, we lay the foundation of future improvement. An object lesson is a systematic exercise in *thinking*; its purpose is to teach the student to *see* nature, to *think* as it observes, to *retain* the impressions made upon the mind, and be able to reproduce them at will.[44]

This method was in use at Friends in 1871, several years before the famous educational reformer, Francis Parker, began using it in the schools of Quincy, Massachusetts.[45]

At the same time methods changed, academic standards improved. Prior to 1879, Lamb informed the Education Committee, "it was determined to raise our standard and to endeavor to establish our school as a regular high-grade preparatory academy . . . ." Academic excellence was clearly Lamb's goal. But he may in fact have raised the standard too rapidly and too high to satisfy some parents. When the school received criticism in 1879, Lamb replied to the Education Committee that

> We introduce nothing into our requirements which will not contribute to the development of the human being into a perfect man or woman. Our object is the welfare of our pupils in every sense. We impose nothing to overtax, withhold nothing that may be required to strengthen them either intellectually, morally or physically. When we find that pupils are not able to do as much as their classmates we require less, and when circumstances seem to

make it proper we are prepared to substitute others for such studies as seem unnecessary or out of place in individual cases.[46]

The criticism Lamb referred to was probably from the parents of children in the college preparatory program. The class of 1879 was the first to finish the two-year preparatory course that was established in 1877. By June of 1879, however, Lamb reported that although the class had done all expected of them, they had not completed all the work; therefore he delayed their graduation six months.[47] It is hard to imagine that students accepted the unexpected extension of their work or that their parents agreed to pay more tuition without complaining to the principal and Education Committee.

Certainly the students due to graduate that year were not dullards, for in the fall term of 1878 they published the first issue of *The Oracle*, a quarterly magazine of student essays. The first number, edited by Robert M. Reese, a senior, contained short stories, poetry, translations of Latin and German literature, and several original essays. The final piece was a humorous comment on the competition between Friends and the local public schools. While all of the contributions have an appeal to juvenile tastes of the nineteenth century, the quality of the publication suggests that Eli Lamb was indeed successful in educating his pupils.

By 1879 the basic pattern of education in the school directed by Cousin Eli had taken shape and would remain much the same for the rest of the century. Physical education classes and music were later added to the curriculum, and there was a constant effort to replace and improve the school's supplies of books, maps, globes, and laboratory apparatus for teaching science. But the goals of preparing students for college by giving them a classical education, and of preparing other students for the business world by supplying them with a solid foundation in the liberal arts and sciences remained largely unchanged.

It was, however, time for another change in location. By 1884 the Lombard Street school and meeting house were becoming victims of urban growth. Located in what was now Baltimore's central business district, between Eutaw and Howard streets, the school suffered from the intrusions of the city environment. The school and parents alike believed that the number of saloons along Lombard Street were becoming a hazard to young boys and girls walking to school. Also the noise of city traffic and of nearby industries created too many distractions for fidgety scholars. Teachers and parents demonstrated their frustration and concern when they urged the Monthly Meeting to go to court to silence the boiler factory built next to the school.[48] Moreover the Lombard Street buildings were simply out of date. In 1884 the Education Committee complained of a defective furnace that blew dust and smoke into the classrooms, and they requested the permission of Baltimore Monthly Meeting to search for better quarters.[49] By July of 1885 Eli Lamb reported that he had found a suitable house at the corner of McCulloh and Preston streets near what is now called Bolton Hill.[50] It lacked a lecture hall and was generally not as spacious as the old school, but it was in a much more pleasing neighborhood.[51] And besides, the area was becoming one of the prestige neighborhoods of Baltimore where many prospective pupils lived.

Illus. 5-1   When the Lombard Street property was sold in 1887, Friends School moved to 1005 and 1007 McCulloh Street, at the corner of Preston Street. This building housed the Intermediate and High School.

CHAPTER 5

Friends Divided and Renewed

The relocation of Friends School from Lombard Street to McCulloh Street in the 1880s was a reaction to the changing pattern of Baltimore's social history, just like the move from Old Town had been in 1805. The earlier move reflected the westward shift of population and commercial activity as Baltimore improved its harbor and its inland transportation routes. The move in 1886 was likewise a consequence of population growth and economic development. West Lombard Street after the Civil War was in an area of commercial and industrial expansion. As Baltimore's population approached half a million, shops, stores, small factories, and warehouses demanded more space and pushed outward from the harbor to form an ever-larger, non-residential, commercial district. To meet the demands of the thousands of workers and employers who travelled daily from their homes to their jobs near the center of the city, urban technology provided several new methods of transportation. At first horsecars that ran on fixed iron tracks replaced the old, red, rough-riding omnibuses. After the Civil War residents could ride the horse-drawn cars for as little as five cents. In the 1880s the new electric-powered streetcars, which were cleaner and faster, replaced the horse-cars. The tracks stretched out through most of the city's neighborhoods, reaching as far as Towson, Pimlico, and Catonsville.

Most of the Quaker community, however, preferred neighbor-hoods that were not so far away from the meeting house and their places of business. The Bolton Hill area, which still had an atmosphere of openness and country freshness, was an attractive choice. Built on a hill overlooking downtown Baltimore and the harbor, the neighborhood had grown out of several large estates. Each decade after the Civil War saw the tastefully designed rowhouses spread toward the north and west to the boundary of the new Druid Hill Park. Like the Quaker mer-chants, many families of Baltimore's business and professional class found these brick homes and tree-lined streets suited to their social and residential needs. Many Virginians and ex-Confederates moved there after the Civil War because they found the neighborhood attractive to their tastes and sympathetic to their past.

The appeal of the neighborhood increased in 1876 when The Johns Hopkins University opened its doors nearby along Howard and Ross streets. In fact, in the last quarter of the nineteenth century this northwest part of the city from Mount Vernon Place at one extreme and Druid Hill Park at the other became the home of many of Baltimore's private schools. Loyola College began in 1852 at Calvert and Madison streets and Baltimore Female College was located at Beethoven Terrace. Bryn Mawr for girls, and Boys Latin and Marston's University School for boys were opened just a few blocks to the east. This northwest area had become one of the finest residential sections of the city and the home of many prospective students.[1] It was no surprise, then, that Eli Lamb sought suitable quarters for the Quaker school on McCulloh Street. Lamb himself, in fact, lived at 187 McCulloh.[2]

In 1886, a year after Bryn Mawr opened and the same year Cardinal Gibbons dedicated Corpus Christi Church on Mount Royal Avenue, Friends Elementary and High School moved to a four-story rowhouse with an enclosed brick yard at the corner of the block. The modest-size rooms of the former townhouse were equipped with the furniture from the Lombard Street school and were lit by gas chandeliers that gave them a slightly yellowish tint on dark, cloudy days or in the early evening. Lamb and the school committee tried to keep the facilities up to date in order to compete for students with the other private schools. The science rooms, for example, were outfitted with the specimens, chemicals, and apparatus needed to teach meteorology, geology, physical geography, zoology, physics, and chemistry. No longer bound by archaic methods that required only memorization and recitation, students were allowed to conduct experiments and examine real specimens. Laboratory work was now a part of science teaching. A large display case of over one hundred stuffed birds helped students understand ornithology, and seniors were encouraged to work in the chemistry laboratory that Lamb had thoughtfully located on the top floor where explosions from chemical accidents would at least not bring down the whole building.[3]

A source of pride in the McCulloh Street school was the well-equipped gymnasium. Housed in a separate, nearby building, Lamb and the teachers filled the gymnasium with all the barbells, rings, ladders, parallel bars, mats, and Indian clubs needed to turn Friends' scholars

Illus. 5-2   Friends Kindergarten and Primary departments, as well as the Gymnasium, were located at 1007 McCulloh Street after 1887.

into healthy young men and women. By the 1890s the school had accepted and encouraged the belief that physical education was an appropriate part of the curriculum and that physical development was important for mental progress. To further promote fitness and to maintain the general health of the larger number of students, the school committee approved the designation of a medical examiner, usually a physician who was an active member of Baltimore Monthly Meeting. Unfortunately the school physician did not preserve any medical records that would reveal whether the collection of barbells and gymnasium apparatus caused more damage than good for the young students.

The pupils who came to the new school at the corner of McCulloh and Preston streets were from much the same background and homes as previous students. Only a small number of the 235 students who attended classes in 1884 were the children of Quakers. The others came from the families of middle- and upper-middle-class Baltimoreans. Like the parents of the Quaker children, their fathers were businessmen, professionals, foremen, bookkeepers, and skilled laborers such as carpenters and masons. Few came from outside the city limits and most lived in northwest Baltimore along Park Avenue, Charles and St. Paul streets, and in or near Bolton Hill. Others lived to the west in the direction of the B & O's Mount Clare station. And there were many too, mostly Quakers, who continued to live in Old Town where the original meeting house still stood.[4] The families of the pupils were seldom among Baltimore's wealthy elite, but they had usually achieved the prestige of non-manual or white-collar status. The slowness with which Friends School turned to manual training as part of its curriculum may be a hint that most of its clientele expected their children to be employed in occupations where they worked with their heads instead of their hands. Manual training had become popular in many American schools by the 1880s, but was adopted by Friends only after 1900. Parents in Baltimore who wanted their children to learn special skills could send them to the new Manual Training School (Baltimore Polytechnic Institute) on Courtland Street, which opened in March, 1884. Besides, at a cost of $600 to $800 to send a child to eight years of school at Friends, few working-class families would have been willing to pay the cost of private education.[5]

As the school's standards and reputation gradually rose, the number of graduates who achieved position or recognition in the Baltimore community increased. Alcaeus Hooper, for example, who gave an address at his graduation from Friends in 1876, later became mayor of Baltimore in 1896. Dr. William I. Hull became one of the most respected faculty members at Swarthmore College; E. Stanley Gary became a member of Baltimore's business elite; and others served as judges, physicians, and teachers. When The Johns Hopkins University opened in 1876 many of the faculty sent their sons and daughters to Friends.[6]

This middle-class and upper-middle-class orientation of Friends School in the late nineteenth century was typical of private schools throughout the nation. Parents who could spare the children from working and earning wages usually saw the advantage of sending them to school at least into their early teens. Even if they did not complete a full course of study or receive a diploma—and many did not—they acquired enough formal education to enable them to compete in an increasingly white-collar society. The students learned not only the basic knowledge and skills needed to succeed in an urban environment, but they also learned the behavior and discipline demanded by business and society. Although corporal punishment was not used in the Quaker school, there was still an emphasis upon order and obedience. In nearly every report to the Education Committee Eli Lamb commented at length on the exemplary behavior of the children. Awards were given for perfect attendance and for "Perfection in Observing Rules and Deportment."[7]

Friends School was typical of Quaker education in the nineteenth century in its appeal to the student's conscience. Rather than relying on an excess of external rules and regulations as the Puritans did in earlier days, the Quakers tried to direct the child to proper behavior. While the public schools relied on "rattaning" until the 1880s, Lamb's faculty corrected disobedience with verbal rebukes and additional work. Instead of keeping students after classes, teachers required them to attend school on Saturday.[8] For those who refused to conform, dismissal from school was the common solution. "To be firm, without being severe," and "to *prevent* trouble and encourage a healthy degree of emulation in well doing . . ." were the guiding principles of the Quaker teachers. The two offences that most concerned Cousin Eli were the use of tobacco and vulgar or profane language. In nearly every annual report he commented on the presence or absence of these "evils" as an indication of how orderly and obedient the pupils had been. Eighteen-seventy-two was an unusual year because Lamb dismissed two students for using profanity.[9] And no one was given a diploma who used tobacco or vulgar language.

The growth and prosperity Friends Elementary and High School enjoyed by the mid-1880s was due to its enlarged curriculum, which offered classes from primary to high school in a single institution, and to its emphasis on preparing students for either the business world or for college. Part of the school's success, however, probably came from the reputation of Eli Lamb and his staff of teachers. As the faculty increased in size, the credentials that new instructors brought with them became more impressive. Initially in 1864 Cousin Eli was assisted only by his sisters, Philena and Rachel. Both taught for nearly two decades at Friends and specialized in teaching English, handwriting, history, and geography, but neither held any formal college degrees. By 1884, however, the number of teachers boasting degrees had increased. Professor Edward Deichmann, for example, instructor of German and Greek, held a Ph.D. from Leipzig; Sidney Frost, who taught natural science, had an A.M. from Amherst. Others had attended Haverford,

67

Illus. 5-3   Classroom, McCulloh and Preston streets, ca. 1890

Dickinson, and the Pennsylvania Academy of Fine Arts. Thomas W. Sidwell, who later founded a Friends school in Washington, D.C., also gained much experience and reputation by teaching several years at the school in Baltimore.[10]

By 1884 Lamb's faculty had developed a pattern or profile that was to change little over the next twenty years. Out of a staff of fifteen or sixteen, usually about a dozen were women. Women were preferred as teachers of the younger children in the primary and intermediate departments, but they were customarily paid about half what male teachers received. The salaries, which ranged between $350 and $500 for female instructors and between $600 and $1,000 for men, were, in the last quarter of the nineteenth century, typical of salaries in most urban American schools.[11] In the high school women taught English literature, French, painting, and drawing; the mathematics, history, geography, philosophy, German, and classical languages were offered by men. These divisions of labor and inequities in pay were a reflection of the prevailing attitudes towards the roles of the sexes in nineteenth-century society and suggest that despite their religious belief in the equality of men and women, the Quakers did not differ greatly from the rest of the community in the employment of females.

Besides the male-female pattern of the teaching staff, it was also characteristic of the school in the last quarter of the nineteenth century that all but two or three of the teachers were members of the Society of Friends.[12] Even though the school's administration secularized the curriculum in its attempt to prepare students to enter the larger community, the faculty were still expected to hold firm to the traditional values and beliefs of the Quaker society. That the school was always able to retain the Quaker influence without placing religious demands on the students and parents made it attractive to those who preferred a school with a greater emphasis on moral education than the public schools offered. The delicate mixture of emphasis on Quaker values and academic excellence that became characteristic of the school in the twentieth century had its origins in this post-Civil War era of Eli Lamb.

To credit Lamb and his faculty with all the success of Friends School in the nineteenth century, however, would be to make them larger than life. It is less heroic but more accurate to point out that the growth of Friends, as well as Bryn Mawr, Gilman, Boys Latin, and other independent schools that appeared before the end of the nineteenth century, benefited from the weakness of Baltimore's public schools.

Despite the city's relatively early start in public education compared to southern cities, the school system seemed to be floundering in the last third of the nineteenth century. In 1873, the assistant superintendent of schools reported that teaching was generally poor. Teachers required students to memorize rules of grammar or numbers in arithmetic without encouraging understanding. Classes of sixty to eighty pupils with one instructor were not uncommon and some taught over one hundred. As one historian of the public schools described these years:

> The schools were caught in a maze of municipal politics and the professional educators and those commissioners who were not pawns of political bosses were faced with endless frustrations. . . .
> The school facilities throughout the era were miserably inadequate, and overcrowding pupils in unhealthy quarters. . . was the rule rather than the exception.[13]

Teachers, who were not always well trained in the first place, had a high turnover rate. In 1890 nearly forty percent of the city's public school teachers had less than three years' experience. Since salaries tended to be low compared to other white-collar occupations or even to teachers in other urban areas, the large majority of instructors were women whose job opportunities were limited in the nineteenth century. When they married or had children, they usually left the profession permanently or for an extended period of time. Much of the teacher's effort was spent preparing students for examinations, because promotion to the next class was by testing and teachers were rated by the percentage of their pupils who passed. Overall, the public school teachers of that period have been described as "underpaid, lacking opportunities for training, burdened with oversize classes, dependent on ward politicians for appointment and promotion, and nevertheless expected to be paragons of virtue, models of citizenship, and incarnations of high ethical consciousness...."[14]

Not only did low-quality teaching retard the development of the public schools, but the erratic attendance and high dropout rate of pupils also disrupted the system. Too, many Baltimoreans gave in to the temptation to take children—especially boys—out of school at an early age and put them to work to increase the family income. The Federal census of 1900 found 20.6 percent of the boys and 14.5 percent of the girls in the 10–15 age group to be wage earners for their families. Other statistics showed that only 6 percent of those who began the first grade in the public schools ever graduated from elementary school. These figures did not improve until after Maryland passed its first compulsory education law in 1901.

At the same time the public schools were struggling against overcrowding and erratic attendance, there was also a tendency toward manual training in the city schools. The Manual Training School (Polytechnic) opened its doors in 1884 and Baltimore established the Colored Manual Training School in 1892. This movement to manual training in preparation for future occupations was common to public schools throughout the nation. The consequence, however, was that those parents who hoped to push their children toward college began to look more frequently to those schools that retained the classical and college preparatory courses of study. By the 1890s the competition for students of the middle and upper class was between the private schools like Friends and Boys Latin, and City College, which offered both a classical and a commerical course of study.[15] The demand was great enough and the private schools responded well enough that most of them entered the twentieth century financially sound. Friends School,

Illus. 5-4   Laboratory, 1005 McCulloh Street, ca. 1890.

however, had to pass through difficult times before it found stable conditions again in 1899.

Although the school's move from Lombard Street to Bolton Hill seemed at first to be the right thing to do, it proved instead to be the beginning of a major disruption in the school's history. Baltimore Monthly Meeting owned the building on Lombard Street where the school had been held, and the Education Committee received the principal's report, approved expenditures for enlarging or repairing the school, and regularly visited the classrooms to observe the teachers. But Eli Lamb was directly responsible for collecting the tuition from the pupils' families and for handling the daily financial affairs of the school. In return for this privilege, he paid Baltimore Monthly Meeting $800 rent per year for the school rooms on Lombard Street. Even though this relationship between the Meeting and the principal was a delicate one that required cooperation and trust, it was typical among Quakers at that time. In fact, earlier generations had found that it was often financially preferable both to the Monthly Meeting and to the teacher to let the latter collect the tuition and pay the daily expenditures. As long as everyone was agreed that the purpose of the school was to provide a guarded education for the children of members of the Society of Friends, there were seldom any differences that interfered with the relationship.

But the purpose of the school had begun to change after the Civil War. No longer set up exclusively for Quaker children, Friends Elementary and High School was by 1886 competing with other private institutions for a broader group of students. The school had expanded its purpose both because the Society of Friends itself had become more open and because modernization made many new demands of all the existing schools. Consequently the older, informal agreement between principal and Baltimore Monthly Meeting had become obsolete by the last quarter of the nineteenth century. The failure of the old arrangement was not obvious to any of the contemporaries, however, so long as the school stayed at Lombard Street. The physical proximity of school and meeting house—essentially in the same building—protected the Quakers' "gentlemen's agreement." Once the school moved, the inadequacy of the old relationship was exposed.

Specifically the issue that caused the break in the association between Eli Lamb and Baltimore Monthly Meeting was the discount allowed for children of Quaker parents. In order to encourage parents who were members of the local or neighboring monthly meetings to send their children to the school, Lamb and the Education Committee had offered tuition discounts of between forty-three and seventy-two percent.[16] In addition, a small number—seldom more than five or six—who were unable to pay anything at all were allowed to attend the school free of charge. The money for these discounts usually came from two sources: the Fair Hill Fund, which was an education fund within Baltimore Yearly Meeting, and the rent charged to Lamb for the use of the school building.[17] In 1886, however, when the School Committee presented Baltimore Monthly Meeting with a bill for $52, which was the balance of tuition of five pupils for one term, the Meeting rejected the bill saying they did not want "to incur any greater expense in educating the children above alluded to than can be met by the amount furnished from the income of the Fair Hill Fund. . . ."[18] Having lost the $800 per year rent of the school building, the Monthly Meeting decided by August 9, 1888, that "it was making too much of a debt for it to carry and the fact that the school was not on the grounds of the monthly meeting it decided to relinquish any connection with the school. . . ."[19]

The request for greater funding came at an inopportune time since Baltimore Monthly Meeting had just sold the Lombard Street property and was preparing to move into a new meeting house being constructed on Park Place. The Quakers who contributed to the new building project probably were feeling the bottom of their pockets and were in no mood to take on new expenses for the time being. Consequently from 1888 until 1899, when Baltimore Monthly Meeting formally purchased Friends Elementary and High School, the Society of Friends had no control over the school administered by Eli Lamb.

For the next eleven years Cousin Eli's school on McCulloh Street continued as before with little change in purpose or structure. Even many of the teachers remained the same, although the number of new instructors who had formal degrees continued to increase.[20] Young instructors like Stephen Harry, a graduate student studying mathematics under Dr. Frank Morley at Johns Hopkins, joined the faculty by the 1890s. Others came with degrees from Michigan, Bowdoin, Swarthmore, Washington College, and the Pennsylvania Academy of Fine Arts.[21] The most significant change was the addition of a kindergarten department for children, ages three to seven. With this improvement, Lamb continued his efforts to be competitive with Baltimore's best private institutions, and to provide a completely integrated course of study for his students. The severing of the relationship with Eli Lamb and the move to Park Avenue did not mean the end of Baltimore Monthly Meeting's interest in education or the end of their school. It only meant the end of a relationship in which they were not in complete control. No sooner had they broken with Lamb and moved into their new meeting house than they formed another school committee and opened their own school on April 1 of the following spring of 1889.[22] Their purpose was not to compete with Lamb's school but rather to provide for the needs of the Quaker community. In two rooms of the second floor of the spacious new building on Park Place they opened a kindergarten with nineteen pupils. Hannah Yardley took charge of the school at a salary of $500 and hired one assistant. The following fall the committee hired Louisa P. Blackburn to be the head of the primary department that opened in rooms above the library and the men's meeting room.[23] In both cases "The school [was] to be under the oversight of this committee, the teacher being responsible for any pecuniary obligations."[24]

In a sense the Monthly Meeting was reverting to its traditional concept of education in which the school would be self-supporting

Illus. 5-5   Gymnasium, 1007 McCulloh Street, ca. 1890.

financially and its primary purpose would be to educate the younger Quaker children during their value-forming years. High school and preparation for college were left to Eli Lamb and the other established schools. This new school—called Friends School at first and then Friends School and Kindergarten in 1890—concentrated on elementary education; and its main clientele were the children of Quaker parents, although non-Quakers were also invited to send their children.[25] Its location in the rooms above the meeting house of the new building was also a reaffirmation of the desire to keep education under the "care" of the Monthly Meeting.

What was new or different about this school was the kindergarten. Whereas Lamb had concentrated his efforts on developing a strong secondary level of study, the new school emphasized the education of younger children. The faculty was never large—only six by 1897—but they offered a full range of subjects at the elementary levels, including French and German, painting, drawing, and calisthenics.[26] The teachers added instrumental music and "voice culture" in the 1890s, indicating that the old Quaker restrictions on the use of music had weakened. The school purchased its first piano for $165 in 1894.[27]

Illus. 5-6   Friends Meeting House, Park Avenue and Laurens Street, ca. 1889.

The location of the school on the second floor of the meeting house was apparently intended to be a temporary arrangement, for by 1892 the Education Committee spent $7,000 to purchase an adjacent lot for the purpose of eventually building a school there. In 1895 they began a subscription for construction and within a year had over $19,000. That was barely one-fourth of the amount they needed and meanwhile the pressure to enlarge the school increased. The primary and kindergarten classes now had six teachers and almost sixty students. Moreover, by 1897 Louisa Blackburn, principal of the primary department, raised the issue with the Education Committee of the need for higher classes or grades beyond those offered.[28] Convinced by her arguments, the committee wrote to Baltimore Yearly Meeting appealing for funds and justifying the construction of a new school:

> Many Friends believe that a well-managed, graded school, under the care of the Society, preparing the young for the active business of life or for Swarthmore College, would prove of such inestimable advantage to all concerned, that it would receive substantial financial aid in the nature of Endowment Funds from members of the Society having means.[29]

At this point it was logical to consider a renewed relationship with Eli Lamb's elementary and high school. The old dispute between Lamb and Baltimore Monthly Meeting was apparently no longer a disturbing issue and Cousin Eli was still, after all, an active and respected member of the Quaker community in Baltimore. Who took the first step is not clear; but by October, 1898, the leaders of the schools were discussing the possibility of a merger between the Park Avenue school and Lamb's school.[30] They spent the fall and winter of 1898-99 organizing funding and on March 24, 1899, committees from each of the schools sat down to negotiate the final details. Baltimore Monthly Meeting purchased most of the usable equipment and furniture from Lamb's Friends Elementary and High School, and agreed to pay Cousin Eli ten percent of the gross income "from the pupils attending his school at this time for transferring the same to the Park Avenue school."[31] This was profitable to him since he had 132 pupils and a gross income from tuition of $10,250.[32] In addition Lamb was to be the associate principal, helping the new principal, John W. Gregg, whenever needed, and otherwise was to assume the regular responsibilities of a teacher. For these duties he was to receive a salary of $1,200, which was in addition to the money received for agreeing to the merger.

Baltimore Monthly Meeting was confident the merger arrangements would be acceptable to Lamb because they had already chosen Charles E. Cassell as the architect and granted a construction contract to Morrow Bros.[33] Cassell was a well-known architect who had designed the Greek Orthodox Church at Preston Street and Maryland Avenue, and the Graham-Hughes House at Washington Place.[34] With the help of a donation of $5,000 from John Jewett and $6,000 from the Fair Hill Fund, Baltimore Monthly Meeting raised enough money to lay the cornerstone on April 24, 1899, and the following September opened the doors of the new building to 154 pupils.[35]

Because Jewett had insisted that the new school be a large one, there was plenty of space in the Park Avenue school. Separate classrooms for the Intermediate and High School departments filled the main part of the new building. For the first time the school had rooms especially constructed for particular uses. The science laboratories were fully equipped with large tables and apparatus for experiments, and the art room was designed with a skylight. A large gymnasium, showers, lockers, and a separate library for the school's 3,000 books gave Friends some of the best facilities available in the city.[36]

The small school taken over by Eli Lamb thirty-five years earlier had come a long way by the end of the nineteenth century. Besides the new building in a choice location on Park Avenue, Friends School could quietly boast that its graduates were now accepted without examination at Swarthmore, Women's College (Goucher), and The Johns Hopkins University. Its coeducational basis, a strong faculty, and its special Quaker character were also a part of the school's advantages as it began the twentieth century in Baltimore.

*Illus. 6-1   The faculty (ca. 1900), after the school had moved to Park Avenue, included (seated, l. to r.)
Emily Steiner, Louisa Blackburn, Rachel Lamb, John Gregg (appointed Principal in 1899), Eli Lamb
(Associate Principal, 1899–1910), Bertha Baugher, Emma Broomell Newman, Anna M. Berger;
(standing, l. to r.) Roman Steiner, William Pike, Helen Eley, Hannah Yardley, Mary Broomell Hull,
Frances Hartley Shoemaker, Stephen Harry.*

CHAPTER 6

Emergence of a Modern School

As he had done so many times before, Eli Lamb stood at the entrance to the school and greeted each child who arrived on the Monday that school opened, September 18, 1899. Still dressed in a somber black suit faintly smudged with chalk dust here and there, he had been greeting students in the same manner on opening days for thirty-five years. His hair had grayed and he wore small frameless glasses now, but he still had the same warmth and dignity. Each student might have been a little awed by his serious appearance, but each knew that Cousin Eli respected his students. To them he was the figure of authority and the representative of scholarship and education. For the returning students Cousin Eli's presence was reassuring even though it was a sign that the leisurely days of summer were over and that a new school year had begun.

But this year would be different. To symbolize the transition to the new school, the teachers had assembled the pupils at Lamb's old school at McCulloh and Preston streets and marched them in two columns to the new building on Park Avenue at Laurens Street. The late-summer morning was clear and cool and the students must have looked forward with excitement to the adventure of exploring the new, spacious building. It was different, too, for Eli Lamb who stood on the steps awaiting them. For the first time in more than a third of a century Lamb would not be greeting his students as their headmaster. As part of the merger agreement, Cousin Eli handed over the principalship to a younger man, John W. Gregg, and assumed a new position as associate principal. At the age of sixty-four Cousin Eli was apparently ready to lay down part of the burden of administering a growing school. His new responsibilities as associate principal included teaching mathematics whenever needed and supervising the Intermediate Department study hall where "the natural dignity and kindly austerity of the old gentleman usually sufficed to keep perfect order."[1] He was neither in retirement nor was he the major moving force he had once been in the school. Lamb was still consulted on issues of importance, but the fact that none of the members of the school committee from his old institution at McCulloh and Preston streets were included on the new governing committee for the Park Avenue school suggests that his power was definitely diminished.

Perhaps it was just as well that Eli Lamb was willing to step aside and let younger men and women pick up the burdens of leadership. It was not that he was too old to carry out the responsibilities of the principal or that somehow youth was better than age in the role of principal; rather, it was simply that the world had changed considerably since Cousin Eli took over in 1864 and new ideas and new leadership were now needed. The foundations of the modern Friends School had been laid under Lamb's tenure. Future headmasters, teachers, students, and alumni would have to acknowledge the significance of this dedicated man in the school's development. He had broadened Friends beyond its narrow purpose—that of providing a guarded education for Baltimore's Quaker children—and made it into one of the city's best private institutions. Parents who wanted their children to be accepted into Johns Hopkins, Goucher, Swarthmore, and other first-rate colleges and universities knew that graduation from Friends would assure them of admission. The basic goals of college preparation and a broad, liberal education for all pupils had been firmly established under Lamb's leadership. Moreover, parents knew that Cousin Eli symbolized the Quaker values that permeated an education at Friends. Whether they lacked faith in the quality of education in the public schools or sought the prestige of a private institution, parents knew that their children would be exposed at Friends to teachers and administrators who possessed desirable social and moral values. The time seemed right for change and improvement in the school.

The Education Committee, made up of several women and men like Jonathan K. Taylor, a successful insurance agent, and other businessmen and professionals, recognized the need for new leadership as the twentieth century approached. For one thing the competition for students was more intense. Alongside advertisements that announced the opening of Park Avenue Friends Elementary and High School (the name was shortened to Friends School in 1900) were notices of opening classes for more than twenty other private institutions. In addition to the older competitors like Bryn Mawr, Boys Latin, and Marston's University School for Boys, there were the newcomers like the Country School for Boys (Gilman) and The Calvert School, both opened in

1897.[2] Professor Deichmann, who had once taught at Friends, now had his own college preparatory school on North Howard Street; and there were many others like the Baltimore Academy of the Visitation, the Milton Academy on West Hoffman Street, Franklin University School for Boys, and Miss Gover's School and Kindergarten on Carrollton Avenue. Already many of these schools had begun to adopt new and "progressive" methods of teaching that were attractive to parents. If Friends were to grow and compete for students, it could not cling too rigidly to the ways of the past. Some of the Quaker traditions could be preserved, but much of the curriculum, teaching methods, and financial operation of the school would have to keep pace with the rapid changes that were occurring in society.

Baltimore and the nation at the beginning of the twentieth century presented a far different environment from the one Eli Lamb found when he arrived in the decade of the Civil War. Both the city and the nation had grown and matured in the last half of the nineteenth century. Industrialization was in full swing, and the United States was now the leading economic power of the world. Baltimore, whose early wealth had come from trade, was turning more and more to manufacturing by 1900. The Pennsylvania Steel Company opened its Sparrows Point mills in 1887 and by 1915 Bethlehem Steel, which had bought out the older company, was one of the largest in the United States. Along the Jones Falls in the Hampden and Woodberry sections of the city were a diversity of manufacturing establishments, many of which produced cloth and ready-made clothing. By the beginning of the twentieth century, close to a quarter of Baltimore's working force was employed in some type of industry.

The continuing role of commerce was easily seen downtown at the inner harbor and along the wharves of Light and Pratt streets. Oyster boats bringing in their daily hauls moved in and out of the congested harbor alongside the steamers and sailing ships. The larger ocean-going vessels carried bananas and coffee from South America and took away flour and grains from western Maryland and central Pennsylvania. On shore the Light Street wharves were jammed with hundreds of horse-drawn wagons being loaded and unloaded. Hogsheads of tobacco lined the streets waiting to be auctioned off. Scores of workmen moved about along the bumpy, Belgian-block streets and wooden wharves counting cartons, shouting orders, and keeping the cargoes moving. The typical larborer wore the accepted uniform of the day, complete with vest, rolled–up sleeves, derby or straw hat, and often sported a mustache. It must have been a strong temptation for school boys and girls to slip away from classes for an afternoon to enjoy the excitement, smells, and noise of the harbor at the turn of the century.

More likely, however, when the children who attended Friends went downtown near the harbor it was with their parents to shop. Preparing for the fall school term usually meant a trip into the heart of the city where the large department stores were located. If it was too far or too hot to walk, streetcars delivered shoppers at the doors of Hutzler Bros., O'Neill's, Solomon's, Posner's, or Gutman's. The fare was only six cents. To the congestion of electric streetcars, pedestrians, and horse-drawn vehicles would soon be added noisy gasoline-powered automobiles in the first decade of the twentieth century.

Besides the excitement of the waterfront and the shopping districts, the Baltimore of 1899 had other enticements for school children. Whether they went by streetcar, horse-drawn carriage, or automobile, children and parents could enjoy a variety of entertainments and recreation. Electric Park, off Belvedere Avenue near Reisterstown Road, featured a swimming pool, boating, band concerts, two roller coasters, and a carousel. Big league baseball was also popular in Baltimore. During the week school opened in September, 1899, the Orioles were in fourth place behind Brooklyn, but earlier in the 1890s they had been National League champions three times with stars like Wee Willie Keeler and John McGraw.[3] Picnics in the city parks and cemeteries, excursions down the bay to Tolchester and Annapolis, train rides to the ocean, and bicycle trips—all were popular diversions at the turn of the century.

Baltimore, with over a half-million people, now could offer the best, and sometimes the worst, to its inhabitants. Evidence of the prosperity of the late 1890s was seen in the steady construction of new homes, offices, and public projects. The city had finished the North Avenue Bridge over the Jones Falls three years earlier and was planning the Court House on Monument Square. A good system of roads and streetcars encouraged construction of new homes in the suburban areas of Mount Washington, Catonsville, and Walbrook. East Baltimore was also rapidly expanding as the number of new immigrants from Europe, especially Germans, Russians, Poles, and Irish, settled in the brick rowhouses beyond Patterson Park.

Such rapid growth, however, carried with it problems. Health standards were still low and the lack of a unified sewerage system caused frequent epidemics of typhoid and yellow fever. Only after the great fire of 1904 did Baltimore build a modern system of sewers and storm drains. The disastrous fire also accelerated the trend toward the suburbs by convincing many residents that the crowded central city was not a safe place to live. Likewise the greater social diversity brought by the increase in the number of immigrants and southern blacks moving into the city created an atmosphere for conflict and potential violence. A glance at the headlines of the daily papers on the day the new Friends School building opened indicates the social intolerance that was prevalent in the nation. In Georgia a local railroad was indicted for breaking state Jim Crow laws by letting whites and blacks ride in the same passenger car. In Illinois six blacks were killed for the offense of merely entering a town to take a train. Abroad, the Dreyfus case involving anti-Semitism was still going on in France; American troops were crushing the movement for independence in the Philippines; and the Boer War was about to break out in the Transvaal.[4]

Externally, the United States was expanding its trade and enjoying its new-found power. Within a few years, during the presidencies of Theodore Roosevelt and Woodrow Wilson, and after World War I, the country would begin its reign as the most powerful and influential nation in the world. Domestically, the progressive era, which reached from the urban reform movements of the 1890s to the national political and social reforms of the next two decades, would bring the modernization of American life into full swing. It was indeed a new world that the leaders of Friends School were preparing students to face, one that held promise as well as apprehension.

The man the Education Committee hired to take charge of the new Park Avenue school during these changing times was John W. Gregg, only twenty-nine years old but with experience as the principal of Friends High School at Moorestown, New Jersey, and before that as a teacher at George School in Bucks County, Pennsylvania. With a salary of $1,200—about the average for school administrators at that time—he settled into a rowhouse at 2014 Park Avenue, only three blocks from the school.[5]

Except for the distinction of being the first principal of the enlarged school, however, Gregg made little impression on the institution's development. Instead, for the first few years the real guiding force was the Education Committee of Baltimore Monthly Meeting, and particularly its chairman, Jonathan K. Taylor. From the opening of the school in 1899, this committee of fourteen showed an interest in the administrative details that went beyond that of any previous committee. As Kirk Brown, a member of the committee who had previously served when the school was on Lombard Street, described the duties of the group, it was to provide "general supervision of the schools, education and financing matters. . . ."[6] To carry out these duties the members of the committee created about a dozen sub-committees to deal with books, admission, tuition, teachers, lecturers, property, decoration and hygiene, and other basic issues. The minutes of the whole committee show that no question was too large or too small to be excluded from discussion. They reviewed the credentials of new teachers, evaluated the performance of employed teachers, discussed salaries and the duties of janitors, and decided on the purchase of everything from classroom books to roller towels in the restrooms.[7]

The leader in the discussions and decisions was Jonathan K. Taylor, an educator who had been forced to turn to business. By the end of the century, Taylor was sixty-two years old and a successful agent of the Provident Life and Trust Company of Philadelphia. His first love, however, had been teaching and school administration. Failing eyesight forced him to give up his initial job as a teacher and later cut short an attempt to open and run his own school. It was natural that he should take an active part in governing the affairs of Friends School. His residence in fact was a large double rowhouse at 1615 Park Place, within a block of the school. He was well-liked and respected in the Baltimore Quaker community and for years gave his time and money to the school. Each year the student who won the Jonathan K. Taylor Debate was awarded a watch by the chairman himself.[8]

The other members of the committee were all active in Baltimore Monthly Meeting and were firm believers in the validity of the Quaker traditions. Surprisingly, eight of the fourteen members were women; but it is clear from the records that the men were dominant. Besides Taylor, other leaders were Richard Thomas, Treasurer; Seneca Broomell; Edward Stabler, Jr.; and Kirk Brown, who described his occupation as "collector and genealogist." Most who served on the committee in the first quarter of the twentieth century were merchants or businessmen, and most of them lived in the neighborhood of the school and meeting house.[9] These men and women kept a close watch on the school's affairs. They visited the classes regularly each month and discussed their impressions at the committee meetings.

Under their supervision the school prospered. By the third week of school there were 150 students enrolled in the four different departments: kindergarten, primary, intermediate, and high school. Fifteen teachers, including Gregg and Lamb, were hired by the school

Illus. 6-2 The Education Committee, ca. 1900: Jonathan K. Taylor, Chairman (seated, center); *Anne W. Janney, Secretary* (seated, third from left); *Seneca P. Broomell* (seated, left).

to give the most careful training to those entrusted to its care, that they may be prepared to enter upon the duties of later life with the spirit of independence developed and with the habits of industry and integrity established.

Further, it will aim to give a course of instruction which will afford an education at once practical and liberal for those not intending to do other scholastic work, and to those expecting to enter colleges or universities it will offer the most ample opportunities for preparation.[10]

No longer was mention made of providing a "guarded education" for children of Quaker families. Even in the minutes of the Education Committee the purpose of the school is specifically described as preparing students "for business or college."[11]

To all appearances the school entered the twentieth century in a strong position. By 1900 the name had been shortened to Friends School and both teachers and the Education Committee agreed that the "school is now in a most prosperous condition."[12] Nevertheless within three years the committee felt the need to make a change by firing John Gregg.[13] They recorded no reason for the dismissal, but the enrollment which reached 211 by 1901 declined each of the next two years to 201. The decrease was not great, but it must have been a disappointment to Jonathan K. Taylor and others who expected the enrollment to grow.[14] It might also have been a case of removing Gregg to make way for a man whom Taylor was enthusiastic to hire. In less than four weeks after the decision to dismiss Gregg, the committee hired Edward C. Wilson.[15] For the next quarter of a century he would be the steady Principal of the prospering Friends School.

At thirty-three, the same age as the departing John Gregg, Wilson had a dozen years of experience in Quaker schools. He graduated from Swarthmore in 1891, then taught at Barnard School in New York, next at Sidwell Friends School, and finally served as the head of the science department of Friends Central School in Philadelphia before coming to Baltimore.[16] A rather short man with a broad forehead, thin brown hair, and glasses, Wilson was a distinct contrast to the taller, bearded Mr. Gregg. His rimless glasses and three-piece suit gave Wilson a sturdy, serious appearance that could have passed for that of a banker or businessman as well as a school principal.

In fact, in some ways Edward Wilson was a very good businessman. From 1903 to 1927 Friends School grew in enrollment from 201 pupils to nearly 550 and its income increased from about $15,000 to over $150,000.[17] Always keeping one eye on the future, Wilson was keenly aware of the private school competition for students in Baltimore and urged the Education Committee to plan ahead. Within a short time after he was hired he clearly took over the leadership of the school from the committee. In monthly reports and meetings with the whole Education Committee, Wilson took charge by reporting on every detail of business related to the school and by making specific recommendations that were usually accepted. From hiring and firing teachers to planning the purchase of more property or making improvements in the buildings, Wilson was a strong, confident leader. No doubt his friendship with Jonathan K. Taylor and other members of the committee helped to solidify his position. But he received the same respect when he dealt with the business community in Baltimore or with the headmasters of other schools. Typical of Wilson's manner and attitude was his urging of the Education Committee to stay up-to-date in 1916: "We have prospered because we have delivered the goods. We must keep well abreast of market conditions, sort with sanity the new educational

Illus. 6-3   Primary Department, Park Avenue, 1904–05.

ideas that are coming before the public, adopt them when they are proved right and avoid them when they are merely fads."[18]

Those students and teachers who remembered Edward Wilson in later years describe him as a "good administrator," one who commanded dignity and respect. Felix Morley, who attended Friends from 1903 to 1911 and who knew both Wilson and Lamb, believes that Wilson was a major figure in the development of the school. Selma Levy Oppenheimer, who graduated in 1915, remembers Wilson as "very stiff." Others remember Lamb as more "Quakerly" and Wilson as primarily interested in the school. Under Wilson there were no prayers or weekly meeting for worship required of the students or teachers.[19] The principal was still a Quaker who cared about Quaker values, but he was first of all a modern, professional educator.

This same shift toward professionalism occurred among the men and women who taught at Friends during Wilson's administration, from 1903 to 1927. When the merger occurred in 1899 those teachers with the strongest credentials were most likely to stay on. At least thirteen of the faculty at Lamb's old school were not rehired, but the younger faculty with one or more college degrees moved on to Park Avenue. Stephen C. Harry, who had been an undergraduate and graduate student at Johns Hopkins, was retained; and William S. Pike, a graduate of West Chester State Normal School with two more years at Harvard, was hired to teach science. Both of these young instructors would become an important part of the faculty in the next third of a century. Others who had been teachers at the previous Baltimore Monthly Meeting school on Park Avenue, like Louisa P. Blackburn, the former principal there, were retained after the merger.[20] The majority (twelve of eighteen) of those who made up the faculty in 1899 were members of the Society of Friends and had attended Quaker schools.[21] By 1915 the proportion who were Quaker had declined to less than one-third, but the number who were graduates of Hopkins, Goucher, Swarthmore and other east-coast colleges had increased.[22] In fact as early as 1908 Wilson boasted to the Education Committee that "the school now possessed a corps of teachers with a fine unity of purpose and force of action, with no weak spot apparent in the faculty." He worked hard at encouraging cooperation and a positive attitude among his staff. Besides weekly teachers' meetings, "Tea was served each day in the Office at 2:30 P.M., with Elizabeth Wilson presiding and on each 6th day evening [Friday] the Faculty was invited to the principal's home for a social and very informal commingling, by which means it was thought a good and close fellowship might be engendered."[23]

Wilson's success in building a strong faculty was echoed in the appreciation of both parents and pupils. Maurice U. Cahn, for example, whose son, Edgar, attended Friends, gave $1,000 to Wilson after the 1918 commencement to be divided among Edgar's teachers for the last two years.[24] Felix Morley recalled that there was no generation gap between the students and teachers when he attended Friends before 1912: "you didn't regard your teachers as being of a different world or a different climate or a different breed of human being."[25]

Among the best remembered and most capable teachers who made up the core of the faculty in the early twentieth century were Stephen C. Harry and William S. Pike. These two, along with Roman Steiner, were soon known as the "Old Guard" since they were on the original faculty of 1899 and remained after all the others were gone. Stephen Harry had actually begun as an assistant in mathematics in 1890 at Lamb's school at McCulloh and Preston streets. After the merger he was well enough respected to be made head of the High School Department at Friends.[26] Whether students loved or hated mathematics, they remembered their classes with Mr. Harry. A tall man with short, light hair, parted down the middle, he was a sober and precise teacher. Many a student in the small classroom behind the second floor study hall sat quietly in his seat hoping Mr. Harry would not call him to the blackboard to work out a problem in algebra or trigonometry. When students failed to come up with the correct answers, Mr. Harry was likely to chide them in stern Quaker language: "I can see thee did not study thy lesson today." Or to a young Felix Morley, whose propensity was more to literature than mathematics, he wryly lamented, "Thee makes my hair curl." But Harry had his warmer, lighter moments too when he coached teams on the athletic fields or took it upon himself to teach students how to dance. He was also recognized as the "champion top-spinner in the school yard...."[27] Eventually his reputation as a mathematics teacher spread throughout the state and he moved to City College in 1921 after thirty-one years at Friends School.[28]

William S. Pike was another of the "Old Guard" who won an affectionate place in the memories of Friends students. His career was synonymous with the opening of the merged school at Park Avenue and Laurens Street. In the small classroom laboratory at the south-west corner of the third floor Mr. Pike cheerily greeted his students each day to his chemistry and science classes. A short, stocky man with thick, dark hair, glasses, a heavy black mustache, and distinct dimple in his chin, William Pike quickly developed a strong bond with most of his students. Like Harry he had a ready reply for the slow-witted or unprepared student: "If thee can't get it for thyself, I guess I will have to feed thee with a spoon."[29] Carefully supervising each student's experiment in chemistry or physics, Mr. Pike usually mixed a little of his homey Quaker philosophy with his science. Barely a week passed, for example, without his reminding pupils that the money he saved by not smoking and drinking paid for a nice family vacation each year. He was also remembered as the first teacher to buy an automobile, a Ford, which he used to commute to school each day from his residence outside the city at Paradise and Prospect avenues in Catonsville where he lived with his bride. But most of all he left his mark as a teacher. "Pike was the best natural teacher I ever saw," recalled one graduate, "and could teach anything from handwriting on up. All he needed was to be two jumps ahead of the students and he could go from there."[30] Unfortunately his talents were lost to the classroom in 1927 when Edward Wilson retired and Pike was made headmaster by the Education Committee. He was a conscientious administrator, but his true talent was teaching.

The third member of the "Old Guard" was Roman Steiner. Like Pike, Steiner came to the school in 1899 and was put in charge of manual training. From then until he died in 1952 (on commencement day), many generations of Friends students filled their parents' homes with the woodcarvings, bookends, stools, magazine racks, and chests made in Roman Steiner's woodworking classroom in the basement of the school. He was also an art instructor and was placed in charge of the school chorus, which all students were expected to attend. The woodwork his students produced suggested that he had considerable talent for teaching the practical arts, but those students who attempted to be more freely creative found Steiner's instruction too rigid.[31] He was excellent in teaching pupils mechanical drawing and the proper use of handtools, but some thought him too conservative to allow them to develop their talents in painting and sculpture.

Music was Steiner's first love, however, and he was active in a number of capacities. He composed the music for the school Alma Mater, sang in the choir at St. Ignatius Church, taught music part-time at Sidwell Friends School in Washington and at McDonogh School, directed the music at Corpus Christi Church, formed the Handel Choir, and was assistant conductor of the Baltimore Opera Society.[32] Despite his dedication to the arts, however, his classes were sometimes chaotic.[33] Knowing he was not a disciplinarian, students occasionally "cut up" in his modeling classes or in chorus practices. In 1924 the Education Committee acknowledged both Pike and Steiner for twenty-five years of service to Friends School; the latter received a $250 gift and the former was given $500 in gold.[34]

But these were not the only notable teachers who shaped the course of education at Friends in the first quarter of the twentieth century. There were others too who, through professional expertise in the classroom or through the force of their personality, left their marks. Two fascinating individuals whose reputations reached beyond Friends School to the broader Baltimore and Maryland communities were Louis E. Lamborn and M. Letitia Stockett. No student who had the good fortune to come into contact with either of these two outstanding teachers ever forgot the experience. In many ways they were quite different personalities, but their impact on pupils and colleagues was nearly equal.

Louis Lamborn was one of the most dynamic teachers ever to teach at Friends. Born at Still Pond on the Eastern Shore of Maryland, he grew up in a free and open atmosphere that gave him a love for the outdoors, for horses, athletics, and what Teddy Roosevelt would have applauded as the "vigorous life." After managing a ranch in Idaho and finishing a degree at Dickinson College, with a few years of teaching experience in between, he was invited to join the Friends School faculty in 1916 and was placed in charge of boys' athletics. Headmaster Wilson described him to the Education Committee as "a man of splendid personality and character and I believe will succeed."[35] He was an immediate hit with the school children, especially the boys who named him "Doc" Lamborn—the "Doctor of All Those Things That Make a Man a Boy Again."[36] When he left temporarily after only one year to join the army at the start of World War I, the students dedicated their yearbook to him.[37] The power of his personality was also reflected in Wilson's reports to the Education Committee, which revealed an uncharacteristically Quaker pride in Lamborn's rise to a captaincy in the Reserve Officers Training Camp at Fort Meyers, Virginia.[38] After the war, when Pike turned down the principalship of the High School Department at Friends, Lamborn accepted it in 1921 with full faculty endorsement.[39] In this administrative position and in his coaching, "Doc" Lamborn revealed his love for military-style discipline among his pupils. When he lined up the high school students in neat rows along Park Place in front of the school for exercise each morning, no one objected that these quasi-military drills might be contrary to the pacifist Quaker tradition. In 1925 he left Friends to take over as headmaster of the faltering McDonogh School where he put his military principles of discipline to full use. Friends lost more than a good teacher and administrator in Lamborn, since a number of boys withdrew from Friends and followed him to McDonogh.

Letitia Stockett was in many ways the antithesis of Louis Lamborn. What he was to athletics and the "masculine image," she was to English literature and the budding writer. Described as an "outstanding teacher," a "wonderful, inspiring," and even "thrilling" lecturer, she was highly regarded by her pupils, but unlike Lamborn she held herself slightly aloof.[40] Her warmth and sensitivity came out in her published poetry and in her witty classroom style, but she was not one to become "pals" with her students. Besides giving them a love of poetry, literature, and English history, she drilled them persistently in language and grammar. Once again Edward Wilson's judgment of character and his ability to recognize superior talent were evident when he evaluated her in her first year at Friends: "Her students are very enthusiastic about her. She is alert, keen, and sympathetic, and I believe will prove to be

one of the best all-round cooperators we have had in a long time."[41]
Eventually her reputation reached beyond the school to the city and
state where she was known as a popular speaker, poet, and author of
several books, including the witty and lighthearted *Baltimore, A Not
Too Serious History* and *America First Fast & Furious*.

For the most part Wilson continued to build a solid staff of
teachers. His expectations were firmly stated in the school catalogue:

> That which we are we shall teach, not voluntarily, but
> involuntarily, and . . . therefore the instructors of our youth should
> be exemplary in habits and speech; that thus only may they hope
> to lead and mould the lives of youth aright.
>
> We seek the services, as instructors, of men and women who
> shall as far as is humanly possible serve these ends and who have
> chosen teaching as their permanent work; who are willing to
> forego any practices or habits not desirable in youth; who are
> vigorous and positive in presence and personality; who are trained
> to do one thing well; who are young in spirit and understand the
> problems of boys and girls; who have faith in God, in themselves,
> and in the righteousness of their profession.[42]

Many of the teachers hired to fulfill these goals were graduates of
Friends School in Baltimore or of Quaker schools elsewhere, although
by World War I the majority were not members of the Society of
Friends. The greatest number of teachers attended Goucher, Hopkins,
and Swarthmore, but their colleges also included Cornell, Wellesley,
West Chester State Normal School, and Maryland State Normal
School (now Towson State University).[43] Those with prior experience
usually had taught in private institutions, although there were notable
exceptions like William R. Flowers, who became head of the Intermediate Department in 1914 after being principal of Public School No.
49 on Cathedral Street. He eventually went back to the public system
when he accepted the principal's position at Eastern High School in
1921.[44] A few others had unusual backgrounds. For example, Elizabeth
C. Remmert, a native of Germany, was hired by Wilson after she was
dismissed from Western High School at the start of the war for failing to
become a U.S. citizen. She was a popular teacher at Friends and she
spent the rest of her career there teaching German, French, and
Spanish.[45]

Wherever they came from, these teachers who built the solid
reputation of Friends School in the twentieth century were not at-

tracted by monetary rewards. Most salaries of teachers during the Wilson years from 1903 to 1927 were only slightly better than the national averages. In 1904, for example, William Pike earned $1,250, which was close to the national norm for city schools.[46] By 1920, with more than two decades of experience behind him and having achieved a reputation as one of the school's best teachers, he was paid $3,000, compared to the national average for men of about $2,200. The only person earning more was the headmaster. Edward Wilson was handsomely paid, especially after 1905 when he received an attractive offer elsewhere and hinted of leaving Friends. In order to hold him Jonathan Taylor and the Education Committee offered Wilson $3,500 plus 40 percent of the net profits after expenses and repairs. It was an offer Wilson could not refuse, and it certainly must have been an incentive for him to promote school growth for the next two-and-a-half decades.[47]

Like other institutions and like the larger society itself, Friends School discriminated against women. Female teachers usually made about half what men made, regardless of their years of experience or quality of teaching. Caroline Norment, a popular English teacher who wrote the lyrics for the *Alma Mater*, made only $875 in 1914, while Wilbert Martin, the Latin instructor, was paid $1,800. Louis Lamborn in 1920 received twice as much as Letitia Stockett.[48] The same attitude prevailed in administration. Women were assumed to be "unambitious, frugal, and loving," and therefore understanding of students, but men were expected to be in charge of the institution.[49] None of this condemns Friends School; it was simply typical of its time despite its history as the pioneer in coeducation in Baltimore. By the 1920s sex discrimination was coming into greater criticism, but significant change was still a half-century away.

On the whole, Friends' growth during the Edward Wilson era from 1903 to 1927 was representative of a number of changes in the nation and in Baltimore. Compared to earlier decades and certainly to the Great Depression that followed, those were prosperous years. By 1910 the Education Committee reported that income had increased 100 percent over the previous seven years, and that type of growth continued into the inter-war decade.[50] By 1922 Edward Wilson proudly announced that Friends had a financial surplus while its competitors like Bryn Mawr, Gilman, and Park, all of whom charged higher tuition, did not. Even so, the following year he concluded that the years of expansion were over for Friends. Enrollments could not grow much larger and tuition increases could not be made too frequently.[51] These concerns would eventually be a part of the argument for moving the school out of the city, following the trend to country day schools.

Undoubtedly, Friends had continued to prosper in the early twentieth century from the inadequacies of the public school system. In 1898 the city revised its charter and made improvements in the school system. The new document reduced to nine the number of commissioners appointed by the mayor and empowered them to select a professional supervisor for the schools. While this change eliminated some of the political cronyism among the people directly in charge of the schools, it apparently did not resolve all of the problems; and parents continued to seek other alternatives. In 1912 the Park School was formed by supporters of Dr. James H. Van Sickle, who was fired as superintendent after a dispute over new programs. Dr. Hans Froelicher and other disgruntled parents established this new private school not far from Friends on Auchentoroly Terrace near Druid Hill Park. There it soon gained a reputation as a leading proponent of progressive education. Edward Wilson commented on the occasion of Park's opening that private schools were prospering because the public schools "are demoralized." He attributed part of the independent schools' success to their ability to offer full responsibility or full care throughout the school day for children.[52]

The number of parents who abandoned the public schools grew in 1921, when a survey revealed that about half of the 140 elementary schools then in use ought to have been closed because of poor or unsafe conditions. Many of the others were in need of renovation. About 4,500 students were taught in makeshift annexes, and thousands of others were on part-time shifts or had portable buildings, halls, and cloakrooms for classes.[53] With conditions like these, parents readily sought the private school alternatives.

By 1926 when Edward Wilson's health failed and he began to make plans for his retirement, he urged the Education Committee to study the prospects for the future and warned them about the need to stay competitive. By then the competition he felt was not so much with the public schools as with the other private institutions. The following year, 1927, he retired and turned the principalship over to the school's most respected teacher, William S. Pike. But Wilson knew that he had brought the school a long way. On the foundation that Eli M. Lamb had laid, Wilson constructed a modern institution staffed with professional teachers who served a prosperous portion of Baltimore's population.

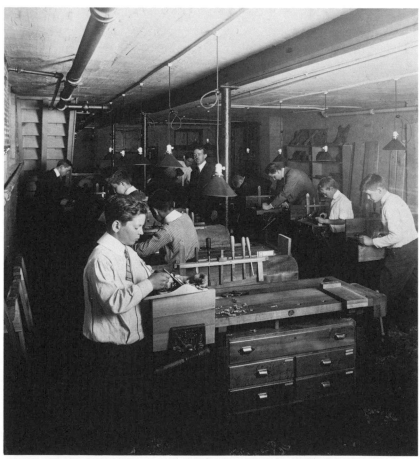

Illus. 7-1   Roman Steiner (center, rear), *Woodworking Class, ca. 1912.*

CHAPTER 7

School Life at Park Avenue

The students who attended Friends during the period of Edward C. Wilson's headmastership, from 1903 to 1927, were there at a time of rapid change. Since 1784 Friends had undergone several stages of development, the last one before the twentieth century being the evolution from a small Quaker school to a respectable academic institution under the guidance of Eli M. Lamb. Now in the first third of the new century, Friends made another incremental step toward maturity. Once again the changes in the school mirrored the changes in Baltimore and the nation. Rising from the destruction of the 1904 fire, Baltimore regained its position as the country's seventh largest industrial center by World War I. Charles Schwaab had purchased Sparrows Point for Bethlehem Steel, and Canton, Curtis Bay, and other areas along the outer harbor were the sites for more expansion. Another annexation of county land in 1918 reflected the growth of Baltimore and clearly indicated the movement of population toward the suburbs. The 1920s, when H. L. Mencken was at his height, was an exciting but restless time; it was the decade of automobiles, jazz, and radio, as well as the period of prohibition, anti-Semitism, the KKK, and youth rebellions. In this first urban decade, when a majority of Americans now lived in cities, new burdens and responsibilities fell upon the nation's public and private schools. Expansion was rapid because school attendance was now the norm, rather than the exception. For Friends School the changes were evident in the students who attended and in the routine of their school day.

In the classroom an expanded curriculum and new methods of teaching prepared more students for college and readied more of them for careers in the Baltimore business and professional community. Outside the classroom extracurricular activities and a variety of sports programs began to dominate the students' free time and became a factor in the growth of school spirit and identity. Even for the observer unaware of John Dewey's progressive educational ideas or G. Stanley

Hall's writings on adolescence, it was obvious that youth were becoming the center of attention. Teachers, administrators, and education committees might still teach the classes, set the curriculum, and pay the bills, but the students' needs and desires were requiring more attention. As F. Scott Fitzgerald, a resident of this same neighborhood, later wrote of youthful rebellion, the students of Friends School on Park Avenue, in a more mundane way, experienced the realities of these decades of change.

At eight-thirty in the morning, when the building opened, students began arriving at the large stone structure facing Park Place. For those who lived nearby in the surrounding neighborhoods now called Bolton Hill, Eutaw Place, and Mount Royal Terrace, it was a short walk to school. They often came in groups or with a few friends, like the "Reservoir Street Girls" who lived just a few blocks to the north.[1] Even without a required dress code, the boys were all dressed in jackets, white collars, and ties. The younger ones wore knickers, but the high-school boys wore long trousers like the faculty. Girls wore dresses with long sleeves and high collars in the turn-of-the-century style. By 1921, however, after two weeks of discussion, the students voted in favor of uniforms for all girls above the second primary class. Most came to like the blue serge outfits with white cuffs and collars.[2]

For those students who dawdled too long on pleasant spring days or who were perpetually slow getting ready in the mornings, it was a short run rather than a walk to school. To be late meant to face Miss Alice Farquhar, Edward Wilson's assistant. Excessive tardiness would result in Miss Farquhar's sending the procrastinator back home where surprised parents were expected to remedy the situation.[3]

When the weather was decent, walking to school could be a pleasant experience—even interesting. Besides the classmates and other students from Friends that one could meet, there was a variety of other people along the streets. After World War I, when the automobile began to take over as the principal means of transportation, there were still plenty of businessmen and clerks on their way to work in downtown offices, and usually a few professors and scholars going to class at nearby Johns Hopkins or the Maryland Institute. Earlier, Woodrow Wilson had been a Hopkins student boarding a few blocks away; and several of the university's world-famous physicians were local residents. In later years during and after World War I these same streets were inhabited by such luminaries as Gertrude and Leo Stein, Dr. Claribel Cone and her sister Etta, writer and educator Edith Hamilton,

Illus. 7-2   Friends School, Park Avenue.

and, for a short time in the 1930s, by F. Scott Fitzgerald. In truth, however, the schoolchildren were probably more interested in their own peers than in Baltimore's famous residents. In addition to their classmates, there was also the pleasure of meeting pupils from other schools like Bryn Mawr, Marston's, or the public institutions.

For those in high school who had a crush on someone, the thing for a boy to do was to walk his best girl home in the afternoon and to stop by Fiske's Confectionery at 701 West North Avenue. Even if one wasn't in love, it was worthwhile to stroll past Fiske's because Miss Marion, the short, plump clerk with the rosette in her hair, gave out cookies on occasion.[4]

But as Friends grew from an enrollment of 154 in 1899 to over 500 by 1927, there were more and more students who lived too far away to walk. For them the streetcar and later the automobile or bus was the answer. At fifteen cents for the roundtrip, the streetcar was cheap enough in those pre-Depression days. Coming from the east or west, the streetcars dropped pupils at the intersection of North and Park avenues. A few came long distances from near Clifton Park or even from East Baltimore, and others came from communities like Walbrook and Forest Park. After World War I, when the city expanded to the north, more children came from Guilford, Roland Park, Homeland, and Govans.

It was also after the war that Friends added bus service to its facilities. The school purchased three Reo buses to carry kindergarten and first primary pupils to school, and to transport older students to the athletic field in West Forest Park. These vehicles, which looked like large boxes set on spoked wheels, were driven by men in scarlet and gray uniforms, with puttees, and "FS" monogramed on their caps. One route ran west toward Forest Park and Arlington, and the other brought students from the Charles Street and Roland Park areas.[5]

As the bus routes suggest, Friends drew its enrollment from the middle- and upper-middle-class neighborhoods of Baltimore. Alumni Office records, schools committee records, and oral interviews with former students indicate that while Friends' students were seldom from the ranks of those in the social register, they came from parts of the city where families lived above the average standard. In 1907 Edward Wilson twice reported to the Education Committee "that the average class of pupils appeared to be constantly improving, being drawn more and more from the most desirable people."[6] The "desirable people" were businessmen and professionals of various types: they owned or ran insurance, printing, and roofing businesses, five-and-ten-cent stores, funeral homes, department and clothing stores, or were physicians, lawyers, teachers, and other professionals. Baltimore writer Gerald Johnson described the residents of Bolton Hill, many of whom sent their children to Friends, as being "what they call in Boston 'comfortably off' and in North Carolina as 'well heeled.' "[7] A graduate of 1912 put it simply when he described the families of his classmates as "distinctly middle class with a strong professional lacing . . . ."[8] The Friends School of World War I days and the 1920s was not where the rich or the social elite sent their children—there were boarding schools and more expensive prep schools which served that class—but it was a school attractive to a rising business and professional clientele who sought a sound moral and academic education for their offspring. The alumni rolls from these years show names like Hutzler, Hecht, and Kohn, all familiar to Baltimore department store shoppers, or like Jonas Friedenwald and Lawson Wilkins, men who would become prominent physicians at The Johns Hopkins Hospital. As the sons and daughters of this pre-Depression generation succeeded and prospered, the reputation of Friends School continued to grow. In the post-World War II period Friends was firmly established as an academically sound institution with particular appeal to the professional and business class. As one respected authority on Baltimore's private schools in the 1970s put it, while "patrician . . . families with daughters to educate, . . ." might go elsewhere, "The college-bound daughter of a successful intown lawyer would be prone to choose Roland Park or Friends. . . ."[9]

But if Friends was able to appeal to an increasingly prosperous clientele, it also retained a diversity of students on its rolls. Continuing the tradition established in the nineteenth century, Baltimore Monthly Meeting provided financial assistance to children of Quaker families who could not afford the tuition. Moreover, the number of scholarships available to all students, regardless of religion, increased. By 1915, with gifts made by John Buffington and several anonymous donors, Friends gave scholarships to about twelve students each year. Jonathan K. Taylor added to the endowment with a bequest in 1923. This tradition of assisting students continued through most of the twentieth century. In 1976 when Dr. Otto Kraushaar compared Baltimore's private schools, he concluded that the institution "using its scholarship funds most effectively to recruit a diversified student body is the Friends School."[10]

The recruitment of children from a wide range of families was made easier by Friends' comparatively low tuition. In 1899 annual tuition ranged between $50 for the kindergarten classes and $125 for high school. Extra charges were required for music and art classes, and students were responsible for buying their own books and supplies.[11]

Sixteen years later kindergarten costs were still the same and high-school tuition had risen to only $175.[12] That same year Bryn Mawr charged $250 tuition. The clearest comparison of Friends' financial advantage over its competitors was in 1926 when Edward Wilson carried out a study of private school fees. Among the seven schools that Wilson reviewed, all were more expensive than Friends.[13] Part of Friends' advantage was that all the others were more recently founded and were still paying off large construction debts.[14] These were prosperous years for Friends, and low tuition kept the school within financial reach of many Baltimore families.

The diversity of students who attended Friends was social and religious as well as economic. When the new school opened on Park Place in 1899, not only were the Quaker children a minority, but there was a significantly large proportion of Jewish students. Exact statistics on the number of Jewish pupils at Friends before World War I do not exist, but it was certainly high, perhaps as much as 20 or 30 percent.[15]

Illus. 7-3   Primary Classroom, Park Avenue, ca. 1912.

This high concentration was the result of two factors: the tradition of acceptance among Quakers of "all God's children" and the proximity to the school of Jewish families. The Society of Friends had a long history of respect for minorities in Baltimore, dating back to the days of Elisha Tyson and the antislavery activities of the early nineteenth century. School catalogues in the 1870s reflected a positive attitude by announcing to prospective parents that students who could not attend Saturday activities because of religious beliefs could make other arrangements.[16] Jewish and Protestant students mixed freely in the classrooms and on athletic teams, though there was less social exchange after school hours or when students dated.

The enrollment at Friends also benefited around the turn of the century from the many Jewish residents in nearby Eutaw Place. Successful German-Jewish immigrants and their descendants had settled in these neighborhoods of spacious three- and four-story rowhouses. Eutaw Place, a broad, tree-lined street with serpentine walkways in the center park and attractive monuments and fountains, was one of the more elegant neighborhoods of turn-of-the-century Baltimore. It was within walking distance of the downtown business district, and of several academic and cultural institutions, such as The Johns Hopkins University and The Maryland Institute.

By World War I, however, Jewish enrollment at Friends sharply declined, mainly because of the opening of Park School. Dr. Hans Froelicher, a leading academician and former acting president of Goucher College, opened the school to apply the newest progressive ideas of John Dewey, and to protest against discrimination in public and private schools. Friends' Jewish enrollment fell to only 22 students out of a total of 499 by 1921, a proportion of only 4 percent.[17] Nevertheless this loss was not lamented by the administration, for it coincided with the notorious Red Scare at the end of the war, when Americans, still suffering from wartime propaganda and fear of foreign influences, attacked the rights of anyone they considered to be less than 100 percent American. Anti-Semitism, anti-Catholicism, and racism settled upon the American society, contrasting with the appeal for justice and human rights voiced by Woodrow Wilson at the peace conference. Even those who recognized the inequalities were not immune to the temptation to follow the will of the majority. Headmaster Edward C. Wilson remarked to the Education Committee that while "Personally I feel that our boys and girls ought to come in contact with other boys and girls of good character of many nationalities and religions and that character should be the determining test," he believed "that our Gentile enrollment has grown and improved to some extent because of the large decrease in attendance of Jews."[18] Such sentiments are not commendable, they are merely a disappointing reminder that even the strong tradition of the Quakers was not sufficient insulation against the power of prejudice.

Such serious thoughts, however, were probably not on the minds of the schoolchildren as they arrived for their first classes at nine o'clock. The school was the newest part of the large, U-shaped, stone building facing the fountains and walkways of Park Place. The oldest part of the building, covered thickly with ivy, was the Quaker Meeting House, which occupied the entire north wing along Laurens Street. The school, added on in 1899, consisted of the central portion of the building, set back from the street, leaving room for a lawn and a small cinder playground. A south section housed a gymnasium on the ground floor and large study halls and classrooms on the upper floors. In 1909 the appearance of the building changed slightly when the old gym was turned into a swimming pool and a new gym was added to the third floor. The entrance was enlarged later in 1922 and new offices were built for the principal and his assistant. It was an impressive building, not for any outstanding architectural feature, but for its size compared to the rowhouse homes around it, and for its location atop the hill at the head of Park Place.[19]

In 1911 the pressure of expanding enrollment encouraged the Education Committee to recommend the purchase of the adjacent rowhouse at 1712 Park Place. This became the classroom building for the kindergarten and early primary students, leaving the main school to the intermediate and high-school departments.[20]

Inside, this main building was one of those grand, spacious, old schools with lots of nooks, crannies, backstairways, and unique spaces that are fascinating and memorable to a schoolchild, regardless of age. As the children entered the building they passed the principal's office on their left. When the door was open students got a brief glimpse of Mr. Wilson's rolltop desk and the statue of "Winged Victory" that stood on the bookcase. If they were on time and were not intercepted by Miss Farquhar or her successor, Mrs. Wood, they passed on into a large hallway with a black slate floor and a stairway leading to the second and third floors. The pipe railings on the stairs were excellent for sliding down, but that had to be done after school or when there were no teachers or adults around. Directly to the back in the center of the building was the library and to the right, behind the Meeting House, was the lecture room where special assemblies and dramatic performances took place.

The first stop for high-school students, however, was the study hall, which filled the front of the left wing of the building. This large room, and the one directly above it for the intermediate students (grades 5, 6, 7, and 8), served as a "home room" as well as a study hall. Each student was assigned one of the hundred or more desks where he or she stored books and supplies. Boys sat on one side and girls on the other. When not off to class in another part of the building, students were expected to be in their seats at work. Eli Lamb finished the last dozen years of his career at Friends School as the supervisor of the intermediate study hall. A stern look from Cousin Eli was usually sufficient to maintain correct order. Few of his successors were quite as successful with later generations of students. Mr. Harry, for example, had to call in "Old John," the janitor, for advice when students smeared limburger cheese on the bottom of several desks.[21]

To the rear of the building, along the alley, were the classrooms where English, history, mathematics, geography, and foreign languages were taught. These were small rooms with wainscoting waist high and plaster walls above painted a light buff or similar color.[22] Each room had several windows for light and was equipped with rows of armchairs, chalkboards, and stereopticons, maps, or whatever other aids the teachers needed. The electric lighting installed in 1908 was barely adequate, leaving the rooms somewhat dark in the evenings or on cloudy days.[23] A unique feature of the second floor was a roofgarden, which was really a porch above the entrance and the headmaster's office. It was built for the primary students in response to the early twentieth-century fad of providing a fresh-air environment. It soon fell into disuse as a classroom, however, when teachers learned that students had more fun throwing things into the yard below and found it hard to concentrate.

On the third floor, which housed the gymnasium after 1909, were the chemistry and physics laboratories and the art and biological sciences classrooms. From this top floor students, either with permission or surreptitiously, could ascend a small staircase into the cupola above the roof for a spectacular view of Baltimore. Since the school was built on a high point of ground, it was possible to see west as far as Catonsville and all the way to Towson on the north. This was the kind of unique feature that made the Friends School on Park Place a memorable building.

By nine o'clock the school day began. First was a brief assembly or what much later came to be called "collection." Primary students gathered in their respective classrooms, but the intermediate and high-school students sat in the large halls. The daily routine varied: sometimes a reading or song was presented, sometimes it was a story or talk by a faculty member, or a recitation by a student. Following the assembly, teachers and pupils moved to the classrooms for the first lessons of the day. From 1899 until 1931 the schedule was essentially the same: five class periods in the morning, a short break for lunch, two more class periods, a long play time of about one and one–half hours and a final class period. By 2:10 P.M. the younger children were dismissed and the intermediate and high-school students used the gymnasium, swimming pool, science laboratories, or study halls until after four o'clock.[24] The curriculum gradually changed over the years as new subjects, new teaching methods, and new extracurricular activities were added, but the schedule of the day remained much the same.

Illus. 7-4   Lecture Room, Park Avenue, ca. 1912.

In this first third of the twentieth century, as the theories of progressive education, of intelligence and aptitude testing, and of training students for business and industry became more popular, the educational program and methods of teaching gradually changed. The evolution of a more modern approach in these years is easily seen in the kindergarten. In 1899 the school's maid and horse-drawn coach delivered the young children to the Park Avenue building at 9:30 A.M. Hannah Yardley and her two assistants greeted them and directed them to their classroom. Once there, the pupils followed a regular schedule of "Morning Talks, Froebel's Gifts and Occupations, Kindergarten Games, Marching, Calisthenics, and German."[25] In all of these activities, especially the marching, calisthenics, and German, the students were required to learn order and discipline and to accept the direction of the teacher.

The school explained to prospective parents that the goal of the kindergarten was "systematically" to develop the students' minds and talents in preparation for beginning the regular primary classes. Even the photographs in the school catalogue show the children seated in orderly rows around two tables and watched over by two teachers.[26]

Another photograph from 1918 advertises a neat and orderly kindergarten, with all the chairs carefully arranged in a circle.[27] But by 1927 the scene, and apparently the teaching philosophy, had changed. Instead of children lined up in symmetric rows, they are shown seated on the floor around the room, playing and working at a variety of activities. The only teacher in sight, Miss Jane E. Williams, is seated at the piano, and the accompanying statements emphasize that "Happiness is the right of childhood . . . ." The school goes on to state that at Friends, "children are given opportunity for the carrying out of their own ideas and thus grow in purposive activities, initiative, and independence."[28] Very clearly the emphasis seems to have shifted from the order and authority of the teacher to a concern for the freedom and self-expression of the child. The academic atmosphere of 1927 was much more open and less controlled.

Subtle winds of change were also blowing through the classrooms of the primary, intermediate, and high-school departments. Before World War I when high-school students entered Miss Rachel Lamb's class on Rhetoric and Composition, they knew they would be expected to memorize and recite rules of grammar. When they studied the classic works of English literature that were recommended for entrance into college, they could again expect to memorize large passages. These same teaching methods applied to learning history, Latin, and modern languages.[29] The purpose was "to secure mastery of subject-matter, and through that, not only intellectual growth, but culture and spiritual insight; above all, to inspire a love and appreciation of good literature," or of whatever the subject might be.[30] More than half a century later students who had attended Friends in these pre-World War I days could still recite accurately the poems they memorized for Caroline Norment, and the verses they learned in Wilbert Martin's Latin classes, or could sing the songs taught to them in German by Catherine Schimpf.

The emphasis on memorization and recitation led naturally to an interest in public speaking. For many years every student in the high school was required to memorize a poem or short story, such as *Casey at the Bat*, or Poe's *Tell-Tale Heart*, and to present it in the annual Declamation Contest.[31] The Jonathan K. Taylor Literary Society conducted debates on the last day of school each year, with the winner being presented a dictionary by Mr. Taylor, chairman of the Education Committee.[32] In 1915, two weeks before a German U-boat sank the *Lusitania*, Edward C. Wilson announced that the topic for that year's debate would be, "Resolved that the Further Increase in Armament and the Introduction of Military Training in Schools and Colleges in the United States would be Undesirable."[33] There were other occasions, too, when students were called upon to speak, such as the Ivy Oration at which the senior class planted ivy obtained from Addison Walk, Oxford University. The importance placed on public speaking was, of course, not unique to Friends. In the era before film and radio it was common to turn to various types of oratory and debate as entertainment. Fourth of July speeches and political rallies were well attended by interested listeners. Friends School students must have felt some of the excitement when the 1912 Democratic Convention was held nearby in the Fifth Regiment Armory, or when they heard about the prolonged oratory that finally resulted in Woodrow Wilson's nomination. Public speaking was an honored American tradition, and schools commonly offered various programs as a community entertainment as well as a learning experience for pupils.

Eventually, in the 1920s, the emphasis on memorization and recitation began to decline. It was still the principal methodology for teaching grammar, geography, Latin, and most history, but new methods had begun to appear. Besides drilling students on sentence structure and verb tenses, teachers like Letitia Stockett also lectured and held discussions on material that had been assigned. Others began to use essay examinations more frequently. Louis Lamborn gave a "horrendous" final examination in 1924 when he required students to "tell everything you know about American history from the Pilgrims to the Civil War" and "from the Civil War to the present."[34] More field trips to local manufacturing houses and businesses and the introduction of films, slides, and other visual aids also began to appear among the teaching methods by World War I.[35] In 1914 a unique course was taught on the government of Baltimore, and key city employees and politicians came to the school as guest lecturers. Mayor James H. Preston spoke to the students on "The future of Baltimore," and others discussed city markets, charities, liquor licenses, sewers, and public baths.[36] Community improvement associations, civic clubs, neighbors, and patrons were invited to attend the lecture series.

The most noticeable changes were not so much in how students were taught but in what new courses were added to the curriculum. In 1898 the Education Committee seemed to follow a national trend by approving manual training courses. Roman Steiner was hired at $350 per year to teach clay modeling and carving, as well as drawing and painting.[37] The program at Friends, however, emphasized the artistic aspects of woodworking and handcrafts, rather than attempting to provide practical skills for students preparing to go into industry or some form of manual labor. In this sense Friends was in tune with the philosophy of John Dewey who argued that manual training ought not to be for job training, but instead should be valued because it improved moral character. The use of hand tools was also beneficial to the child because it strengthened his or her powers of observation and coordination. But the main advantage, Dewey believed, was to help children work together, which would eventually lead to the creation of a successful community.

A decade later, in 1909, Edward Wilson urged the Education Committee to expand the manual training program:

> I want eventually to see in connection with the school a department of manual training and domestic science that shall provide for woodworking, metal working, mechanical drawing, care of a house, cooking, etc.[38]

He was in part reacting to the challenge he saw coming from the growth of Baltimore's public school system. In particular he felt that Polytechnic High School, founded earlier in 1884, was offering a unique program that would attract more students in the future. He warned:

> If we want to make this school a different kind of school and possessing advantages that will stand out in marked contrast to those about us, we must provide city children with hand as well as brain work, and equip them for the ordinary daily routine tasks of their lives as well as the strictly mental side of their future.[39]

The public in the twentieth century was demanding more manual and vocational training; therefore Friends should provide what parents required. Wilson apparently won his point, for over the next few years Friends broadened its curriculum. In a new domestic science laboratory, high-school freshmen and sophomores learned cooking, sewing, and other household skills. By 1915 mechanical drawing, shop work, and "household arts" were made requirements for graduation.

The influence of social and economic change on the curriculum of Friends was clear in this acceptance of manual training as a part of each student's education. Even if few of the graduates of Friends expected to find work on the assembly line, the school was acknowledging the importance that industrialization had come to play in the American economy, and particularly in Baltimore. After World War I Baltimore's industrial capacity grew rapidly, with new factories and plants springing up everywhere. While Lever Brothers was constructing a new factory at Canton, Procter and Gamble was building at Locust Point, and McCormick was financing a new plant on Light Street near the harbor. Montgomery Ward invested in a massive new structure on Monroe Street, Stieff Silver had a new factory near the Cedar Avenue bridge, and Western Electric was spreading out on its new 125-acre site.[40]

The boom in Baltimore's industries also meant a growth of services that accompanied them and in general fostered an expansion of the whole business economy. It was not accidental that Friends began to offer business education courses to prepare students to enter the competition for white-collar jobs. Even before the election of Warren G. Harding and Calvin Coolidge, when the heyday of the businessman reached its peak, Friends hired Mrs. J. Garland Turner, a former business college principal, to teach stenography, bookkeeping, and typewriting on Saturday mornings. Edward Wilson argued before the Education Committee that business education ought to be made a part of the regular curriculum, since it would be another step in preparing graduates for employment. The business courses, he said, will offer "work that will serve constantly to connect strictly scholastic activities with the years that immediately follow graduation."[41]

By the 1920s, then, the curriculum of Friends School was as broad and as "up-to-date" as any similar institution in Baltimore. A typical high school of the post-World War I period offered thirteen subjects: six academic (English, foreign language, mathematics, science, history, and social studies), and seven non-academic (business, manual arts, agriculture, home economics, art, music, and physical education).[42] With the exception of agriculture, Friends provided courses in all of these areas. In fact they even offered one subject not taught in many other Baltimore schools at the time—sex education. Whether or not Wilson was confident of his decision, or whether he feared resistance to his action, he did not inform the Education Committee until after he hired Laura B. Garrett and Dr. O. Edward Janney to lecture to the high-school students on sex. Each of the instructors gave five lectures to the girls or boys. Since this was in 1912, Wilson perhaps had reason to expect some objection to the introduction of sex education classes, especially in a coeducational institution; but none was recorded.[43]

The World War I era also saw the introduction of individual testing of each pupil. Like other schools, Friends was quick to adopt the intelligence or IQ test popularized at that time by Lewis Terman.[44] They

Illus. 7-5   Domestic Science Classroom, Park Avenue, ca. 1912.

had enough confidence in the ability and intelligence tests that by 1920 Mr. William Flowers, principal of the Intermediate Department, announced that all classes would be reorganized according to the scores of the students.[45] By 1926 each student in the primary and intermediate classes took the Otis tests and the Stanford Achievement Tests.[46]

More fun for the students and faculty than any of these standard ability tests, however, were the "General Information-Observation Tests" given to the high school each January. Every year the principal and a faculty committee would collect 1,000 or more suggested questions; from these they chose the best 150 and arranged them in categories. For days students would read the daily newspapers carefully, trying to prepare themselves for questions like "Who is the present German Ambassador to the United States?" or "Name two of the four U.S. delegates to the Paris Peace Conference." They reviewed their literature and geography books, and quizzed each other on "Who wrote *The Tale of Two Cities?*," "Who said, 'All the world's a stage'?," or "Where is the Field Museum?" The winner of the contests usually answered more than 100 correctly and some, like David Robertson, the

𝕱riends 𝕾chool

𝕭altimore

General Information Test

January 1924

High School Department

Locate by country:
1. Moscow.
2. Flanders.
3. Vera Cruz.
4. Lands End.
5. Mt. Everest.

Who lived first:
10. Jefferson or Henry Clay.
11. Christ or David.
12. Lord Baltimore or Columbus.
13. Confucius or Mohammed.
14. Julius Caesar or William the Conqueror.
15. Tom Sawyer or Mark Twain.
16. Queen Victoria or George Washington.

Name the author of:
22. Pilgrim's Progress.
23. The Gettysburg Address.
24. Nicholas Nickleby.
25. Caesar's Commentaries.
26. Treasure Island.

Locate by state:
32. Mineola Flying Field.
33. Pike's Peak.
34. Muscle Shoals.

Why is each of the following well known:
6. Dr. F. G. Banting.
7. Milton Hershey.
8. Edward W. Bok.
9. Sir Christopher Wren.

Name the painters of the following pictures:
17. The Sistine Madonna.
18. The Angelus.
19. The Blue Boy.
20. The Horse Fair.
21. Mona Lisa.

Explain briefly:
27. Seismograph.
28. Mah Jong.
29. Adam's Ale.
30. f. o. b.
31. S. P. C. A.

Locate by city:
35. The largest Stock Yards in the U. S.
36 Manhattan Island.
37. Westminster Abbey.
38. The Kodak Factory.

The Bible:
44. Name the first five Books of The New Testament.
45. Who wrote the Epistle to the Romans?
46. Who is usually named as the author of the Book of Proverbs?
47. Quote the first verse of the 23rd Psalm.
48. Who wore a coat of many colors?
49. What king saw the hand-writing on the wall?
50. Who was thrown into a den of lions?
51. In which Book of the Bible is the story of the Flood?

Local Questions:
52. Who painted "The Argosy?" (In front hall of Friends School.)
53. Locate the Baltimore Museum of Art.
54. What is Baltimore's largest market?
55. Name the Mayor of the city.
56. Name the much beloved classical scholar of Baltimore who recently celebrated his 92nd birthday.
57. Name one well known Baltimore sculptor.
58. Name the Director of the Peabody Conservatory of Music.
59. Who owns the largest private art collection in Baltimore?

Illus. 7-6   General Information Test, 1924.

son of the president at Goucher College, was right on 136 out of the 150 questions.[47] It is doubtful that today's students (or their parents) would be able to improve much on the scores of their predecessors.

But student life was not all tests and homework. One graduate of 1908 remembered the junior prom of that year: as the girls entered the gymnasium where the dance was held, the faculty who were chaperoning checked to insure that there were no low-necked gowns, no dresses with hems more than three inches from the floor and, when the couples danced, that there were always at least four inches between partners.[48] Stephen Harry, the head of the high school, probably saved many of his students from embarrassment and perhaps a few from injury by insisting that these young novices learn to dance properly. In the week before each school dance, he gave dancing lessons in the lecture room next to the library. Since there were few couples who "went steady," Mr. Harry also laid down the rules for inviting partners to the dance: "1. A boy should ask a girl if he might escort her to the dance. 2. A girl must accept the first invitation she receives. 3. After a specified time, if a girl has not been invited, she is free to invite a boy not enrolled at Friends."[49] These rules reflect the school's strong sense of responsibility and control over the students' behavior.

By the decade of the "Roaring Twenties," however, the students of Friends School must have been influenced by that same rebellion of youth so vividly portrayed by F. Scott Fitzgerald. Whether or not they were attempting to dance the Charleston and Black Bottom in this new age of Jazz is not known, but headmaster Wilson occasionally expressed concern about the "character" of the dancing.[50] Moreover, the students were less willing to accept rigid control of their activities. In 1925 Edward Wilson reported to the Education Committee that the seniors had requested the opportunity to give a play and a dance to raise funds for a student publication. They asked the administration to extend the time limit for dances until 12:30 A.M., and if denied, they suggested that they might hold the dance somewhere other than the school. Wilson, who was certainly not a weak administrator, confided to the committee that he "would regret this and consequently want[s] to be just as liberal as possible. . . ."[51] On the whole students were not rebellious and seldom complained about too much interference from faculty or parents, but they were no longer afraid to assert their will from time to time.

The students organized or ran a variety of activities largely by themselves. As early as 1913 the first student government organizations appeared in both the intermediate and high school departments.[52]

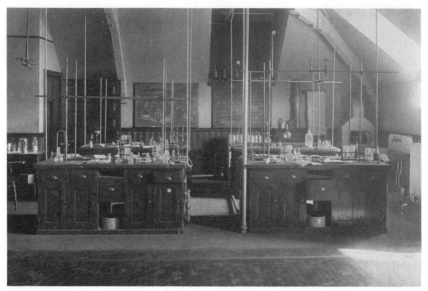

Illus. 7-7   Chemical and Physical Laboratory, Park Avenue, ca. 1912.

Wilson remarked that the discipline handed out by the students under the authority of these organizations was often harsher than that issued by the faculty. The Alpha Honor Society for boys and The Square for girls were other societies open to students by invitation. And there were several school publications for which students had responsibility. *The Friends School Quarterly* began in 1901 with the objective of producing "a truthful record of all events worthy of remembrance connected with the school."[53] It was followed by *The Scarlet and Gray* in 1908, a lively literary and school news journal in which all departments, from the primary to the high school, participated. Both the intermediate and primary classes produced "papers" also, and an athletic news sheet appeared by the time of the Depression.[54] *The Quaker* was the annual "yearbook," similar to those of other schools, which chronicled the achievements, antics, and hopes of the graduating class.

Nor were drama and music neglected at Friends School. Besides local performances at the school, such as the "Folk Song Fantasy" by the Girls' Glee Club in 1923, the girls were good enough to be the only private school group asked to perform at the childen's concert of the Baltimore Symphony Orchestra at the Lyric Theater in January, 1925.[55] For the younger children, Isabel Woods, who led the glee club and taught dramatics, organized a kazoo orchestra among the fourth grade class and gave concerts.[56] These musical performances, as well as plays, were held in the lecture or assembly room behind the main part of the meeting house. It was there on the portable stage, complete with footlights and curtains, that audiences saw plays like *Seven Old Ladies of Lavender Town* or William Dean Howell's *An Unexpected Guest.*[57]

There was usually a dramatic presentation as part of the annual fall Bazaar and Doll Show. The purpose of this popular affair was to raise money for local charities and for refugees of international conflicts. Funds for school improvements also became a part of the event's objective, and for many alumni it would become one of their primary attachments to the school long after graduation.

Motion pictures became a part of the Friends School scene as early as 1917, only two years after D. W. Griffith filmed *Birth of a Nation,* the first full-length feature film. Initially films were shown to primary and intermediate students on the ground that they might be instructional. Wilson reported showing "industrial" and other types of movies on a weekly basis. But the childen, and soon the faculty, considered motion pictures as entertainment. Enjoyment was clearly the purpose in 1926 when a Mr. Depkin of the Metropolitan Theatre supplied *Rin Tin Tin.* The Primary Department was occasionally rewarded with extra films for good attendance.[58]

The outstanding entertainment and education program of Friends School, however, was the Friday evening lecture series that began about 1900 and lasted until 1916. Students, parents, faculty, and the interested public of Baltimore purchased tickets and gathered in the large meeting house to hear the notable Senator Robert La Follette speak on "Representative Government," writer Hamlin Garland discuss "Joys of the Trail," statesman Thomas Nelson Page on "America as a Peace Maker," reformer Jacob Riis explain "What Makes Pure Americans," and Judge Ben Lindsey, a leader of juvenile reform, describe "The Misfortunes of Mickey."[59] Over a decade and a half some of the most prominent public figures on the national and local scene appeared at Friends School. The students probably enjoyed the illustrated lectures best, like Commander Robert E. Peary's "Nearest the North Pole—and Plans for the 1908 Expedition" or Arthur Peck's "Storm Heroes of our Coast," but they also were impressed by seeing and hearing some of the major figures of the day. In the spring of 1914 Governor Phillips Lee Goldsborough helped make the arrangements for ex-President William Howard Taft to speak on "American Ideals in

Illus. 7-8   May Fête, West Forest Park, 1913.

Statesmanship."[60] Taft actually arrived early enough to visit briefly a few of the classrooms before his evening lecture on March 27. Being able to bring speakers of this stature to Baltimore must have contributed significantly to the reputation of Friends. On the other hand it had little immediate financial value, since the 1913–14 series netted only $88.02 in profits. At the end of the school year the commencement exercises were another occasion that brought prominent figures to the school, like Governor Edward Warfield in 1904.[61]

Probably more exciting for the students were the outdoor events held on the school's athletic grounds and the excursions to parks. The May Fête, for example, began in 1913 as a celebration of spring. The girls dressed in white gowns and hats and carried or wore bunches of spring flowers as they paraded around the Maypole. The whole school would turn out for these affairs held at the athletic field in West Forest Park, on the Hallowell Lawn of the Taylor Home, and later in Homeland. Each child went home with special memories of the day, such as Eleanor Dilworth Mace, who forever remembered losing her wand when she was Queen of the Fairies.[62] More vigorous and less decorous was Field Day. All the classes were divided into two teams matching the school colors, scarlet and gray, and pitted against one another in

Illus. 7-9   The 8½ acres in West Forest Park, purchased in 1912 for athletic fields, became known as the "Friends School Country Club."

athletic competitions. Over the years these celebrations and sports events changed as new activities were added and old customs fell into disuse. In 1936 a Spring Carnival to collect funds for a new gymnasium included races, pony rides, a dog show, an alumni lacrosse game, a tennis tournament, and a merry-go-round in the afternoon, while in the evening a large crowd was entertained by a fashion show, a musician, movies, and dancing to a forty-piece band.[63]

All of these extracurricular activities became a significant part of the school because they broadened the social experience of the students and because they were essential to the development of a school "spirit." As the public school system expanded and the number of independent schools increased, the Wilson administration began to recognize that a sense of unity and identity with Friends was an important ingredient in the continued strength of the institution. By 1923 Wilson was prematurely predicting that "The years of expansion are a matter of history"; nevertheless, by building a strong sense of loyalty to the school through sound academic programs and a variety of other activities that involved students, alumni, faculty, and the neighboring community, he believed that Friends could hold its own and prosper.[64]

This growing awareness of competition with other institutions was partially responsible for the gradual enlargement of the athletic program from a few limited facilities to a variety of sports that typify modern schools. In 1900 Theodore Kistler was hired as the "gymnasium instructor" for $300 per year. The "gym" was on the lower level of the Park Avenue building next to the property at 1712 (which later had a small gymnasium on the top floor for younger children). Like the old gym at Eli Lamb's school, this room contained ladders for climbing, balance beams and rings for gymnastic exercises, and served as a small but adequate basketball court. It was here in 1900 that Friends launched its competitive basketball program with its first game against Baltimore Polytechnic Institute. The score was 2–0 in favor of Friends at halftime, and the final margin was a decisive 8–0; whether the low score was the result of a conscious "stall" is unknown. The parents, faculty, and students crowded the edge of the small court and leaned over the balcony to cheer the team to victory.[65] The setting, if not the team, improved in 1909 when a new, larger gymnasium was built on the third floor of the school. The team also had new uniforms by then, made up of gray jerseys with a scarlet band running from the left shoulder to the right hip and showing the letters FS.[66] A sense of the school spirit that basketball encouraged was evident in a student description of a 1910 game against Sidwell Friends School of Washington, a team that had defeated Loyola, the Baltimore City champions of that year:

> From the minute the ball was tossed up at center it was a contest of skill between the two teams. Both sides were up to the mark in snap and team work, and the audience was kept on edge from beginning to end by the closeness of the score and the spectacular playing. With only a half minute left Carson Moore shot a foul goal, and as the ball dropped through the basket the whistle for time blew, giving us the game 16 to 15.[67]

As expected the 200 spectators who lined the court in chairs or sat perched on the high window sills "went wild."

When the gym was moved to the third floor the Education Committee recommended construction of a swimming pool where the old gym had been. There Mr. Kistler, who could not swim himself, taught swimming and coached the team. The first lesson for beginners took place on a stool in the gym, where the pupil learned the breaststroke; later in the pool Kistler would follow his novices along the edge with a long pole. The older boys showed off their bravado by leaping over the pipe railing into the pool or by dropping into the water from the low ceiling beams.[68] In summer the pool was made available to the local neighborhood, which improved the school's image among the local residents.[69]

Outdoor exercise was of two types: daily exercise for all students in the street or park in front of the school, and competitive sports at various athletic fields rented or purchased by Friends. At about 10 A.M. each morning, Louis Lamborn and Marian Bentley Millard led the intermediate and high-school students in deep-breathing and stretching exercises in the street, which the police allowed them to block off temporarily.[70]

The first athletic field used by the school for track and field events and other outdoor sports was near the corner of Park Avenue and Mount Royal Terrace.[71] Because that field was so small, the school rented the Mount Washington Club facilities in 1906. By 1912 they had purchased eight and one-half acres in West Forest Park, which was about a thirty-minute ride from the school by streetcar. Later the Education Committee used the school's Reo buses to transport the athletes. At the West Forest Park grounds Friends constructed a baseball diamond, tennis courts, a club house, and a grandstand. It was there that Friends fielded its first football team in 1912 and three years later won the Baltimore Preparatory School Championship.[72] Friends enjoyed equally quick success when it added lacrosse to the athletic

Illus. 7-10   Mid-Morning Exercise, Park Avenue, ca. 1919.

Illus. 7-11   Baseball Squad, West Forest Park, 1913.

Illus. 7-12   Girls' Gym Class, Park Avenue, ca. 1919.

program in 1924, and four years later defeated defending champion Poly for the Maryland Scholastic Championship.[73]

Just as Friends had madé a reputation as the first coeducational school in Baltimore, it was among the first to develop sports programs for girls as well as boys. When the Girls' Athletic Association was formed in 1915 among the high school, intermediate, and fourth primary students "to discuss athletic affairs and to arouse enthusiasm and school spirit," the girls' teams were already successful.[74] The high-school girls basketball team won the City Championship in 1913–14, the same year that Miss Alpine Parker introduced field hockey. In the 1920s and after, under the capable leadership of Marian Bentley Millard, the field hockey teams would win wide respect. Lacrosse for girls began in the spring of 1927.[75] Even those girls who did not star on any of the varsity teams usually could recall vividly many years later the gray bloomers they wore with the sailor blouses and the scarlet flannel collar. Often the boys tried to peek through small holes in the glazed windows of the gym to see the girls in these exotic uniforms.

By 1927, when Edward C. Wilson retired and was replaced by William S. Pike, Friends School was a much different place than it had been at the beginning of the century. The expansion that Wilson thought at an end had not yet run its course, though the coming depression years brought temporary decline. The movement of the school from Park Avenue to Homeland, which began under Wilson and would be completed by his successors, eventually provided the space and stimulus for another stage of growth. The children who attended the new suburban campus in later years would know little of the old Park Avenue school, but the continuity and tradition of Friends would bind them to these earlier generations.

Illus. 8-1   William S. Pike (front left), a member of the faculty under Principal Edward Wilson (front center) when this photo was taken in 1914–15, became Principal in 1927.

From Park Place to Homeland

One late November day in 1936 H. L. Mencken grumbled about the growth of Baltimore's suburbs:

What wrecked the older Baltimore was what wrecked all other American towns of its age and size: the invention of the automobile. As soon as people could get into the remoter suburbs cheaply and quickly, they began to move there, seeking more room and less taxes. But soon or late, I believe, they will be driven back. For one thing, the discomforts of suburban life are numerous and dreadful, and people always tire of them eventually.[1]

The leaders and patrons of Friends School, however, were not deterred by Mencken's opinion and in that same year completed a move of the entire school to a new suburban campus. Like the generations who preceded them, they recognized the changes occurring in Baltimore and were willing to adjust. After the city's last annexation in 1918, which tripled Baltimore's area to ninety-two square miles, more and more of those residents who were most likely to send their children to private schools began to leave the old social center of the city around Mount Vernon and Bolton Hill for the newer suburban neighborhoods of Roland Park, Guilford, and Homeland. North Charles Street became the axis for a "green wedge" of residential developments that stretched out toward Towson and the Green Spring Valley.[2]

Even before the end of the nineteenth century developers and institutions had already begun to select sites in the rolling hills of Northern Baltimore and the nearby county. Architect Stanford White designed First Methodist Episcopal Church on St. Paul Street in 1882 and four years later Goucher College built a new campus on adjoining property. Horsecars and, later, electric trolleys provided reliable transportation to the middle- and upper-middle-class families who were attracted to Charles Village and the new homes being constructed beyond North Avenue. By World War I the movement northward began in earnest, and the annexation of 1918, which permitted the extension of city streets and other services to suburban neighborhoods, encouraged the exodus. The attractive new single homes built by the Roland Park Company proved irresistible to the families who found the older city too crowded and noisy, or who sought a less "urban" environment. By the time the automobile became a common means of transportation in the 1920s, the scattering of Baltimore's population into the suburbs had become a familiar and expected pattern.

For Friends School the movement to suburbia began in the fall of 1924 when Edward Wilson became alarmed by the changing population in the vicinity of the West Forest Park athletic field, and observed the movement of students' families to the north. Concerned over the theft of athletic equipment and by the disruption of athletic programs by "undesirable neighbors," primarily newly arrived immigrants from Russia and Eastern Europe, Wilson urged the sale of the West Forest Park property and the need for a new "out of town" location.

> The neighborhood is changing rapidly and we are drawing less and less from it. It appears now that the increase is coming from the northern section of the city, Charles, St. Paul and Guilford Streets and from Roland Park and Guilford. With the development of the new suburb, Homeland, we learn on good authority that scores of our people formerly resident in Forest Park, West Forest Park, Arlington, etc., have purchased lots and contemplate building homes.

Recognizing and taking advantage of the shift in population was a question of survival in Wilson's view:

> The next 5 years are to be test years for our own as well as other private schools in the city not having well established and proper out of town location for athletics and other purposes. We have reached our peak in income. The budget will always increase. I see no way of avoiding it even to hold our own which was a comparatively simple matter a few years ago.[3]

Not one to hesitate once his mind was made up, Wilson inquired of the Roland Park Company whether they "would favor having the school locate, at least for athletic purposes, on ground near one of their developments." At first he got no encouragement, but when he turned to James Carey Martien, a member of the Executive Board of the

Roland Park Company and a patron of the school with four children enrolled, he began to get a positive response. Martien, the real estate agent who originally sold the West Forest Park property to Friends, now offered to help with the sale of that property and the acquisition of an appropriate tract of land on North Charles Street.[4]

If Wilson had no trouble convincing James Martien of the wisdom of the move, he had a more difficult time gaining the consent of all the school's patrons. Those who lived in the western residential areas of Baltimore preferred that the school be moved there rather than farther north to Homeland. Others raised serious objections to the expense involved. They saw a large piece of property on Charles Street as both too expensive to buy and too expensive to build on. It would lead to a large debt for Baltimore Monthly Meeting, they said, would increase tuition charges, and perhaps necessitate the reduction of teachers' salaries.[5]

But such opposition was no match for Edward Wilson and the proponents of the move to the northern suburbs. The most frequently cited justification for moving was that Friends needed to join the

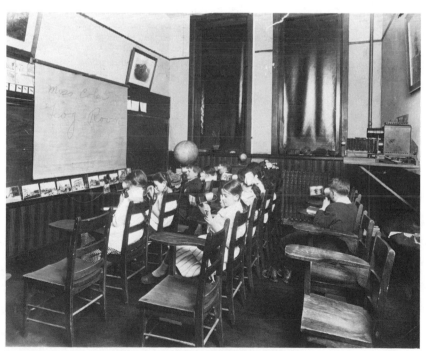

Illus. 8-2   Miss Coale's Geography Class, Park Avenue, ca. 1917.

country day school movement in order to compete with other private schools in Baltimore. Once again responding to changing urban conditions, schools had begun to seek the healthy air and uncrowded playing fields of suburbia. According to Wilson the city had become detrimental to pupils because of "1, the afternoon movie, 2, the danger of street traffic, and 3, the increasing distraction of various artificial and unwholesome daytime recreations." The cure to these ills, he felt, "lies in getting as much of God's out of doors into the lives of children as we can. We feel that we owe it to childhood."[6]

Wilson's desire to acquire more space in the outlying suburbs may have come partly from his educational goals of providing a fresh air environment for the children, but he was also reacting to the social changes in the city. The Baltimore fire of 1904 had been a dramatic factor in increasing the desire of some businesses and many residents to push outward away from the crowded center of the city. The movement of new immigrants and larger numbers of blacks into Baltimore was also a part of the explanation for the flight to white, Anglo-Saxon suburbia. And of course the arrival of the inexpensive, personal automobile by the 1920s made it all possible. As the families who sent their children to the private institutions moved closer to the country, it was only reasonable that the schools would follow.

That Friends School would move to the northern suburbs instead of the western caused a sharp but brief disagreement among members of the Education Committee. Specifically, Wilson suggested three possibilities: a site on Charles Street, a twenty-four acre plot on Bellona Avenue, or the purchase of property in Mt. Washington.[7] Perhaps because of the encouragement of Mr. Martien or simply because it was the most attractive site, Baltimore Monthly Meeting in 1925 purchased twenty-six acres on North Charles Street formerly known as Fahey's Meadow and later the Roland Park Company's nursery, for a little over $80,000.[8] The land sloped gently to the west away from Charles Street and was filled with a variety of trees and shrubs. On the far western edge of the property was Stony Run, the small stream that gave its name to part of the area. On the whole it was an attractive piece of land that Baltimore Monthly Meeting had purchased for the eventual relocation of its school.

The initial purpose of this property was for use as an athletic field, but Wilson and others quickly saw its potential as a future campus for Friends School. The headmaster planted the seed as early as May, 1925, when he mentioned to the Education Committee the possibility of

Illus. 8-3   Friends School Bus, Park Avenue, ca 1919

building a primary school there.[9] While Baltimore Monthly Meeting paid the bill for the purchase of the land and while Wilson finished his last two years as principal, the seed took hold. When William S. Pike became the new head of the school at the beginning of 1927 he strongly recommended that a new primary building be constructed on Charles Street. The Monthly Meeting responded positively and by June a building committee was busy planning and raising funds. The Olmstead Brothers of Boston, the landscape architects who planned Roland Park, were hired to study the grounds and the location of buildings, and the firm of Mottu and White was selected as the architects.[10] After extensive study of many local school buildings, the building committee selected a Gothic design as the most attractive and appropriate plan. Mrs. William Byron Forbush, the mother of Bliss Forbush and an artist, was also influential in encouraging the adoption of the Gothic style which was popular among private colleges. The relative quickness and ease with which the Quaker community was able to make a major purchase of property and begin new construction was a tribute to the leadership of Edward Wilson and the Education Committee that served during his twenty-four years as principal. As mentioned earlier school income had increased tenfold and the value of the Charles Street property alone had grown to $140,000 in just two years.[11]

On May 22, 1928, school officials, faculty, and students gathered to lay the cornerstone for the new primary school. Because of heavy rains and muddy grounds, the ceremony was held at the Park Avenue building. Professor Frank M. McKibben, of the Education Department at the University of Pittsburgh, addressed the participants on "Symbols and Ideals in Education," and William S. Pike presided over the filling of a copper box with school documents and current newspapers that were sealed in the cornerstone.[12]

Four years later, on May 6, 1931, Pike again led the ceremonies when the cornerstone was set for the next principal building at Charles Street.[13] The Intermediate Department moved to the Homeland campus after Pike argued successfully that the urban location of the old school below North Avenue was limiting enrollment growth. Parents had complained that they did not like starting their children at the Homeland primary and then having to move them to the Park Avenue building when they entered the fifth grade. Moreover, Pike pointed out, Calvert School, Girls Latin, Bryn Mawr, and McDonogh had all established suburban campuses. Friends could no longer stay in the city and continue to compete with other private schools, especially during the Depression when new students were hard to come by.[14]

Once the Primary and Intermediate departments were established in new buildings on Charles Street, it was inevitable that the High School should follow. The Education Committee, echoing earlier arguments, observed in February, 1936, that the "number of students drawn from the immediate vicinity of the Park Avenue school seems to have been gradually decreasing as the large center of residents appears to be moving toward north Baltimore."[15] The following fall, high-school classes were moved to the suburban campus. When a new gymnasium opened there on December 30, 1937, Friends School had completed its relocation once more.[16]

The movement of Friends School to suburbia coincided with the first change in principals in a quarter of a century. Faced with failing health, Edward Wilson had retired as principal in 1927 and gave the office over to one of the school's most loved and faithful teachers, William S. Pike. Hired at a salary of $7,500, Pike took up the duties of principal in January, even though Wilson officially finished out the academic year as head of the school. Having begun as an instructor of science and "physical culture" for $800 in the fall of 1899, Pike had taught at Friends for twenty-eight years. In 1926, when Louis Lamborn resigned to move to McDonogh, Pike began his administrative career as the Principal's Assistant in charge of boys, and as Principal of the High School Department.[17] From beginning to end in his long career he was a favorite of students and fellow teachers. A stocky man with a round face, twinkling eyes, and a large black mustache [later a handsome gray], he was remembered by one student as both "dignified and jolly"—a perfect type for the role of Santa Claus which he often played at Christmas.[18] When he married Miss May Henry, also a teacher at Friends, in the meeting house, the pupils and faculty shared in the happiness of their favorite instructor and colleague. Few teachers in the history of the school achieved the popularity of William S. Pike.

Upon becoming principal of the school in 1927, Pike took on a role for which he was less well suited. Following in the shadow of Edward Wilson, Pike felt somewhat uneasy in his new position. His early reports to the Education Committee reveal a man self-conscious of his lack of administrative experience but eager to serve the school.[19] The primary difference between him and his predecessor, which he readily acknowledged, was that whereas "Wilson was good at ideas...," he, Pike, was "better at system and working out detailed work."[20] After teaching for twenty-eight years he admitted that "It is a little hard for me to keep my hands off as I have been so used to routine school work for such a long time, but I think on the whole it is best for me not to dip into the small things, but rather spend my time looking after the larger aspects of the school."[21] Despite this determination to stay away from dealing with details, Pike was unable to change his habits of three decades. His reports to the Education Committee steadily grew in length as he informed them carefully on many topics such as a new fire door for the boiler room, the purchase of Christmas cards, new tires for the buses, and uniforms for the drivers.

Pike's devotion to detail stemmed largely from his complete loyalty to Friends School as well as from his belief that teachers and staff should be fully committed to their work. In a candid assessment in 1928 of why enrollment was declining in the Intermediate Department, Pike laid the blame on "Teachers who do not feel the need of getting to school early in the morning nor remaining after school hours." He also cited their "lack of co-operation" or "lack of loyalty" to Mr. Warren B. Dunham, the Intermediate Department principal. In particular, with a bit of male chauvinism that Pike displayed from time to time, he singled

Illus. 8-4   Kindergarten Class, Park Avenue, ca. 1921.

out the female teachers of the Intermediate Department. Not only were there "Too many women teachers in the department," but "some of the women teachers [were unwilling] to do reasonable sized day's work." He concluded that "For the betterment of the department we must have teachers who are willing to take an interest in our boys and girls beyond the classroom."[22]

A few months later Pike was still pondering the question: "What kind of teachers do I want around me? I will tell you," he replied, before the Education Committee. "I want those who have been brought up under fine home influences, who have a splendid background of parent training, church training and the like. In other words, those who have culture and refinement. These things, I believe, count big for success." He then added, "What we want is the real man or woman."[23]

Fortunately Pike inherited a good faculty of "real" men and women from Edward Wilson. Besides Letitia Stockett and Roman Steiner, there was Franklin Kuller, who taught Latin and ancient history; Lawrence Peacock, German instructor and director of athletics for boys; Catherine Schimpf, a tutor in languages; and M. Eleanor Starr, the librarian. Elizabeth C. Remmert, the German-born teacher of foreign languages, often gave students a ride to school, but en route she required them to recite a full sentence in whatever language they were studying. Her pupils forgave her for her demands for hard work when she brought German-style gingerbread houses to school.[24] She was a good example of Pike's ideal of a teacher whose interest in the students went beyond the classroom. There were others who were brought to Friends by Edward Wilson, like Isabel Woods, the dramatics coach who wrote her own plays and operettas, or alumna Marian Bentley Millard, the devoted and capable director of athletics for girls. Having begun in the 1920s and remaining until the mid-1960s, Mrs. Millard was one of the most influential and remembered teachers at Friends. Eleanor Dilworth was another example of the strong character among the teaching staff that Pike inherited. A graduate of Friends, "Miss Dilly" returned to the school as head of the Intermediate Study Hall in 1926 and stayed on for thirty-six years as a teacher of history, Dean of Girls, Assistant to the Headmaster, and finally Principal of the High School with an important role in determining school policy and decisions in the 1950s and 1960s. To this strong core of teachers William Pike added others like Ruth C. Dibert, who persuaded several decades of Friends pupils that English grammar was actually important to know; or Oliver W. Melchior, head of the Intermediate Department, who once jumped up from his desk in an English class while his feet were still in the wastebasket; and Merrill Hiatt, long-time principal of the High School. Only about one-third of these teachers were Quakers, but they all had the qualities of personality and the commitment to education that made them a sound faculty from the viewpoint of administrator, student, or parent.

William Pike's greatest problems as head administrator of Friends School from 1927 to 1935 came not from his teachers nor even from the disruption of moving piecemeal from Park Avenue to the Homeland campus; his most serious difficulties had root in the national depression that followed 1929. Like other cities, Baltimore did not escape the effects of the stock market crash or the prolonged decline in production and employment. Nevertheless it was not as severely affected at first because its economy was diversified with workers scattered throughout a broad range of industries and businesses. By 1931, however, the unemployment rates climbed to 20 percent and by 1933 over 23,000 Baltimore families were on some form of government relief.[25]

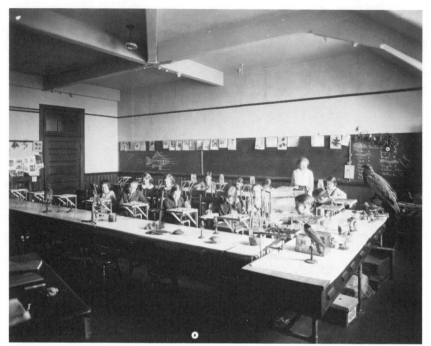

Illus. 8-5   Zoology Lab, Park Avenue, ca. 1921.

Both the Baltimore Trust Company and the Chesapeake Bank had closed their doors under the pressure of economic decline and there were nagging fears that public riots might return the city to its turbulent days of the nineteenth century when it earned the label of "Mobtown." Thousands of workers at major companies like the B & O Railroad or Bethlehem Steel at Sparrows Point were either laid off, worked sporadically, or labored for much reduced wages. The earnings of taxi drivers had shrunk to only eight or nine dollars a week.[26] Needless to say, most Baltimoreans drastically cut back their consumption to those things they felt were necessary. Even for the white- or blue-collar laborers who were not out of work, either the decline in wages or the fear of unemployment made them more conservative in their financial commitments. For Baltimore's private schools this meant a loss of enrollment and of revenues.

Between 1930 and 1934, the worst years of the Depression in Baltimore, Friends School's annual income dropped 37 percent, leveling off at about $107,000 per year until 1937. Enrollment declined from around 450 in 1930 to a low of only 288 in the 1936–37 school year. Not until the end of World War II did either revenues or the student population return to the pre-Depression levels.[27]

In fact even before the 1929 crash Pike had begun to worry about expenses and enrollment. He noticed in March, 1929, that expenditures had increased because two new teachers had been hired, and he recommended that with the new Homeland school they could take in 100 more students and slightly increase tuition.[28] His plans for growth, however, soon turned to strategies for survival as financial conditions worsened in the next few years. Income fell as parents took children out of school or failed to pay their bills. By February 1, 1930, midway through the school year, parents still owed $23,000 and Pike admitted that prospects for collection were not good. Teachers' and employees' salaries were reduced by as much as 20 percent, the number of buses was reduced from four to three, and all "frills" were trimmed from the budget. Through it all William Pike urged the Education Committee members to appear to be cheerful and optimistic in order not to convey the truly bleak atmosphere to the teachers and parents.[29] Camouflaging the obvious was impossible, of course, since the teachers saw their paychecks reduced and, most disturbing of all, saw several of their colleagues released. The Friends School faculty dropped from forty-seven in 1930 to thirty-nine two years later. Only by such drastic measures were Pike and the Education Committee able to finish each year without an excessive debt. The principal debt that the school had in these years resulted from the purchase of the Homeland property and the construction of new buildings there. The fact that they continued with plans to build a new Intermediate Department building in 1931 and to move the High School into it in 1936 actually illustrated shrewd planning. Since prices of material and laborers' wages were low during the Depression, there could not have been a better time for an institution like Friends to carry out major capital construction plans. Moreover, if they had not built in the suburbs and instead had clung to the old facilities on Park Avenue, the enrollment probably would have dropped more sharply than it did. Perhaps the knowledge that the school run by the Society of Friends had already survived for a century and a half gave them the confidence that it would also survive the economic upheaval of the 1930s.

On the whole the quality of education at Friends during the worst years of the Depression probably did not suffer noticeably because of the dedication of the teaching staff. Although Pike felt he should not

Illus. 8-6   Primary Class, Park Avenue, ca. 1921.

discuss plans for salary reductions or retrenchment of positions with the faculty because "They get so excited and upset when such things are considered that they are unfitted to carry on in the best manner possible the work for which they are responsible," they nevertheless agreed peacefully in 1932 to take a second 10 percent decrease in pay rather than see several of their colleagues fired.[30] Few faculty complained, realizing that they were fortunate still to be working, and there is no indication that the economic worries of the school ever had any adverse effect on the children in the classrooms.[31]

No doubt there might have been more discontent had the teachers heard some of the statements made by William Pike to the Education Committee. In 1930 for example he belittled those teachers who requested support for summer travel projects or even for tuition to attend summer school. "The school is not in such a position to be able to grant extravagant requests." Yet Pike requested and received full expenses to attend the NEA, Progressive Education, and other conventions, and even asked for and received $125–$150 to buy movie film to take on his summer vacation. At least his films, and lectures on

Illus. 8-7   Art Class, Park Avenue, ca. 1922.

America's natural wonders such as the Grand Canyon, were shared with the whole school.[32]

The steady decline of the school's enrollment and financial health was apparently the motive for a change in leadership in 1935. Meeting in November, 1934, at the home of Bliss Forbush, chairman of the Education Committee, the group agreed that while William Pike, now in his thirty-sixth year at Friends, had "wide knowledge of student needs," and that "his careful management, and his keen desire to improve the work of our school was never more needed than now," it was nevertheless time "to appoint an executive officer who would be able to make contacts, and approach the general public, in a manner not possible by anyone on our present staff."[33] In January, 1935, the Education Committee notified Pike that after a one-year paid leave of absence, he would return to the school as a science teacher with no administrative duties.[34] Pike graciously accepted the offer and was probably happy to return to the classroom where he was so outstanding.

His successor was Edwin Cornell Zavitz, a Quaker of Canadian origin, educated at the University of Michigan and Teachers College,

135

Illus. 8-8   Aerial View, Homeland Campus, ca. 1932.

Columbia University, and most recently the headmaster of University School of Cincinnati.[35] Earlier he had been an assistant professor of education at Antioch College and the headmaster of several schools, including Chateau de Bures at Villennes near Paris. Unlike Pike, who had become head of the school because of his local success in the classroom, Zavitz came to Friends as a professional administrator trained in educational theory and familiar with ideas at a number of schools outside the Baltimore experience.

Almost immediately Zavitz instituted changes in Friends School. First of all he decentralized part of his authority by increasing the roles of the three principals: Ruth Wrightson, in the Kindergarten and Primary grades; Guy Beetlestone, head of the Intermediate classes; and Merrill Hiatt, of the High School. He officially changed his own title from that of principal of the school to headmaster. He also delegated authority to a Dean of Girls, Eleanor Dilworth, and appointed a Superintendent of Buildings and Grounds, Otis E. Mace, a responsibility that had absorbed a large amount of William Pike's time as

Illus. 8-9 The faculty at Homeland Campus, 1936–37, under Headmaster Edwin C. Zavitz (1935–43): (back row) Edwin Zavitz, M. Margaret Rawlings, Ann C. Corckran, Lucy T. Willis, Margaret J. Tyson, Eleanore S. Lewis, Franklin A. Kuller, William S. Pike, John L. Etter, L. Lawrence Peacock, Guy C. Beetlestone, Roman Steiner, Jean H. Thomas, Elizabeth D. Steuart, Eileen Turk, Lucinda M. Primrose, Merrill L. Hiatt; (front row) Katherine I. Gorsuch, Lillian Griscom, Mary S. Rowe, Elizabeth C. Remmert, Marian B. Millard, Ida Schmeiser, Elizabeth S. Stimson, M. Eleanor Starr, Isabel Woods, Letitia Stockett, Ruth C. Dibert, Eleanor M. Dilworth, Margretta Cauffiel.

principal.[36] (Later, Miss Dilworth married Otis Mace.) The following year, 1936, when the High School moved to the Charles Street campus, Zavitz changed the organizational structure of the school that had existed since the days of Eli M. Lamb. He replaced the old system of three departments—Primary, Intermediate, and High School—with a Lower School of grades one through six, and an Upper School of grades seven through twelve, each housed in a separate building.[37] In 1937 the former clubhouse on the Homeland property was remodeled and opened as a nursery school and kindergarten.

Beyond this structural reorganization, Zavitz made few dramatic changes in the curriculum of Friends School. Significant departure from past practices seemed unnecessary, since the basic objective of sending a large percentage of well-prepared graduates on to college was already being accomplished. In the Lower School students studied the traditional subjects of reading, spelling, writing, arithmetic, history,

Illus. 8-10   Intermediate Study Hall, Homeland Campus, ca. 1932

geography, and art, as well as a coordinated science program that began in the first grade. In the high school the concentration was in six major fields: English, Latin, modern languages, mathematics, history, and science.[38]

Any meaningful changes that occurred in this pre-World War II period were more likely in the methods of teaching than in subject matter. The 1930s was the heyday of the progressive education movement, and Edwin Zavitz was a follower of that philosophy.[39] He attended most of the annual meetings of the Progressive Education Association, occasionally appeared as a speaker on the program and several times urged his teachers at Friends to attend the conferences by closing the school and providing them with expense money.[40] Even so, Friends would not have been labelled as strictly a "progressive" school as others in the city such as Park School, which under the leadership of its first headmaster, Eugene Randolph Smith, was widely recognized for its experimentation with new educational ideas.[41]

Progressive education, as it was popularly extracted and simplified from the writings of John Dewey, Francis Parker, and others, proposed

Illus. 8-11   Football Squad, Homeland Campus, 1932.

to instruct the children in three types of subject matter: first by teaching the necessary skills for employment as an adult, second by teaching the background of social life (e.g. through teaching history, geography, and economics), and third by teaching communications and inquiry through reading, grammar, and arithmetic. This basic subject matter was to be taught in an informal classroom setting where the child's natural abilities and interests were used to draw him or her into a variety of activities. Children would learn from observation and laboratory experimentation, as well as from the more traditional methods of reading and recitation. The child would learn to cope with his own environment as well as to develop his own talents or creativity. Extracurricular activity became increasingly important in the effort to produce the well-rounded child.[42] All of these methods were suggested in a flyer prepared in 1941 by Zavitz entitled "Objectives of Junior High School."

While there was no formal policy to make Friends a progressive school, individual teachers were nevertheless influenced by the discussion of progressive education ideas and methods. Miss Anita Biemiller, for example, who studied at Goucher College and Columbia University, used informal ways of encouraging individual learning among her intermediate level students. Even before the arrival of Zavitz, Ruth Wrightson, head of the Primary and Kindergarten Department, visited other schools in Baltimore and Wilmington, Delaware, to compare them with Friends. She concluded that her kindergarten was "progressive" because the children were taught to do things for themselves in order to promote independence and creativity.[43] Margaret Tyson [Bouchelle] taught her first grade primary students with several experimental methods, but emphasized individual reading and even began to work with dyslexic students as early as 1937. She objected to the curriculum that took her first grade pupils out of class for conversational French lessons; she believed they ought to be using that time for learning to read.[44]

Individual intelligence and achievement testing were also a part of the progressive trend followed at Friends School. Public interest in IQ tests and aptitude tests rose during World War I when the government attempted to evaluate its military personnel more accurately. By the late 1920s Friends had adopted a policy of administering IQ tests to all entering students and followed that with achievement tests to determine the placement of students. In 1929 Friends was paying a Johns Hopkins psychologist $1,000 a year to test the children and verify their classification. Apparently the teaching methods at the school were successful, because the Stanford Achievement Tests given in 1931 showed most classes to be one to one and one-half years ahead of the standard.[45]

The methods of grading students in the classroom did not change significantly under Edwin Zavitz. Pike had instituted a system of giving students numerical ratings on both their scholastic achievements and their personal character. Zavitz changed the numbers to letters but the methods were essentially the same. (See a typical report card in 1931-32 in illustration 8.12.)

Apparently the young Harry Scott was having a more enjoyable year in the third intermediate class (7th grade), for the previous spring he had passed a note to his classmates demanding: "We, the undersigned, upon the famous date of May 29, 1930 do demand more study periods, less book reports and tests, longer recesses, better lunches, etc." The note was signed by fifteen others, including Richard Hutzler, Evelyn Robinson, and Katherine Deming, who hedged by writing "may-be" after her name.

Name **Harry Scott**

INTERMEDIATE SCHOOL REPORT—19 **31** —19 **32**

CLASS **4A**

| | 1ST SEMESTER | | | | | 2ND SEMESTER | | | | | | |
| | 1 | | 2 | | | 3 | | 4 | | | | |
	CLASS AVER.	EXAM.	CLASS AVER.	FINAL EXAM.	GRADE	CLASS AVER.	EXAM.	CLASS AVER.	FINAL EXAM.	GRADE	GRADE FOR YEAR	RESULTS
Algebra								76	94	84		
Arithmetic	77	92	81	60	78	84	85					
Oral English	98		90		94	96		85		88		
Drawing												
French	89	72	92	80	88	85	95	88	99	92		
Geography												
Grammar	85	95	75	85	83	75	70	85	90	80		
History	92	90	89	88	90	90	90	92	96	92		
Latin	80	83	80	76	80	85	79	85	76	82		
Literature	80	60	85	85	79	80	85	85	90	84		
Manual Training	80		90		86	98		100		98		
Music												
Physical Training	70		90		80	90		90		90		
Physiology												
Science												
Spelling	90	95	95	95	93	90	95	98	98	95		
Writing	85		90		88	95		95		95		
Sewing												
Bible	90	87	93	94	91	94	97	85	90	91		
Days Absent	0		6			5		0			av. 87.50	
Times Late	0		0			0		0				
No. in Class												
Class Average											86.77	

PARENT'S SIGNATURE

FIRST REPORT *Harry A. Scott* | THIRD REPORT *Harry A. Scott*

SECOND REPORT *Harry A. Scott* | FOURTH REPORT

Illus. 8-12   Intermediate School Report for Harry Scott, 1931–32.

Zavitz's tenure as headmaster marked the increased involvement of adults in the school, both as parents and as students. In October, 1936, the Friends School Association was formed "to meet the need for a closer relationship between the school and its patrons, alumni, former pupils, and friends."[46] This group, which chose Dr. John C. Baldwin as its first president, produced a newsletter, *Contact*, and planned activities at the school, its first being a children's concert on homecoming day. But adults were also drawn closer to the school through courses offered by the faculty. These "Winter Courses," beginning in January and running one evening per week for six weeks, included academic as well as handicraft lessons. Letitia Stockett had no trouble filling classes entitled "Cavalcade of English Literature" or "An American Roundabout." Roman Steiner taught wood carving, John W. Tottle, Jr. discussed current events, Conrad Geblein put together an "orchestra," and Ronald Levy offered "Badminton for Beginners."[47]

By the end of Zavitz's administration in 1943 the Homeland campus of Friends School had become an active community center. Besides the evening courses and programs involving parents, there were several athletic clubs and social events that attracted a large number of participants from the community. The Racquet Club used the tennis courts in the summer months, the Archery Club and two women's hockey clubs enjoyed the green playing fields, the University of Baltimore rented the gymnasium for its basketball games, and neighbors in the community used the playgrounds, auditorium, and lecture rooms on a regular basis. The faculty agreed with Zavitz "that the school should be a local center of recreational and educational nature for the community in which it is located."[48] Alumni affairs and fundraising activities for charity also increased during these years. The Bazaar, which had started in 1904 as the Doll Show, was held each December to raise money for several charities. From the sale of cakes, candies, and other items the school was collecting over $1,200 a year by the 1940s.[49]

If the level of activities at the school increased for adults and neighbors, it also increased for the students themselves. One of the tenets of progressive education was to educate the whole child through a variety of experiences that included physical and social actions as well as academic lessons. The trend toward more extracurricular activities that began to grow significantly under Wilson and Pike continued under Zavitz. The student newspaper, *The Quaker Quill*, listed a steady diet of plays, concerts, lectures, proms, banquets, field trips to Washington and Philadelphia, and many new organizations such as literary or debate societies and a history club. Primary students enjoyed these experiences as fully as their elders in the high school. In 1931, for example, the younger pupils were directed by Isabel Woods in "A Pageant of Folklore adapted from *Grimm's Fairy Tales.*" With Bliss Forbush, Jr. as Herr Jacob Grimm and Marjorie Forbush as the Fairy

Illus. 8-13 Lower School Lunchroom, Homeland Campus, ca. 1936.

Godmother, the characters from Cinderella and other tales delighted the audience. Often the songs and music were written by Miss Woods. Her operetta, *The Sorcerer's Daughters,* drew an audience of 550 in 1941.[50]

The newest activities during Zavitz's tenure were ice hockey, the orchestra in the Upper School, volunteer work with the Red Cross, and the creation of a student council.[51] On the other hand, Zavitz eliminated those events or traditions that emphasized individual competition. The annual Information Contest ended and even the special listing of students who had perfect attendance records was discontinued because the headmaster believed that pupils should perform as part of a group or as a community, rather than compete as individuals.[52]

One way students could still fulfill any competitive urge they had was on the athletic field. More than ever before, under headmasters Pike and Zavitz athletic teams became an important part of the students' lives and a significant factor in the image of the school in Baltimore. By the time Pike became head of the school in 1927, all the athletic fields were at the Homeland property. Three scarlet-and-gray

Illus. 8-14   Lower School Classroom, Homeland Campus, 1936.

school buses shuttled students to the Charles Street grounds where they played field hockey, lacrosse, and baseball, ran races, and participated in other outdoor activities. Basketball, swimming, and other indoor sports continued at Park Avenue until 1937 when a new gym opened on the surburban campus. In justifying the growing importance of athletic teams in the school, Pike warned the Education Committee: "We must make a prominent place in athletic games if we expect to hold our big boys and attract others. We must be careful that we do not become largely a girls' school, and indeed we are tending that way at the present time."[53] Pike's emphasis seemed to begin to pay off when Friends put together winning basketball and swimming teams in 1928–29. As a consequence he felt the school was developing a strong school spirit. Nineteen thirty-one was an even better year when the boys won the MSA B Conference Championship in football and the girls won the City Swimming Championship. And Pike was so proud of the unde-feated lacrosse team, with All-Maryland players Frank and John Christhilf and Tony Rytina, that he showed game films to the Education Committee. He was certain that it was the finest high-school lacrosse team in the country.[54] Pike's pride and enthusiasm obviously influenced his evaluation of the team, but there was no doubt that Friends, from time to time, was able to field athletic teams that were the match of any in the city. During Zavitz's administation there were more championships such as the 1938 boys' lacrosse team that ended City College's thirty-seven game winning streak and finished with an unblemished season record. Later they hosted an all-star team from New York. In 1940 Bliss Forbush, Jr., a Baltimore *Sun* all-star, led the football team to another B Conference title.[55]

It is unnecessary to record every victory or to cite every championship team; the point is that Friends School, like its private and public competitors, was building a stronger self-identity and school spirit through its social and athletic programs. From time to time each successive headmaster or Education Committee would worry that there was too much or too little emphasis on sports or extra-curricular activities, but never was there a doubt that these were important parts of the curriculum.

By 1940 any changes that Edwin Zavitz was going to make had already occurred and his influence in the school began to decline. In June of that year he was asked by the American Friends Service Committee to go to France to survey Quaker refugee work going on there. Since he had taught in France twenty-five years earlier and still had a good command of the language, he was a logical choice. And Zavitz wanted to go. While he was on leave for the 1940–41 year the school was administered by a committee consisting of Merrill Hiatt, Martha Parsons, Eleanor Dilworth Mace and Alice Farquhar, with Bliss Forbush as chairman.[56] Zavitz returned for the next school year, but in September he requested permission to accept the headmastership of Sidwell Friends School in Washington on a part-time basis.[57] He proposed to divide his time between the two schools. The committee at first agreed, but it was apparently an unpopular arrangement in the eyes of the faculty and among some members of Baltimore Monthly Meeting. When Zavitz reported an offer in January 1943 to move to Sidwell full time, the Education Committee quickly accepted his resignation and enthusiastically offered the position of headmaster to Bliss Forbush. Years later when those who knew Edwin Zavitz recalled his tenure at Friends, they remembered him as an administrator who was oftentimes too idealistic and not always practical. Some old hands, like Letitia Stockett simply refused to let Zavitz interfere with their classroom teaching. Although he was generally liked by the teachers, he apparently did not measure up to the popularity of William S. Pike nor did he have the confidence of the teachers that Edward Wilson had. With the end of his administration in 1943 a new era would begin, one in which the Forbush name became predominant.

Illus. 9-1   Bazaar in the Gymnasium, Homeland Campus, November 1958.

CHAPTER 9

An American and Quaker Dilemma

Shortly after 2:00 P.M. on December 7, 1941, Friends School students first heard the news that would affect their lives for the next few years. Some of the older boys heard the Mutual Broadcasting System announcement that broke into the play-by-play coverage of the Dodgers-Giants football game at the Polo Grounds in New York. Others didn't learn of Pearl Harbor until their parents turned on the radio at three o'clock that Sunday to hear the CBS broadcast of the New York Philharmonic. Some heard the war news from neighbors or friends who spread the information as quickly as it was known. And younger children remembered the day war came to America only by the serious and sometimes angry way their parents talked about the Japanese threat.

For Baltimore's Quaker community war was a particularly unwelcome event. Strong in their patriotism and loyalty, and outraged like other Americans by the unexpected attack on Pearl Harbor, the Quakers nevertheless tried to refrain from condemning the Japanese and from calling for revenge. Since the time of George Fox, the Society of Friends had faced the dilemma of maintaining the principles of peace while their nation went to war. For American Quakers the Revolutionary, Civil, and First World wars had been difficult times that saw the loss of many members who chose to fight and thereby reject or compromise the principle of nonviolence. Now in 1941, when the nation seemed so unjustly attacked, the reconciliation of patriotism and religious values strained the resolve of even the most ardent Friends. At home children heard their parents and relatives agree that the United States ought to "crush the sneaky Japs and give them what they deserve." They watched fathers, uncles, and older brothers proudly enlist in the armed services to defend the nation. How then would these students respond to their school when teachers and administrators talked of the importance of peace and world cooperation. How tempt-ing, too, for the school simply to de-emphasize its pacifist scruples and to join enthusiastically in the war effort on the home front. Without careful leadership, Friends School faced the danger of losing its most precious possession—its Quaker character.

This problem of defending the principles of peace in a nation at war was only the first, and perhaps the least troublesome, of the dilemmas the school would face over the next two decades. Potentially more damaging than the war was the issue of desegregation. In the 1940s and 1950s Friends School would be launched upon a difficult course as it became one of the first of the independent schools in Baltimore to racially integrate. The public and Catholic school systems preceded it in this significant change. Partly by choice, behind firm leaders who became increasingly uncomfortable with the hypocrisy of segregation in a Quaker institution, and partly compelled by national events that demanded greater equality in American life, Friends School confronted the racial questions that threatened either to destroy it or thrust it into the forefront of integration in Baltimore's private schools.

Less dramatic and more subtly pervasive as a dilemma for the postwar society was the new prosperity that carried the nation away from the memories of the Great Depression. A mass consumer life style, ushered in by the postwar recovery and the greatest baby boom in history, threatened to rewrite the traditional values and codes of behavior that Americans were familiar with before the war. While an older generation looked over its shoulder at the uncertainties of the depression years, a new generation eagerly welcomed the unpre-cedented growth of the 1950s. The accumulation of consumer goods that was pursued so ardently in the new suburban shopping centers may not have been America's new "religion," but it was at least a new attitude which suggested that personal affluence could be an end in itself. Friends School, which took pride in trying to educate the "whole child," would have to confront the challenges the new spirit of con-sumerism brought.

In some ways Friends School might have been better prepared to deal with the beginning of World War II than other schools in Baltimore. First of all several teachers had been in Europe in the summer of 1939 and they brought back strong impressions of a world preparing for war. Elizabeth Remmert, who heard one of Hitler's speeches in August just before the war began, felt fortunate to have escaped Europe without harm. She left Germany "for Copenhagen on a black-out night, changing trains five times, unable to use American money," and forced "to pay a special levy of $70 per passenger to cover war risk insurance for the crew." Eleanor Dilworth Mace was another teacher who arrived in Paris just as the agreement between Hitler and Stalin was announced and she saw the French making hurried preparations for war.[1] Bliss Forbush, Chairman of the Education Committee, had also returned in June from assisting Jewish families escape from Germany. This war-consciousness on the part of the faculty, combined with the Quaker tradition of providing aid to distressed peoples throughout the world, led to the school's early involvement in a refugee program. Before the end of 1939 Friends School had taken two students into the Upper School who were war refugees from Europe. Several more English and Dutch children arrived the next year and by 1943 there were nearly a dozen pupils attending Friends after their flight from England, Holland, Spain, and even Germany. Some came through the actions of the American Friends Service Committee, while others came because of direct contact with specific individuals, such as the Hamilton Davis family whose members had attended Friends for several generations.[2] Teachers encouraged correspondence with children in France, England, China, and other countries affected by the war, and in the Lower School each class began to collect clothes and make blankets for the refugees abroad.

As long as the war was being fought by other nations, Friends School could encourage its students to support and aid the unfortunate victims without fear of contradicting Quaker principles. The Society of Friends had always been in the forefront of those institutions and organizations that gave aid to the oppressed. But after 1941 when the United States itself went to war, the school administration and the Education Committee had to move carefully so that neither the members of Baltimore Monthly Meeting nor the non-Quaker majority of school families were offended. Military recruiters and speakers for the government's wartime programs were not permitted to address the students at the Homeland campus. Conversely in the post-Pearl Harbor atmosphere of 1942–45, non-Quaker supporters of the school would not tolerate any overt opposition to the war effort. Rather, the wise path the school chose was one that upheld Quaker principles of peace but which allowed each individual freedom of opinion and action. As Bliss Forbush put it simply, each "must come to his position on the war by action. The faculty formed new committees to bring better coordination to the curriculum and improve teaching methods; the Education following his conscience" and all viewpoints must be respected.[3] With this attitude of flexibility and freedom, Friends School adjusted as well as possible to the dilemmas posed by the war years.

In their own way children kept up with the war news. They read letters from fathers and brothers who were away in the armed services and listened to the radio. Boys sometimes played war games and girls played army nurse or Red Cross rather than house. After school they hurried home to hear the latest episode of Dick Tracy, Superman, or Hop Harrigan, which often involved spies or a wartime setting. At the Quaker school on Charles Street, however, the awareness of the war was kept to a minimum. A . . .

> sincere and positive effort was made to keep war hysteria out of the school. No war drives or bond sales were conducted, no service enlistment interpreters spoke in assemblies, and no new courses were introduced. On the other hand the school did not live in isolation from world affairs. Causes of war and peace were discussed in Social Study courses, the progress of the war was intelligently treated in current event periods, and speakers from foreign countries were used when it was known they would present matters from a good will point of view.[4]

Younger children collected books, clothing, and newspapers for the men in the services. Several pupils began riding bikes to school rather than coming by automobile, in order to save rubber. In the high school the Student Council discussed giving up formal dances because they were too expensive during wartime, but mostly because they wanted to show their willingness to make sacrifices. Girls were allowed to forego their usual uniforms in the winter months and wear wool dresses and heavy sweaters since the classrooms were kept cooler to conserve valuable fuel. And all the students were made conscious of the war by the regular air raid drills. When warning bells sounded, students learned to slip quickly beneath their school desks or to march rapidly to the basement areas of the buildings. But the most sobering reminder of the war came when eighteen-year-old senior boys were drafted before their graduation. A few had to leave early for the army or navy, although most were given deferments until after commencement. Even those who weren't yet drafted had to prepare by taking physical and mental ability exams.[5] To aid the Quaker boys and others who were conscientious objectors, Bliss and LaVerne Forbush helped set up the first Civilian Public Service Camp. Some of the boys were housed in the old Friends School building on Park Avenue and bused daily to Patapsco State Park for work. Many of these young men wanted to make their contribution by serving in hospitals, or with the Red Cross in Europe. Instead they were put to work in national and state parks, like Patapsco, or did antipollution work in the city.[6] Whether or not they were drafted or fought, most of the older students were aware of the wartime tensions. Bliss Forbush observed that a few new disciplinary problems arose in those years as young people felt a desire to have a "last fling" at life before joining the armed forces.

In retrospect the Education Committee concluded in 1945 that "actually the school passed through the war years in a favorable condition."[7] With more mothers taking jobs outside the home in war industries and retail stores, the number of applicants for school increased. Certainly the improved wages of the war years helped many to consider for the first time the advantages of an independent school like Friends. Enrollment grew from 366 in 1940–41 to 462 in 1944–45. Economically the worst years were behind and the school had a new administration to carry it into the next two decades.

When Bliss Forbush took over the headmastership from Edwin Zavitz in July, 1943, he came to the position with feelings of anticipation and apprehension.[8] His excitement came from the challenge of beginning a new career at an institution with which he was well familiar. He had taught religion classes at Friends School since 1923 and had recently been a member and chairman of the Education Committee. His brief service as acting headmaster when Edwin Zavitz was away with the American Friends Service Committee was enough to convince him that he would enjoy the new position. Nevertheless, Bliss Forbush had his doubts about the job. It was not a position he had sought and he was reluctant to step down as the leader of the Yearly Meeting, where he had many friends and enjoyed much influence. With resignation, however, he admitted that "Perhaps we had accomplished all we could do at Park Avenue Meeting; we were running out of new ideas, and the committee was finding it more difficult to raise the necessary funds to cover our work." It was time, he felt, that "someone new come on the scene."[9]

Certainly the promise of a higher salary and greater financial security for his family of seven children helped to ease the transition. But if the Friends School position brought personal economic improvement, the overall financial prospects of the school worried him. "I do not see the school position as a bed of roses," he wrote to a trusted friend. "The financial picture is not a too happy one.... We have a large debt, and for the past eight years have either been in debt or had a balance of one or two thousand dollars." Teachers' salaries, Forbush admitted, and Zavitz would have agreed, were a disgrace.[10] There were no retirement or health insurance systems for the faculty, and still more physical improvements and additions were needed at the Charles Street campus. At the same time he would be trying to solve these problems, he would also have to provide the intellectual leadership that would keep Friends School in the forefront of education in Baltimore. To ask him to follow in the footsteps of Eli Lamb, Edward Wilson, William Pike, and Edwin Zavitz, all experienced teachers with degrees in education, was expecting a lot.

But those who encouraged Bliss to take the responsibility of running the school knew exactly the kind of man they were getting and there was not a doubt among them. Forty-seven years of age when he became headmaster, he was one of the most well-known, respected, and loved Quakers in the whole Pennsylvania-Maryland-Virginia area. His position as Executive Secretary first of the Baltimore Monthly Meeting, then of the larger Yearly Meeting, not only brought him into contact with Quakers throughout the Mid-Atlantic region, but also made him well-respected as a religious leader in Baltimore. He was a member of the Board of Directors of the Maryland Council of Churches, Dean of the Baltimore School of Religious Education, Chairman of the Baltimore Leadership Training Council, delegate to the American Section, World Council of Churches, a Trustee of McKim School, and was appointed by the governor in 1939 as a trustee of Morgan State College. Add to these activities the chairmanship of Friends General Conference and leading roles in several other Quaker organizations and programs, and one has a man with exceptional administrative experience and wide public contacts. He was in constant demand as a speaker in churches and community organizations, on college campuses and at commencements, and even on local radio programs. He was already established as a prolific writer by 1943, publishing an article each week for the *Friends Intelligencer*, pamphlets for the General Conference, and eventually would write eleven books.

It was this background in public speaking, publishing, and broad community activities that made Bliss Forbush different from all of his predecessors as headmaster. Eli Lamb was the sober school principal, Edward Wilson the efficient organizer, William Pike the master teacher, and Edwin Zavitz the professional educator. Bliss Forbush in his turn was the beloved Quaker and inspirational public leader. To this can be added that he proved to be an exceptional administrator as well, which Sheppard and Enoch Pratt Hospital recognized years later by calling him out of retirement to serve ten years as its President, and then electing him an honorary member of the medical staff. He was a person who fell quite naturally into a leadership role, regardless of whether he had long experience in a particular field. As he would admit years later in looking back at his own career, he often had to develop the expertise after he had taken the job. He had no experience in mental hospital administration before he accepted the Sheppard-Enoch Pratt position just as he had no experience in education prior to 1943 except for the Bible classes he taught at Friends. A year's study in The Johns Hopkins Evening School was his only formal training in educational methods.

Bliss Forbush's strength was his warm personality, his firm character, his basic common sense, and most of all his deeply-rooted religious faith. None of which is to suggest that he lacked academic credentials, for he had earned an A.B. and an A.M. at the University of Chicago and had completed all of the work for a doctorate except the dissertation when he was stopped by a serious heart attack at the age of 40. Later he would receive honorary doctorates from Swarthmore and Morgan State College. He also wrote a scholarly biography published by Columbia University Press on the great Quaker leader, Elias Hicks. Some of his talent for scholarship and writing no doubt came from his father, Dr. William Byron Forbush, a Congregational minister, President of the American Institute of Child Life, an associate of noted child psychologist G. Stanley Hall, and the author of dozens of books on youth and Christianity. Bliss Forbush then, although he did not fit the mold of the typical school administrator, was a man of immense talent and capacity for leadership. As Friends faced the dilemmas of the post-war years, it was fortunate to have this inspirational Quaker in charge.

The new headmaster had no difficulty in assessing the strengths and weaknesses of the school, for he inherited a long list of "goals for the future" left by Edwin Zavitz, and in 1943 a detailed evaluation of the school by the Middle States Association of Colleges and Secondary Schools. The greatest problem that each of these sources pointed out was the financial condition of the school. Specifically the salaries paid to teachers were so low that Forbush feared a loss of accreditation unless they were raised to the approximate level of public school faculty.[11] A comparison showed Friends School teachers consistently below the average and in some cases far below. At the junior high level, for example, where the maximum salary in Baltimore's public schools was $2,600, faculty at Friends received $1,100 less than the standard. Likewise all administrative and office staff salaries were below public school levels.[12] To make matters worse Friends School had no retirement system for any of its employees. Since many sources predicted a return to the Depression economy once the war was over, the new headmaster had good cause to be concerned. Over the next seventeen years the most consistent policy of the Forbush administration was the effort to raise salaries and to establish security for the faculty. On the whole he was moderately successful. Tuition was steadily raised, which made Friends more expensive than St. Paul's School and Garrison Forest, though cheaper than Gilman and Park.[13]

Much as he hated being a salesman, Bliss Forbush used his strong public image and his personal charm to increase the school's endowment and scholarship fund. Edward C. Wilson, who died in 1944, set an important precedent by bequeathing part of his estate to the school. New buildings, such as the auditorium completed in 1957 at a cost of over a quarter of a million dollars, and improvements to the grounds and playing fields were also the result of vigorous fund-raising campaigns.[14] By 1959, near the end of Dr. Forbush's administration, the total assets reached one million dollars for the first time and income was approaching half a million.[15] Even so, he still lamented in 1960 that "Salaries continued to be a discouraging factor" and good teachers were leaving for better jobs elsewhere.[16]

Dr. Forbush's concern for his faculty also appeared in his creation of tenure and retirement systems for them. He was shocked when Letitia Stockett, probably the best-known teacher Friends ever had in its two hundred years of education, came to his office one spring day to ask if she were to be retained for the following year. The realization that loyal and valued teachers had no sense of security led to the creation of a tenure program in 1949. After seven years of satisfactory service, teachers were designated as "senior faculty" and considered permanent.[17] The system worked well partly because Bliss Forbush was selective in hiring and because he was willing to spend time helping weak teachers. Most of the hiring was done through the contacts he had as former Executive Secretary of Baltimore Yearly Meeting and through his close relationship with other Quaker headmasters throughout the Mid-Atlantic region. The character, ability, and family background of each teacher was often well known to someone within this network.

Illus. 9-2 The faculty at Homeland Campus, 1948–49, under Headmaster Bliss Forbush, Sr. (1943–60): (front row, left to right) Ruth C. Dibert, M. Eleanor Starr, Isabel Woods, Dorothy E. Michel, Marion B. Millard, J. Harold Passmore, Eleanor M. Dilworth, Bliss Forbush, Sr., Martha C. Parsons, Robert C. Richardson, Ms. Moylan, Beth Hanauer, Roma A. Luttrell, Roman Steiner, Mary S. Barnhart; (second row) Marjorie M. Richardson, Claire Walker, Josephine Miller, Ada C. Baldwin, Alice C. Fry, Nancy Carr, Mary K. Wickham, Mildred M. Hetrick, Eleanor W. High, Ethelind B. Anderson, Janette L. Taylor, Eleanor P. Terry, Harriette Procter Van Sant, Hanne-Liese Dahl, Hermann M. Dahl, Nan H. Agle, Muriel B. H. Oster, Laura H. Singewald, Ida L. Schmeiser; (back row) Virginia G. Hurley, Betty Llewellyn, Ruth W. Boatman, Sara G. Barnes, Henry Woodman, Robert A. Nicolls, Jean P. Stuart, Arthur O. Gray, Eugene H. Denk, L. Lawrence Peacock.

Only once did Dr. Forbush go to a professional employment agency for a teacher and that experience had unhappy results.

According to the Middle States evaluation conducted during the 1943–44 academic year and again in 1945 and 1949, Friends was as good as and in some ways better than other Quaker and independent schools of the region.[18] It was judged to be a "good school" with a "progressive" philosophy, an "above average student body," and there was a "friendly feeling...between the teachers and pupils." The overall physical plant was good and the institution possessed high morale, a superior standard of behavior, and generally good manners. Besides the low faculty salaries, the 1943 evaluation pointed to weaknesses in the guidance program, the library, and the need for more courses in the curriculum for those students not going to college. Greater continuity in social science and language programs, broader variety of student activities, and a more diverse athletic program were other suggestions that were made. In each case the school administration responded with Committee authorized an additional $500 for library books and money for a consultant from the Enoch Pratt Free Library; Bliss Forbush and J. Harold Passmore, the business manager, went to work to raise more money for faculty and physical improvements; and the guidance program was improved.[19]

Looked at from historical perspective, most of these criticisms and improvements fall into the normal routine of a typical country day school trying to improve itself and to keep up with its competitors. But beneath the surface the forces of change were at work that would create new turmoil for the school and, some feared, would even bring its long history to an end. A combination of national events and a stronger sense of commitment to social change during the Bliss Forbush years brought the school face to face with its own moral dilemma: how could a Quaker institution, founded on the principle that "there is that of God in every man," refuse to accept children from Baltimore's black families? The dilemma of desegregation, which had for so long been ignored or deftly sidestepped, now had to be resolved. The 1954 Supreme Court decision, Brown vs. the Board of Education of Topeka, Kansas, made it likely that private as well as public schools would have to remove the racial restrictions from their admissions policies. The only real question was when the change would occur. The fact that Friends was among the first of the private country day schools in Baltimore to begin integration was appropriate to its historical and philosophical roots.

From the early days of George Fox, the Quakers had shown concern for the education of black Americans, both free and slave. Among the queries always asked by Monthly and Yearly Meetings were those regarding the welfare and education of blacks and Indians. This concern, however, did not have specific effect until after the American Revolution. Three years after the opening of Friends School in 1784, Joseph Townsend, the school's first teacher and an early Baltimore abolitionist, advertised for a teacher in the newly opened Baltimore African Academy.[20]

This was only the first of several efforts by Quakers to establish schools for the city's black population. When the local abolition society, of which Townsend was president, was dissolved in 1792, after three years of existence, the organization's building on Sharp Street was turned over to blacks for use as a school. It began with only sixteen pupils, but under the guidance of Daniel Coker as teacher between 1802 and 1817 grew to an enrollment of 150.[21] There is also evidence that Baltimore Quarterly Meeting opened a school for free blacks in 1794.[22] Richard Townsend, Joseph's son, wrote in his diary of an evening school led by another Quaker, Evan Thomas, that opened on Fish Street in 1817 with a "very great" number of scholars.[23] As the frequency of these school foundings suggests, none of them was successful for very long periods of time. Even so, the most enduring interest among whites in education for blacks came from Baltimore's Quakers. When there were no formal schools open in some years, individual blacks were informally educated in the homes of Quaker families. At no time were the Quakers willing to integrate the Meeting's school for their own children, but they nevertheless recognized an obligation to assist the black population of Baltimore. This attitude of support continued into the post-Civil War period as Quakers helped set up schools for freedmen through the Baltimore Association for the Moral and Educational Improvement of the Colored People. These later schools were finally taken over in 1867 by the public school system.[24]

Once public schools were established for blacks in Baltimore, Quaker interest waned. No doubt the Quakers were subject to many of the same prejudices and social attitudes common below the Mason-Dixon Line that kept black Americans in a Jim Crow system of segregation from the end of the nineteenth century until after World War II. Blacks in Baltimore were restricted not only in education but also in residence and occupation. They were excluded from most hotels and department stores and were denied service downtown in all but the railroad station restaurant. With the exception of the second balcony of Ford's Theater, most white theaters refused to admit Negroes. Only with the end of the war did a "thaw" in racial separation begin to appear in the city. The gradual change in Baltimore was part of a national change stimulated by the actions of President Harry S. Truman, who desegregated the armed forces, and by the Supreme Court, which began to strike down Jim Crow laws in the early 1940s. The revulsion from Hitler's racism and the positive response to lofty ideals of the new United Nations also helped to push the United States into a renewed effort for equal rights.

These national events, which culminated in the 1954 Supreme Court decision, would have compelled Friends School to desegregate its student body regardless of who was headmaster or who sat on the Education Committee. Once the public and Catholic school systems of Baltimore were desegregated, the independent schools would soon have to follow. The danger in focusing narrowly on the history of a single institution and its leaders is to sometimes grant herculean praise to what in perspective are more common actions and decisions. With that precaution in mind, it is still judicious to conclude that there were those individuals at Friends, in its administration, on its faculty, and among its supporters, who reached beyond the normal expectations to prepare the school for social change and to bring it about peacefully. Bliss Forbush was called to lead the way.

Tracing his interest in equal rights for blacks back to his days in the liberal environment of Oberlin College in Ohio, where the races mixed together in classes and on athletic teams, Dr. Forbush was active in interracial activities from his first days in Baltimore. As Executive Secretary of Baltimore Monthly Meeting, he attended the Third Interracial Conference of Baltimore held at the Park Avenue Meeting House, February 16–18, 1923.[25] Other conferences and interracial activities followed. In 1939 the governor appointed him to the Board of Trustees of Morgan State College and he also became a member of Baltimore's Urban League. In his twenty-one years of service as a Morgan trustee he was always active in the college's development, with his name eventually appearing on the plaques of ten new buildings. His basic philosophy was that found in the Friends' *Book of Discipline:*

> While other races, either within or without our borders, remain in economic, mental, or spiritual bondage, we cannot be true to the obligation which our common brotherhood imposes upon us without doing our utmost to remove the burden from and to give them assistance and cooperation in obtaining an opportunity equal to our own.[26]

"Friends," he believed, "by the driving force of their religious faith, should be leaders in the movements for the emancipation of the Negro, and other minority groups."[27] This attitude brought him recognition by the Baltimore *Afro-American,* which singled him out as one of those whites "who are helping to promote democracy in our city. . . ."[28]

From the beginning of his tenure at Friends School Dr. Forbush promoted that same philosophy of brotherhood and democracy. In his first year as headmaster he recorded that "in the Lower School my weekly assemblies have been devoted. . . , at the request of the faculty, to the problem of creating better attitudes toward other races."[29] His views on race hit a responsive note among some of the teachers, and the war years proved unique opportunities to begin a long-term program in human relations. An awareness of human suffering and social responsibility rose out of the welfare efforts of the students to send food and clothing to the refugees of World War II. But the school learned a new lesson in 1943 when, after debate and disagreement among the Education Committee, they agreed to admit Mary Innui, a Japanese-American pupil.[30] This action, along with the acceptance of European students during the war, encouraged interest in international culture and stimulted a program of foreign student exchange that continued after the war was over. Each year, through the American Friends Service Committee and its School Affiliation Program, foreign students attended Friends and local students went to Holland, Italy, Singapore, Great Britain, and France. Money from the annual bazaar was used to support children and schools primarily in Western Europe. Nor were conditions at home neglected. With the aid of the Parents Auxiliary, children collected hundreds of books each year and forwarded them to the Faith Cabin Libraries in the southern states.[31]

In 1947 the school formed a Human Relations Committee whose purpose was "to discuss the relations of races to each other and try to get an understanding of what is needed in both attitude and action to build better relations."[32] This committee, which included strong faculty members such as Claire Walker, Eleanor Dilworth Mace, Martha Parsons, Robert Richardson, Isabel Woods, Harold Passmore, and of course Bliss Forbush, was at the heart of the activities that prepared Friends for peaceful desegregation in 1955. They encouraged teachers to organize student trips to the United Nations Organization in New York, invited foreign guests to speak to school assemblies, and promoted more of the welfare projects that had started in World War II. Human relations, they argued, ought to be an integral part of the curriculum in a Quaker school, as essential as the three Rs. "When we think of education in human relations with children, we mean practice in thinking well of and getting along well with people everywhere, regardless of race, religion, color, or social and economic status." This type of thinking and behavior can be brought about through direct contact with other people, through the absorption of values from parents and teachers, and through the study of selected books.[33]

The work of Bliss Forbush and the Human Relations Committee in preparing Friends for desegregation gains in importance when put in the perspective of Baltimore's southern racial atmosphere. Social and economic separation between the races had the sanctity of tradition for a large majority of the white population, even within the Quaker community. Baltimore Monthly Meeting had no black members and whenever the question of racial mixing arose there were many who spoke against any change in policy. In 1944 a move to allow black children to attend the Meeting's summer camp was blocked and several Quakers objected when blacks were invited to attend a picnic and square dance at the school.[34] From the mid-1940s on there was a division among members of the Quaker meeting and in the school over the issue of desegregation. Some were indignant that Friends principles were not carried out and that ideals like integration were always put off until the future.[35]

Bliss Forbush argued that the problem of integrating the school could not be resolved as long as the Meeting remained segregated. In a letter to concerned Friends he suggested that a series of steps be followed to bring about change over a period of time. He would start with a closer informal association with blacks and an invitation for them to begin attending events sponsored by the Meeting. Gradually they would be assimilated into the First-day School (Sunday School) and then admitted formally to membership in the Monthly Meeting. Finally, the school and summer camp would be opened to all races.[36] The Monthly Meeting acquiesced by adopting a statement on civil rights, but it brought no immediate change. There were always arguments to delay any action. Conservative members suggested, with a misplaced sense of justice, that it would be unfair to impose Quaker values of racial equality on families in the school who were not Quakers. Others argued very effectively that desegregation would bring financial ruin to Friends School because a majority of whites would withdraw their children. Lacking sufficient support, there was little that the advocates of social change could do but follow a policy of "wait and educate." Forcing change on a majority was not the Quaker way, and the danger that desegregation might indeed bring financial ruin were adequate causes to postpone any immediate action.

In the meanwhile, Bliss Forbush continued to speak for stronger religious values in the school and others worked quietly in their own way. Martha C. Parsons, head of the Lower School, made it a practice after 1949 to interview each new teacher thoroughly on the question of race and to hire no one who was unwilling to teach or accept black children in class. As a consequence, when integration came in 1955, it was accepted more readily in the Lower School than among the Upper School students and faculty.

By 1951 outside pressure mounted. The Urban League met with the headmasters of the Private School Association of Baltimore to urge changes in admissions policies. Major Lamborn of McDonogh said several blacks had applied to his school but none was qualified. Hans Froelicher of Park School, a leader in progressive education, agreed that the time was not yet right for integration, even though his own school had said in theory that no one would be refused admission because of race. And Bliss Forbush reported that the Education Committee of Friends had rejected any change unless four or five of the private schools agreed to open their doors at once.[37] In a private memo written about the same time Dr. Forbush suggested that integration might be successful if a specific future date were chosen and that blacks be admitted into one grade at a time, starting with Nursery School.[38]

The greatest pressure came, however, after 1952 when the first of Baltimore's public schools was integrated on a limited basis. In September, 1952, the Board of School Commissioners voted to admit sixteen black boys to Baltimore Polytechnic Institute because the unique curriculum offered there was available at no other public high school in the city.[39] The publicity from this event and several other attempts to integrate the public schools increased the awareness of the issue in the Friends community.

Among the private schools, several of the Catholic schools had begun to admit Negroes; and Park approved the principle of desegregation as early as 1950, although no blacks enrolled until September, 1955.[40] When the question of desegregation came up in Eleanor Dilworth Mace's social studies class, twenty of the thirty students said that if blacks were admitted they would leave because of their own objection or because their parents would remove them. Aware that these sentiments were still strong among the school's patrons, the Education Committee in the spring of 1953 refused to take any action to change the admission policy.

> The education committee in charge of Friends School is aware of its responsibility to many groups who have created and supported the School in the past and who are concerned in its future. It does not believe that any large number of Friends, alumni, parents,

teachers, or students are prepared for a change in admission policy at the present time. There is no doubt a growing number feel a change should be made in the future. In the meantime, the Committee believes that steps should be taken, neither ill advised nor before proper preparations have been made, to educate all groups interested in the School in the many facets of the problem involved in achieving the ideal of Christian brotherhood.[41]

This refusal to take action caused at least one patron to withdraw his children in protest of the segregation policy.[42]

By this time the friction between the Education Committee and the Monthly Meeting was nearly at its peak. In answer to the increasing demands that the school bring its admissions policy into agreement with Quaker principles, the Education Committee replied that the Meeting ought to desegregate its own membership before pressuring the school into change. Throughout this highly emotional time the Quakers were plagued by their own tradition of what might be called the "tyranny of the minority." No votes are ever taken in a Quaker meeting and any action must have the consent, if not the agreement, of the minority. By refusing consent and continuing discussion on an issue, a small group could delay action on any decision. The position of Dr. Forbush and his fellow integrationists who followed a policy of "wait and educate" was based on an understanding of how Quaker bodies functioned.

When the Supreme Court declared school segregation to be unconstitutional on May 18, 1954, the period of waiting was nearly over at Friends School. The pressure from reform-minded members of the local Meeting, as well as from Quakers in Philadelphia and other northern schools that had already integrated, joined together with the impact of the Court ruling, was enough to push the school officials into action. At the next Education Committee meeting in June, G. Canby Robinson, M.D., the chairman, reported several letters, including one signed by twenty-seven persons and another signed by twelve parents, all urging the school to accept integration. One member of the Homewood Meeting of Friends wrote to offer a contribution of $50 to $100 for each of the next three years in case enrollment should decline.[43] Still moving cautiously, however, the school leaders chose a subcommittee to study the issue and to be prepared to take action in the fall.

By the time September came, tensions were running high in Baltimore. Although the public schools in the surrounding counties delayed desegregation until the following year, 1955, the public school administration of the city was committed to carrying out the Court's ruling and the Catholic Archdiocese announced that desegregation would begin in Catholic schools. At first the reaction was surprisingly mild. The *New York Times* reported that "In Baltimore, the historic change went into effect smoothly and amicably, with the pupils, especially the younger ones, apparently unaware of the importance of their role. White and Negro parents, escorting beginners to school, chatted of common problems."[44] But the calmness disguised the hostility that lay beneath the surface. Within a few weeks violence over integration broke out in South Baltimore. An angry mob of 800 white parents and pupils attacked four black high school students. One Negro boy was punched in the face and the crowd overturned a police car. Later the same day blacks near Cherry Hill were stoned by angry whites. Mayor Thomas D'Alesandro appealed for calm and reason.

At Friends School the atmosphere was more peaceful, but fear and disagreement were evident. Fortunately for Dr. Forbush he now had the support of a strong and effective chairman on the Education Committee. Dr. G. Canby Robinson, a Quaker and a native of Baltimore, was a natural leader with little patience for inaction. "He was a medical organizer, the founder and first medical director of the Vanderbilt University Medical School, organizer of the Cornell-Rockefeller Center in New York City, consultant to the Christian Medical School in Peking, and at the time connected with Johns Hopkins University."[45] Although he was aware of the financial dangers to the school, he was ready to press forward for integration. On September 10 he and Dr. Forbush met with the faculty to discuss the desegregation issue. The Lower School teachers were ready to accept Negro children into their classes, but many of the Upper School teachers, much to the surprise and dismay of Dr. Forbush, balked at the idea. Some objected because of racial beliefs, but the majority were apparently fearful that desegregation would mean an enrollment decline and a subsequent loss of salary or even of jobs. They were well aware of the cases in other cities where Quaker schools had attempted to integrate a decade or two earlier and had met financial disaster as a result when white parents withdrew their children. No decision was made at this meeting, but the greater portion of the faculty clearly were against changing the admission policy.[46]

The next step was to meet with the patrons of the school. Here was the real test. Would parents resist the effort to change the admission

Illus. 9-3   Roman Steiner, in his 52nd year of teaching drafting and woodworking, Homeland Campus, 1951.

policy? Would they vocally protest on the grounds that it was their tuition money that supported the school and therefore insist that they had a right to influence admission policies? They might even demand a vote since few of them were Quakers and had no experience with Quaker methods of conducting business. Worst of all was the fear that parents might quietly respond by simply not enrolling their children at Friends the next fall. Whatever the outcome, the meeting on September 27, 1954, was a crucial event in the movement for desegregation.

The crowd that filled the gymnasium on the evening of September 27 took their seats with a serious air of anticipation of the discussion to come. At the front of the room along one side were members of the Education Committee: Isabella Jinnette and Harry S. Scott, Jr., Norris Matthews, Harold Passmore, the school's business manager, Philip E. Lamb, a nephew of Eli Lamb and the Vice Chairman of the Committee, Gilbert H. Alford, and several others.[47] As the audience settled down, the first to rise and speak was G. Canby Robinson. A handsome man, well accustomed to positions of leadership, his voice and manner gave an air of authority and control. Dr. Robinson spoke of the "American Dilemma" of racism and of the "Quaker Dilemma" of reconciling actions with principles. Quoting passages from the Friends' *Book of Discipline,* he raised the question "whether we have the right to expect the Society of Friends to conduct in the future a school in which racial segregation is the policy." It was clear that his own sentiments were against segregation, but he went on to add that the Education Committee also had an obligation to consider the viewpoints of the large majority of patrons who were not Friends and who might oppose integration.

Bliss Forbush then spoke, reviewing the school's attempt to prepare children by teaching them about other cultures and races. Until now, he said, Friends had taken pride in trying to be as democratic as the public schools. The failure to integrate would put a weapon in the hands of the enemies of democracy. Besides, he reassured the audience, the experience of Friends' schools elsewhere suggested that when they were opened up to all races, few blacks had actually applied and only the strongest applicants were accepted. He tried to ease the fears of those who warned of a rapid change in the school's constituency. To make the transition a gradual one, he proposed a plan to open the Nursery School and Kindergarten to all applicants in 1955, the first grade in 1956, and one grade each year thereafter until the whole school was integrated. In this way no child currently enrolled in the school would be forced to sit in the same classroom with black children.

When Dr. Forbush finished, Dr. Robinson then opened the meeting to discussion. His commanding figure kept the audience under control, but there were some who threatened to withdraw their children if the admission policy were changed, and others who objected that the school had no right to desegregate after their children were already accepted. A few faculty rose to warn of the financial difficulties that might arise and to argue that the school had an obligation to support its tenured teachers. But there were an equal number who commended the Education Committee and urged them to fulfill the obligations of a Quaker school by integrating.[48] By the end of the evening it was obvious that the school community was divided. It would require courageous leadership to resolve the issue without doing serious damage to Friends. Fortunately that leadership was present.

In preparation for the meeting of the Education Committee on November 16, when a decision would be made, Dr. Forbush reviewed the situation in a memo to Canby Robinson:

> In one way the recent Supreme Court decision makes no difference to the School, in another it does. The School, as an independent institution not receiving State aid, is legally un-affected by the recent decision; but the decision also points up the fact that due to local attitudes of both Quakers and non-Quakers, the Quaker belief in the equality of all men is denied when Negro children are refused admission to the School simply on the basis of race.
>
> As the present School in building, endowment, and invested funds, is primarily due to those who desire to maintain the present admission policies, consideration must be given by right to their feelings in the matter. A sudden change in policy would be unfair to those who have largely created the School, and to the present staff whose numbers would necessarily be reduced. It might also greatly increase the debt of the school as teachers salaries should not be reduced by a change in policy, nor should tenure be abandoned.
>
> The Education Committee gave permission, reluctantly by some, to secure the best person, irrespective of race, to fill the vacancy in the Business Office. This pointed the direction in which the School is going. This first step probably had little effect on the present enrollment, but a shrinkage in new enrollees has already begun, which some believe is the result of the expectation of some Baltimoreans that Quaker Schools will sooner or later admit students of all races.
>
> In any case it would seem only fair to present patrons and alumni to admit Negro children, when the time comes, to the Nursery School first, then to one new grade at a time in the Lower School and so on through the Upper School.

Dr. Robinson agreed with Dr. Forbush's position and together they asked the Trustees of the Baltimore Monthly Meeting to set aside funds for the school as a financial resource in case enrollment should decline.[49] The Trustees agreed and on November 16 the Education Committee took the final step toward desegregation. Even though about one-fourth of the Committee's members preferred a post-ponement of three to five years, they finally agreed to go along with the majority.[50] The Committee announced the new policy in the December issue of the school newsletter and at the same time students were informed in a school assembly.

After years of soul searching, preparation, and cautious discussion, the decision had finally been made. Now attention turned to the reaction of parents, students, faculty and the community. From some, like Carl Murphy of the *Afro-American,* and Irvin Bupp, Youth Director of YMCA, came praise and congratulations.[51] Alan Paton, author of *Cry, The Beloved Country,* who had met Bliss Forbush before returning to his native South Africa, wrote that he left America "feeling very hopeful that this age-long evil is coming to an end. I wish I could say the same of my country, but I cannot."[52] Others were not so pleased with the new policy. One alumnus wrote to request that his name be removed from the records of the school. "I want to go on record as protesting vehemently against such a procedure, which will only serve to encourage the foolish Supreme Court opinion that will prove unworkable among southern people, providing we can rid ourselves of the type responsible for this latest policy at Friends."[53] After a flurry of telephone calls from upset parents, the excitement began to subside in the next few months. At the school itself the students made little noticeable response and the faculty who were concerned about the negative impact on enrollments waited quietly but nervously for the fall enrollment figures.

The next fall Friends School opened its doors to its first racially integrated class. The white backlash that school officials feared never occurred. Only 18 students withdrew because of the desegregation policy, but overall enrollment rose from 514 in 1954–55 to 523 in 1955–56. The next year it went up slightly again.[54] If there were some parents who chose not to enroll their children in Friends for the first time, there were more than enough others who were unopposed to racially mixed classes. Among the new students were six Negro children. One father was a fireman, one a recreation department employee, and four were on the faculty at Morgan College where Bliss Forbush was a Trustee. Usually the black children who were accepted were highly qualified, one starting at age four with an IQ of 165. Since these students were all beginning in the Nursery and Kindergarten classes where children were very accepting and where Martha Parsons had prepared the faculty for integration, there were few, if any, racially related problems. Only later when the Upper School was integrated in the 1960s would more difficult problems of social adjustment arise.

Ironically after 1955 the number of Negro applicants declined. By 1960 Bliss Forbush reported that there were only thirteen in the school, and there were no black children enrolled in the four-year-old nursery group.[55] The problem thereafter would be finding black students who wanted to and could afford to come to Friends, and just as difficult, finding qualified black teachers that Friends could afford to pay.

Certainly the transition from segregation to integration was made easier because of the superb faculty and staff of Friends School during these years. Headmaster Forbush inherited a strong corps of teachers from his predecessors and he was able to add several more in the years between 1943 and 1960. Besides the struggle to integrate the school, Dr. Forbush considered his most important responsibility the recruiting and holding of good faculty. Fifteen of the fifty-two teachers who taught at Friends during his seventeen-year administration were with him during the entire term. When he had to replace faculty he usually tried to hire Quakers, although the quality of the applicant as a teacher and as a person was still the first priority.[56] In a speech given at Pendle Hill and at several other Friends schools, Dr. Forbush described the expectations for new teachers. Above all they should be professional in their attitudes, though the job at times is "tough and tiresome." Not only should they know their subject matter and teaching techniques, but also they should learn the strengths and weaknesses of each pupil. And lastly, whether or not they are Quakers, good teachers should share the basic values of "honesty, reverence, democracy, courtesy, simplicity, and helpfulness."[57]

In addition to setting high ideals for each of his teachers, Bliss Forbush also dealt with the practical matters of administration. He no doubt won many admirers among the faculty by establishing a tenure system and by getting the Education Committee to agree to a retirement plan for teachers and free tuition for their children.[58] In 1946 he reorganized the school's administrative structure, altering the system set up by Edwin Zavitz. He eliminated the principal of the Upper School, leaving the headmaster in charge of academic matters at that level. Martha Parsons continued as principal of the Lower School, Eleanor Dilworth Mace became Dean of Girls and Assistant to the Headmaster, and Robert Richardson was made Dean of Men to handle discipline problems and to interview parents.[59] These four individuals formed an executive council that met each Monday morning to review the past week and to plan for the future.[60]

The two women on this council were both major forces in the running of the school during these years. Martha Parsons, already mentioned for her work with human relations and integration, was described by Dr. Forbush as "the powerhouse of the Lower School and Nursery-Kindergarten." A strong Presbyterian whose moral values were similar to those of the Quakers, she was able to lead and offer criticism of her teachers without making them feel threatened. The Johns Hopkins Chapter of Phi Delta Kappa, a national education honor society, recognized her achievements, and she was granted the first "Best Teacher of the Year" award in Baltimore.[61]

Another influential woman in the governance of the school was Eleanor Dilworth Mace, or simply "Miss Dilly" to most of the students and faculty. An alumna brought back to Friends by Edward C. Wilson in 1926, she became by the late 1940s "the sparkplug of the school."[62] Described as good tempered, loyal to the school and its traditions, a great communicator with young people, an excellent counsellor, and a good teacher, "Dilly" was "the key to the Upper School."[63] In 1953 Dr. Forbush changed her title from Assistant to the Headmaster, to Principal of the Upper School.[64] As a former student and long-time faculty member, she understood the traditions and spirit of the school and could pass on those special attitudes and values to each generation of students.

It was during these years that Friends lost two of its most loyal and outstanding teachers. Letitia Stockett died unexpectedly in 1949 after a bicycle accident while on vacation, and Roman Steiner suffered a heart attack one day before the 1952 graduation ceremony that would have honored his fifty-three years of service to Friends. Neither could be replaced because each was unique.

But there were others who would carry on the traditions.[65] Isabel Woods, for example, came to Friends School in 1918 and taught music to the Lower School children for the next forty years. Her special love was medieval Europe, which was often the setting for the musicals and dramatic presentations that she wrote herself. Usually dressed in a white blouse and grey skirt, with a string of pins around her neck she directed her children and dressed them in a variety of fabulous costumes that she made or collected. She could turn a group of energetic children into fanciful visions of Magi, medieval knights, clowns, or rabbits, cows, and lions. When she was not preparing musicals she served as the school's librarian. And together with Martha Parsons and the Parents

Illus. 9-4   Lower School students participate in one of many Community Service projects, 1960–61.

Auxiliary volunteers she organized the annual collection and mailing of clothes, books, school supplies, food, and other necessities to children in Europe. Between 1950 and 1960 over 500 boxes were sent to families and schools abroad. When she died of cancer in 1960, donations were collected to build an art room addition to the Kinderdorf, an orphanage she had often visited in Imst, Austria (a similar addition was made in honor of Martha Parsons who retired in 1961).[66]

In the Upper School music program Bliss Forbush was delighted with the results Miss Frances Bartley had in arousing the interest of teenage students. Her energetic personality and fine singing talents inspired her pupils in memorable performances of shows like *The King and I* and *The Sound of Music.* Nan Agle, an illustrator and writer of childrens' stories, and Jennie D. Powell, who guided students in painting the stage scenery, rounded out a talented group of teachers who strengthened the school's theater and art programs.

Robert Richardson, another member of Forbush's administrative team, was a stern New Englander who kept high standards for behavior and discipline as the Dean. Students in his French classes, however, knew the twinkle in his blue eyes and recognized the fairness and the respect he held for them. Eugene Denk, a small, precise man with a dry sense of humor, was another of the male teachers whom students learned to admire. His algebra classes and Bob Richardson's French classes were of such quality that many Friends graduates found those subjects to be relatively easy when they got to college.[67] And many students, especially the boys, fell under the spell of Robert Nicolls. "Mr. Nick," as he was usually called, taught history and coached the lacrosse team. He was a natural teacher, for he came to Friends in 1938 with no formal training in education. He only knew that he wanted to teach.[68] He also wanted to coach and eventually became one of the best in the area. Throughout the late 1940s and 1950s, Mr. Nick's lacrosse teams produced quality players and from time to time enjoyed a championship season. Many of his "boys," who later would go on to become leaders in Baltimore's legal, professional, and business communities, could recall their favorite triumphs, such as the victory over Gilman in 1949 that brought their rival's 32-game winning streak to an end, or the 1954 season when Friends defeated St. Paul's for the private school championship and then beat Poly to capture the state title.[69] Stephen Sachs, one of his students and admirers, later recalled that "Mr. Nick's" success among the boys came from his example that it was possible to be both "macho" and interested in history and literature. His anecdotal style of recounting the stories or battles of American history captured their attention and made the learning fun.

Lawrence Peacock was another of the teachers who combined academics with sports. He taught seventh and eighth grade math, coached the younger boys in football and lacrosse, and the high-school boys in swimming, and served as assistant athletic director.[70] Among the male newcomers hired by Bliss Forbush were Frank Shivers and Bliss Forbush, Jr. Mr. Shivers became one of the mainstays of the English department. A wry sense of humor and his college-type lectures made him popular among the students. Many would look back and say it was Frank Shivers who taught them to write.[71] Bliss Forbush, Jr. finished his master's degree in June, 1950, and joined the faculty the next September. Despite the "handicap" of having a headmaster who was also his father, Bliss, Jr. became one of Friends' strongest faculty over the next several decades. His science and mathematics courses were conducted with warmth and interest in his students, and most students felt he prepared them well for college.[72]

Ruth C. Dibert and Marian B. Millard, among the women teachers, made lasting impressions on hundreds of Friends School graduates, both male and female. Miss Dibert's English classes were often the highlight of a student's day, and most girls were coached by "Benny" Millard in one sport or another on the playing fields. She always instilled fairness in her girls and even when the game was on the line she never hesitated to play everyone on the team regardless of ability. The male coaches found Mrs. Millard to be a tough opponent when they had to compete with her for the use of the gymnasium and the prime athletic fields. [73]

One of the more controversial teachers on Bliss Forbush's staff was Claire Walker, who joined the staff in 1947. Dr. Forbush described her as the most valuable teacher he recruited. "She is truly a great teacher, hard-working, imaginative, and idealistic." [74] Over the years she taught geography, English, history, and Latin, but her real love was Russian, which the students had asked her to teach. She was the first secondary school teacher of Russian in Baltimore and one of a handful in the nation. At a time when McCarthyism made teachers and politicians with less courage look over their shoulders, Claire Walker firmly advocated the teaching of the Russian language. She brushed aside the concerns that her actions were "un-American" or that teaching Russian was somehow supportive of Communism. Twice she was elected Vice-President of the American Association of Teachers of Slavic and East European Languages, and she helped to gain national recognition for Friends in Russian language instruction. Later she was the first American to receive the distinguished Pushkin medal. Her enthusiasm for the subject and her demands that students push themselves to their highest potential sometimes brought complaints from disagreeing parents, but Dr. Forbush always defended her and the best students praised her for the challenge she gave them. [75]

Of course it would leave a false impression to suggest that all the teachers at Friends during the years between 1943 and 1960 were great or that even the best didn't have their failings. What one student found inspiring, another might find intimidating. When a member of the Education Committee visited the classroom of one of the most popular male teachers, she found the room "slovenly," the discipline weak, and the teacher poorly prepared. One particular teacher of languages taught by old-fashioned drill methods and learning by rote. In rebellion against her rigid ways, two students locked the door when she went into the store room, and then sat down for a leisurely cigarette. The solution to

Illus. 9-5   Claire Walker's Russian Class, 1959.

weak teachers under Bliss Forbush, however, was not to fire them but personally to counsel them and help develop their talents. With such a positive atmosphere among the administration and with many strong models to learn from on the faculty, most of the less competent teachers usually improved.

Much of the success of Friends School in the post-World War II decades came from the positive and supportive atmosphere that existed there. The school was still small—445 in 1943 and 664 in 1960—and the relationship between faculty and students was close. Teachers and administrators not only helped one another, but they usually knew every child in the school by name. Even the Middle States evaluation teams that visited the school commented on the friendly, family-like atmosphere that prevailed. Discipline was not a significant problem. When a student erred he or she was more often counselled than punished. At worst, the offender might receive a "check" or two and be assigned work in the school on Friday afternoon or Saturday morning. Smoking in Mr. Nick's closet was often the "wildest" thing students could remember happening during their years at Friends and few if any were ever suspended for such a "serious" offense.[76]

Parents, too, were part of the supportive efforts in the school. They had always been involved in the annual bazaar and other activities, but in 1947 they began to organize partly out of a desire to help Martha Parsons and the Lower School pack supplies for overseas refugees. The following year they formed the Parents Auxiliary, which quickly grew to include the Upper School and Nursery as well. The original purpose of the organization was to help parents understand the aims, policies, and philosophy of Friends School and to create greater unity between parents and faculty. By the 1950s the Parents Auxiliary was publishing a bulletin, scheduling lectures and meetings, organizing open houses and teas at the school, helping to transport children to athletic events, and generally helping wherever needed.

Much of the good feeling and cooperation that characterized the school atmosphere came from Quaker philosophy and values. In 1955 Bliss Forbush wrote in the school catalogue:

> As a Quaker School we try to uphold, wherever possible, these ancient testimonies of the Society of Friends which are based on the belief in "that of God in every man." This belief, emphasizing the value of every individual irrespective of race, nationality, color or creed, leads inevitably to the Quaker testimonies on peace, racial equality, and the brotherhood of man.[77]

Although Edwin Zavitz reestablished the practice of holding a meeting for worship for the students, it was Bliss Forbush who made the Quaker influence a basic part of the school atmosphere. Every faculty meeting, every school assembly, every meeting of a parent group began with a reading by Dr. Forbush of a religious or philosophical nature. Besides trying to hire more Quaker teachers, he met with each new faculty member in September and explained to them the meaning and purpose of a Quaker education.[78] Students of all faiths joined together in the activities of a Religious Life Committee.[79] And other teachers picked up on the "tone" set by the headmaster. Bliss Forbush, Jr. developed into one of the best speakers at the weekly meetings for worship.[80]

At the same time Friends was successfully developing its students' academic abilities. By the 1950s over 90 percent of each graduating class went on to the best colleges and universities in the nation. Their SAT scores were well above the national averages and each year they won scholarships to Swarthmore, Wellesley, Washington and Lee, Oberlin, and other schools.[81] Two graduates, Stephen Sachs and Jon Oster, looked back at their Friends' education and credited it with developing their interest in academic subjects and a love of language. The small classes made education more personal and the athletic activities built a sense of confidence and achievement.[82] When the Middle States Association returned to evaluate Friends in 1959, near the end of Bliss Forbush's tenure as headmaster, they were favorably impressed. The school was given a 4.2 rating on a five point scale, well above the 3.7 average for private schools in the region.[83]

By 1960 then, when Bliss Forbush retired, he would look back over his seventeen years with satisfaction. "The faculty was complete, the enrollment was at its highest level, and the spirit of the School was never better."[84] Friends had grown from 391 to 664 pupils, the salary budget had increased from $67,934 to $301,820, and the school's physical plant, with the addition of new athletic fields, a new shop building, three faculty homes, and a new central auditorium, had doubled in value to over $1 million.[85] More important he had won the respect and affection of all who met him. As one mother wrote: "I have known several headmasters who were considered wonderful by parents and teachers, I've never known another man who was so consistently spoken of with admiration and affection by the children."[86] The students themselves thanked him in the school yearbook:

> With his humility of spirit and his great delight in all things great and small, with his interest in each one of us as an individual, and with his great spiritual knowledge and insight, Dr. Forbush has been to us not only a friend and adviser, but a warm example of a vital life. He has carefully upheld the Quaker principle of education and brought each of us a greater understanding of our school's Quaker heritage, at the same time creating and maintaining the best scholastic standards and encouraging athletic achievement. We feel Dr. Forbush—historian, humanitarian, religious leader, teacher—has given us true values for our future.[87]

At four o'clock on May 8, 1960, over one thousand friends gathered in the newly built "Forbush Auditorium" to dedicate the structure and to honor the retirement of its namesake. John E. Motz, chairman of the School Development Committee, presented Friends with an oil portrait of Dr. Forbush by Trafford Klots; and Dr. Richard H. McFeely, headmaster of George School in Pennsylvania, gave an address. The best summation, however, of Bliss Forbush's philosophy of life and of his contribution to the school, is found in his own words written a quarter of a century earlier: "He, who in supreme devotion, sets himself to the doing of God's will, utilizing institutions, assisting great careers, serving individuals, has found an integrating center for his life."[88]

Illus. 10-1   Upper School Collection, 1960–61.

CHAPTER 10

Progress and Prosperity

I t seems appropriate that Friends School began the 1960 academic year with a new headmaster, for that year in history has come to mark the rise of a new generation in American society. The decade of the sixties began with a series of "explosions and shocks." On May 5 the Soviet Union shot down a U-2 spy plane belonging to the United States. Relations between the two superpowers deteriorated significantly which added to the sense of frustration felt by many citizens who were told by officeseekers that a missile gap existed. The space race blended with the older contest for nuclear superiority to keep the Cold War going. John F. Kennedy defeated Richard M. Nixon in the presidential election in part because he promised a tough foreign policy and new leadership in social reform by a younger generation.

At home the battle for desegregation was becoming more violent. Only 6 percent of southern schools were integrated in 1960 and more efforts to secure civil rights for blacks were being met by violence. Harper Lee's new novel, *To Kill a Mockingbird,* captured the sense of injustice and frustration many Americans felt. But President Dwight D. Eisenhower tried to cheer up the voters by predicting that 1960 would be one of the most prosperous years ever. The government had a $200 million budget surplus and the prospects for sustained economic growth were bright. Consumer markets were strong and Americans had much to celebrate. Hawaii joined the union to become the fiftieth state, Floyd Patterson brought the world heavyweight championship back to the U.S. by knocking out Ingemar Johannson, a young Arnold Palmer was capturing the hearts of golf fans, and the Pirates defeated the Yankees in the World Series.

Baltimore, the old port city on the Chesapeake, was beginning to gather its resources in preparation for what would later be referred to as a renaissance. Only the year before, Baltimore's Urban Renewal and Housing Agency had adopted a major renewal plan; and groups of businessmen, bankers, and investors were exploring ways to revitalize

Illus. 10-2   Lower School students attend Meeting for Worship, Stony Run Meeting House, ca. 1965.

the city's economy and to renew its appearance. The shift to the suburbs had already drained much retail and manufacturing activity from the downtown harbor area, and population shifts continued to change the socio-economic characteristics of Baltimore. The non-white population was 35 percent in 1960 and was rapidly growing as blacks migrated into the city from the South and whites moved to the suburban counties. The following decades would be among the nation's most turbulent, but they would also offer expanding opportunities for a school like Friends. With a new headmaster in charge, Friends School was ready to accept the challenges the next quarter of a century would bring.

Actually many of the issues Byron Forbush confronted in the years after 1960 were very similar to those that had faced Bliss Forbush. Quaker pacifism, strained by World War II, was again a subject for debate and action during the Vietnam War. The problems of racial integration continued as Friends tried to understand minority students and help them adjust socially to a white, suburban school environment. Less dramatic but more powerful as a force for change, however, was the tremendous economic prosperity that had begun after World War II and reached its maturity in the 1960s and 1970s. The post-war baby boom that swelled the American population between 1946 and 1964 put heavy pressures on the public schools and created a huge new pool of applicants for Baltimore's private institutions. Coupled with unprecedented prosperity among middle-class consumers, this new generation of schoolchildren created superb opportunities for independent schools to expand and strengthen their financial positions. For Friends the challenge would be to take advantage of the new prosperity without losing sight of its original purpose as a Quaker school.

That Friends would change was inevitable. But then it had always been evolving and changing in every decade of its two-hundred-year existence. Change in fact had been the great constant. No alumnus who ever graduated from Friends in any historical period could come back later and say with assurance that "this is the same school I graduated from." The changes between 1960 and the mid-1980s were many: new structures on the campus, new faces among the faculty and administration, a new middle school, elimination of student uniforms, a broader curriculum, and a Board of Trustees in place of the Education Committee of Baltimore Monthly Meeting. And yet there remained an intangible, difficult-to-describe element of continuity that bound the present to the past and continued to make Friends the same institution. Life now ran at a faster pace and there were more moving parts. But Friends School completed its second century with its heart and soul intact.

For the visitor who returned to the campus, the physical changes would be the first to catch the eye. The Gothic stone façades of the Lower School and the Forbush Auditorium faced west from Charles Street, looking out over the small playground and parking area. To the north Stony Run Meeting House since 1949 stood in a small grove of oak trees, reminding visitors of the Quaker origins and character of the school. Only as the visitor passed along the paved roadway and rounded the southern corner of the Lower School building would the recent growth of the last quarter of a century become obvious. From the interior of the campus several new additions stood out. To the west side of the Auditorium was a modern extension built in 1975 to house the newly created Middle School, grades six through eight. Visible beyond the Upper School, tucked into the woods along the northern edge of the campus, was the new science building, opened in 1967. That same year, a major expansion of the gymnasium was completed, west of the

Illus. 10-3 Upper School Chemistry Laboratory, 1965.

Upper School. In the very center of campus, surrounded by new parking areas and walkways, were the tennis courts, ten of them in all. Since these courts were rented to the Homeland Racquet Club and used by local residents, the sound of bouncing tennis balls could be heard from mid-spring through late fall, even when students were in their classrooms.

Several acres of playing fields stretched out to the west toward the wooded streets of Roland Park. Even if the team uniforms of the 1980s were better looking than those of 1960, the enthusiasm of the students who competed on those fields was much the same. Soccer, lacrosse, and football for boys, field hockey and lacrosse for girls, along with other seasonal sports, were often the highlight of a student's day. Whether or not one was the star of the team or there to cheer the heroes on, the large open spaces of the playing fields were a relief after a day of studying indoors.

On the southern edge of the campus, isolated by distance from the other activities, was the Pre-primary Department. In 1981 the Board of Trustees approved a complete renovation of the large old clubhouse that sat on a small knoll surrounded by trees. Here the three-, four-, and five-year-olds played with wooden blocks and learned their first school lessons in the brightly colored rooms. Amid the pleasant clutter and mild chaos, students got their first taste of life at Friends. Close relationships that began here would last for many years until classmates parted for college.

The headmaster's house and the Business/Development/Alumni Office were the other two buildings of significance on the campus. Located at each corner of the southern edge of the tennis courts, these structures were originally built as residences during Bliss Forbush's administration. The Education Committee enlarged the headmaster's house to meet the needs of the younger Forbush family in 1960, but the other residence (called the "Woodman house" because it formerly was occupied by biology teacher Henry Woodman and his family) was converted to the business office in 1967. As the school grew and its operation became more sophisticated, this house would be periodically renovated or enlarged to accommodate new functions such as development, alumni, and admissions offices.

If Edward C. Wilson could have returned to stroll across the twenty-seven acres he purchased for the school in 1926, he would no doubt have felt gratified. It was an attractive and prosperous-looking campus that housed Friends School by the end of its second century. There were inconsistencies in the architectural pattern of the buildings—like the modern, functional design of the addition to the Auditorium—but Wilson would not have minded. He was a practical man who would have accepted the necessity of deviating from the Gothic style that often wasted expensive space. He would have been proud, too, of the green, terraced playing fields which, in his day, had not yet been fully carved from the wooded and rough grounds. It was a complete and pleasing campus that would have satisfied the old principal.

Besides these highly visible changes in the appearance of the campus, there were many other ways in which Friends School grew and became more complex in the years after 1960. One of the significant changes was in the way the school was governed. Since its founding in 1784, Friends had been under the care and direction of Baltimore Monthly Meeting. The Education Committee, or an earlier version of it, was responsible for the administration and finances of the institution. Until the 1960s the headmaster and the chairman of the committee dominated the school administration. Chairmen like Jonathan K. Taylor and headmasters like Edward C. Wilson or William S. Pike had the most influence in the committee made up of members of the Quaker meeting. But by the 1960s a more sophisticated system of governance was called for. A first step was to divide the responsibilities and assign them to subcommittees where members could develop greater expertise and concentrate on specific issues. Subcommittees on Finance, Personnel, Scholarships, Property, and Public Relations were the principal ones, with various ad hoc groups formed as they were needed. An immediate consequence of this delegation of governance was to bring more members of the Education Committee into a closer relationship with the school. They now had greater knowledge of school affairs and were more involved in the policy-making process. In particular, greater expertise was needed in regard to financial matters. Besides the capital improvements to the campus, there were now long discussions in the Education Committee about salaries and fringe benefits, scholarships, supplies, maintenance, operating expenses, endowments, investments, insurance, and especially fundraising. By 1967 the Education Committee created a Long-Range Planning Committee to consider the major goals and problems of the school over the next five years.[1] Gradually the governing group was broadening and lengthening its view of the school and how it should be run. In 1970, during the time when constituencies everywhere were marching and demonstrating for a greater share of the political process, the Education Committee opened its membership to four new groups: students, faculty, parents, and alumni. One representative from each group was added to the committee. At about the same time others began to put forward the idea that there should be one or more non-Quakers on the Committee.[2]

Two years later, in 1972, there were several persons within the school community who argued that the time had come for a major reorganization of the governance system. Specifically there was a movement to incorporate the school and to separate it at least partly from Baltimore Monthly Meeting. Investigations of other Quaker schools and a meeting with the trustees of Wilmington Friends School, Inc., convinced Byron Forbush and leading members of the Education Committee that the current arrangement had several disadvantages. For one thing there was the nettlesome problem of handling property and the financial affairs of the school in its traditional relationship to the Meeting. Not only were insurance and tax problems confusing, but it was becoming clear that the school suffered financially from being under the legal ownership of the Meeting. Non-Quakers, who wanted to give money directly to the school, were sometimes reluctant to funnel the funds through a religious organization.[3] A separate endowment fund and programs for deferred giving or special funding drives would be necessary if Friends expected to keep pace with its private school competitors. Friends School also desired a separate legal identity, not only to defend lawsuits that might occur, but also for the more routine matters of buying or selling property. The most important reason for incorporation, however, was that the school wanted to be able to call upon the talents and resources of its non-Quaker patrons. It was a simple fact that the school had outgrown the Meeting. Friends had grown to over seven and later eight hundred students with annual budgets of more than two million dollars; Baltimore Monthly Meeting numbered fewer than four hundred members. As in any organization, the number of individuals willing and capable of serving on important committees or taking leadership roles was a small fraction of the total membership. Some argued that there were not enough active members adequately to take care of the affairs of both the Monthly Meeting and the school. Those familiar with the school's governance also knew that there were specific talents or expertise in education or business planning or architecture that could not be supplied by the current membership of Stony Run Meeting. Moreover, there was pressure on the administration of Friends from non-Quakers who wanted to see the governing board broadened to be more representative of the school community. Patrons like Charles Hutzler wrote to Byron Forbush urging the administration to consider adding non-Quakers to the governing board.[4] The support of non-Friends was especially required if fundraising efforts were to improve. In spring 1973 a Subcommittee on Legal Structure studied the issues involved and by April submitted its recommendations to the Education Committee. The subcommittee pointed out the advantages and disadvantages of incorporation, and tried to reassure those who were skeptical that a change in governance would not weaken the Quaker foundations of Friends School.

Although the proponents of incorporation persuaded the majority of the soundness of their ideas, this act of separating the school from the Meeting had a disturbing effect. Under the new charter of incorporation eighteen of the twenty-two members of a board of trustees would be nominated by Baltimore Monthly Meeting (four other trustees were to represent the students, faculty, alumni, and Parents Auxiliary). Fifteen of the trustees must be members of the Society of

Friends, leaving three who could be non-Quakers.[5] Although the majority of this new board would be Quaker, it was evident that the Monthly Meeting's ultimate authority and responsibility were diminished. The movement for incorporation uncovered the feelings of discontent between some members of the Meeting and the school.[6] From the one point of view the Meeting's control of the school had been too limiting and created financial disadvantages. But from the the other viewpoint, one of the primary purposes of the school was to serve the needs of the Quaker community. It was founded in 1784 to provide a guarded education for Quaker children; there were those who now feared that the Quaker influence was slipping away as more emphasis was placed on college preparation. And there were other members too, sometimes with no children in the school, who disagreed from time to time with specific policies of Friends School.

In retrospect the dichotomy or differences between Meeting and school were the result of two institutions serving different constituencies. Although there was a definite overlap between the two in individuals and in Quaker philosophy, there were also differences. Even an individual like Bliss Forbush, who was universally respected and who had been a leader of both the Meeting and the school, was not always able to reconcile the differences. When he was executive secretary of Baltimore Monthly Meeting, for example, his complaints were about the school's lack of cooperation. The two institutions were then occupying the same buildings at Park Avenue and Dr. Forbush felt that the school was not properly taking care of the rooms it used behind the meeting house. Years later, when he was headmaster, he saw the other side of the situation and expressed concern that the Meeting was not always fulfilling its obligations to the school.[7]

Although personalities sometimes clashed, the root of the problem was not the individuals involved, but simply that these were two institutions with different purposes or goals. Both were clearly Quaker and both were devoted to the principles of the Society of Friends. Yet one was a religious institution and the other a college preparatory school with a religious foundation. The fact that over 90 percent of the school's clientele were non-Quakers certainly complicated the relationship between school and Meeting. There were differences also between those who held a more traditional or conservative view of Quakerism and those who were more progressive. The traditionalists insisted that the Meeting should not support a private school, especially one that was expensive and housed in Gothic style settings. Simplicity and plainness were the traditional Quaker values. Those who favored a more modern view replied that the Quaker values were still very much a part of the school's philosophy and were incorporated into students' lives through assemblies, early morning gatherings for children, and other activities. The time had passed, they said, when the Monthly Meeting could support a small school solely for the few youths in Quaker families.

What is impressive, however, is not the differences but the unity and cooperation that prevailed. Despite the fears, the incorporation when it came in 1973 did not seem to weaken the Quaker character of Friends School. Much of the credit no doubt goes to the men and women who served on the Board of Trustees and in the school's administration. The long discussions over the relationship between the Meeting and the school sensitized many to the need to insure the place of Quaker values at Friends. From time to time in the 1970s the Board of Trustees and Byron Forbush took special steps to strengthen the ties to Quakerism. The Board created a Committee on Orientation and Coordination to set up seminars, luncheons, and workshops for Board members in order to improve their understanding of the school and its philosophy. A special "Trustees' Study Day" was held to hear advice from outside experts and to review the responsibilities of the Board.[8] Board chairpersons were particularly effective in reminding the Trustees of the obligations to protect the Quaker influence of the school. And Byron Forbush, through his reports to both the Trustees and the Monthly Meeting, continued to renew and emphasize the close relationship between the two institutions.

In its first decade the new Board of Trustees appeared to be successful. One of its objectives was to enlist a more diverse group of persons willing to become knowledgeable about the school. With the greater size of the Board and the freedom to enlist non-Quakers, Friends School broadened its leadership corps. The recognition of at least nine areas in which the Trustees needed competence helped to identify individuals who could supply valuable resources. These areas included institional planning, education, law, fundraising, investment management, public relations, architecture, insurance, and recruitment of faculty and students from racial minorities.[9] Trustees, with jobs as college professors, lawyers, public school administrators, investment analysts, bankers, government administrators, engineers, and accountants, provided knowledge and advice necessary for a modern, independent school.[10] The new Board also had the advantage of a higher turnover of individuals. Whereas in the old Education Committee

185

leaders like Jonathan K. Taylor or Philip E. Lamb might serve for several decades, the new Board was replenished with new talent and new ideas each year. The initial by-laws restricted the Trustees to service of no more than seven of any nine years, which was sufficient to maintain continuity and stability but still discourage domination of the Board by a powerful few.

Shortly after the Board of Trustees was created, it took an important step toward carrying out its responsibility of policy-making by preparing a ten-year plan for the school's development and goals. The plan was based on four premises: that there would be economic, social, and racial diversity among the students; that Friends would continue to be predominantly college preparatory while offering a broad spectrum of programs; that it would remain approximately the same size (700–800 students); and that it would continue to offer classes K through 12.[11] The principal concern of the plan itself was to establish a strong endowment in order to raise faculty salaries, support new buildings and programs, and increase the number of student scholarships. Without a larger endowment, tuition costs might increase too rapidly and discourage parents from sending their children to Friends. Preserving the diversity of students was an important objective that few were willing to relinquish. The new Board of Trustees was expected to be a major factor in the growing financial stability of Friends.

From a longer perspective it is clear that the creation of the Board of Trustees and the significant increase in financial development were largely due to the leadership of the new headmaster, Byron Forbush. If his father had been responsible for bringing Friends School through World War II and putting it on a sound footing in the 1950s, it was the younger Forbush, more than anyone else, who developed the school's potential in the decades after 1960. Difficult as it would have been for anyone to follow in the footsteps of Bliss Forbush, Byron faced the inevitable comparisons of father and son as headmasters.

Unlike the elder Forbush, who changed careers several times over a long lifetime, Byron had a long association with Friends School of Baltimore. His entire education, from the three-year-old nursery group to graduation from high school in 1947, took place there. He continued for four years at The Johns Hopkins University as a scholarship student, then finished an M.A.T. degree at Harvard and a Doctorate of Education at Columbia University. After being drafted into the army in 1-A-O status and later, after discharge, working as a teacher and administrator at Friends Academy in Locust Valley, Long Island, he returned in 1960 to Baltimore as the sixth headmaster of Friends in the twentieth century.[12]

By the time of the school's bicentennial he had spent most of his life at the campus on North Charles Street. From the beginning it was a story of success and accomplishment. Described by his first grade teacher as a "wonderful" student with "no problems," he went on to be a leader of his high school class, a star athlete on the playing fields, and a sound scholar.[13] Merrill Hiatt, principal of the Upper School, described Byron in 1946 as "a level-headed boy" with "all the earmarks of a successful man."[14] Like his father and his older brother, Bliss, Jr., who became a favorite teacher among science and math students at Friends, Byron Forbush was popular among his peers and elders. At Johns Hopkins, where he was an All-American lacrosse player, star of the basketball team, and senior class president, he was described as genuinely modest: "Forbush combines his talents with a friendly manner, easy smile, and complete humbleness towards his own accomplishments, transforming him from the ranks of the untouchable campus bigwig to the classification of a guy everyone knows, likes, and admires."[15]

Because his personality, education, and background suited him so well for the role of headmaster, Friends School moved quickly to hire him when Bliss Forbush retired in 1960. Actually the retirement came a year earlier than planned, but Byron's father realized that unless Friends acted swiftly, his son might be made the headmaster of the Locust Valley school and therefore not return to Baltimore at all. The opportunity to move to Baltimore Friends appealed to Byron Forbush because he considered it to be one of the two or three Quaker schools best suited to his needs and interests. In a letter to his father, however, he admitted that he was lacking in experience and apprehensive about making the move to headmaster at the early age of thirty. Nevertheless in the end he concluded that "I can administratively handle the job. . ." and felt reassured that there was a strong group of people who would stand behind him.[16] To show their confidence that they had hired the right person, the Education Committee signed him to a five-year contract, promised to enlarge and redecorate the headmaster's house for his growing family (Byron had married Ann Nesbitt Farquhar of Sandy Spring, Maryland, in 1951), and agreed to provide an expense account for professional travel and entertainment.[17]

If Bliss Forbush was the philosopher, Byron was the administrator. When the school was smaller and less complex, Bliss Forbush was able to make students, parents, and faculty feel close to him. Each year the elder Dr. Forbush wrote lengthy, personal letters to each student in the school and to each faculty member. These were typical of his ability to extend his personal warmth and touch to every part of the school community. Fundraising, on the other hand, was a task he did well but never enjoyed. Byron Forbush, however, was much more skilled as a fundraiser and professional educator. Under his guidance the academic and financial structure of Friends became more sophisticated and professionally organized. His strength was in sensing the changes in education and society and helping the school to adjust, while at the same time retaining the Quaker orientation of the institution. Despite the burden of having to succeed a man as greatly admired as his father, Byron Forbush was able, within a few years, to impress his own style on the school. Before long most observers concluded that while the two Forbushes were different, each had brought unique talents to Friends School at the times they were needed.

Both Forbushes were successful in the area of school finances. It was here that the history of Friends reflects the changes of the larger society. The 1950s, '60s, and '70s were decades of unprecedented prosperity and economic growth for the nation, and Friends School prospered during these years. In the first major campaign of Byron Forbush's administration Friends raised nearly half a million dollars to build a new science building and a major addition to the gymnasium. Other capital campaigns to renovate and expand the main buildings on campus and increase the endowment followed. At first the Education Committee hired an outside professional to help raise funds for the school, but thereafter much of the fundraising effort came from patrons who volunteered to help and from the administration. Businessmen like John S. Williamson, Jr., or supporters like John and Catherine Motz gave many hours of work to the early capital campaigns of the 1960s. W. Berkeley Mann, chairman of the Education Committee from 1960 to 1967, was a key member of the development program. And within the administration it was John E. Carnell who worked alongside Byron Forbush to establish a more professional plan for setting up scholarships, creating an endowment, and increasing faculty salaries. Mr. Carnell came to Friends as a seventh grade teacher in 1956 but stayed on as business manager, replacing J. Harold Passmore in 1957. Over the next several decades he was one of the great strengths of the school. Under his direction Friends became financially mature. He helped set up better insurance and pension plans for faculty, improved the school's investment programs, and refined budget procedures. In 1971 Friends hired its first Director of Development, Richard A. Lane, Jr., and three years later set up a Development Advisory Council, which included a number of prominent Baltimore citizens. All of these efforts resulted in attracting several large gifts and increased the amounts given annually by regular contributors. The Ensign C. Markland Kelly, Jr., Memorial Foundation, for example, gave a large sum to construct an additional gymnasium. (Ensign Kelly, killed in World War II, had been a student at Friends from 1923 to 1933.)[18] The Annual Giving Fund, which had raised only a few thousand dollars in 1960, rose steadily to reach about $100,000 by the beginning of the 1980s. After the creation of the Board of Trustees and the legal separation of the school from the Monthly Meeting, the financial status of Friends was improved even more.

The Parents Auxiliary had become an important fundraising organization by the 1960s and 1970s. With over a hundred volunteers and twenty subcommittees, they collected money for specific items, such as a new red curtain for the auditorium stage, musical instruments, playground equipment, and resource books for the library. By 1970 the Auxiliary took charge of the annual bazaar and planned other types of fundraisers.[19]

The principal beneficiaries of these vigorous, new, fundraising activities were the students and faculty of Friends. In addition to the drives to make physical improvements to the campus, there was the firm commitment to increase salaries and to enlarge the scholarship fund. Bliss Forbush had made significant advances in the salary scales by 1960, but it remained for his son to bring Friends into the top 10 percent of private schools in the Baltimore region and in the National Association of Independent Schools.[20]

The interest in increasing the size and number of student scholarships came from several sources. In order to keep tuition costs down and to continue to be competitive with other independent schools, Friends needed a strong scholarship program. But Friends also pursued better financial aid for specific groups of students. There was first of all the obligation to educate the children of members of the Stony Run Meeting. A continuing concern of Byron Forbush and the Trustees was to increase the percentage of Quaker children in the school. This was one way of strengthening the link between the two institutions. The Sharp and Jewett funds, created early in the twentieth century, were by now major sources of support for Quaker children, paying out nearly $16,000 in scholarships by 1980.[21]

In addition to this commitment, Friends believed that one of its strengths was the diversity of its student body. In particular, scholarships were needed to encourage black students and other minorities to enroll.[22] Although the proportion of black students who received financial aid was not much larger than that of other students, this support helped recruit children who otherwise would not have attended Friends. Overall with about 10 percent of its annual budget expended for scholarships, Friends was one of the most generous of Baltimore's independent schools.[23] By the early 1980s financial aid was in excess of $200,000 and new sources of funds were opening up, such as a student loan program from the Clarence Manger and Audrey Cordero Plitt Trust, which was similar to many college plans but unique to preparatory schools. By the end of its second century Friends School was in excellent financial condition. The post-war baby boom and the increase in the standard of living for Americans had enabled Friends to grow and prosper.

One of the dangers of emphasizing the financial and physical growth of Friends School, however, is that other changes of equal or greater importance might be overlooked. As one graduate of Friends stated in 1974: "What makes Friends School important is not its campus but its concept—a Quaker education. In essence, it is a commitment to excellence, . . . total training for a meaningful life. This could not be possible without the school's deep, continuing association with the Quaker Meeting."[24] If Byron Forbush was a key figure in capital development, he was even more important in emphasizing the Quaker values of Friends. Perhaps he was responding to the concerns of those who feared that as the school grew and became more complex it was losing its Quaker character; or perhaps he was conscious that many members of the Meeting would compare his actions to those of his father. More likely, as a lifelong member of the Society of Friends, he was merely carrying out his own personal beliefs. Whatever the reason, the religious influence in the school did not diminish with the departure of Bliss Forbush. In fact, W. Berkeley Mann, chairman of the Education Committee, commended Byron Forbush for having "continued a growing emphasis on Quaker Testimonies in the school which make it even more a 'Friends' school that it was when you came to head it."[25]

One of the ways Quaker values and concepts were taught to students was through the Meeting for Worship. It became policy that all students, grades three through twelve, were required to attend with their classes once each week. In a letter to parents explaining the purpose of Meeting for Worship, Dr. Forbush explained, "Participation is...a seeking openness, an interweaving of listening, prayer and meditation carried on in an atmosphere of trust and expectancy. Think of Meeting for Worship as one of the windows opening on the Truth, a great window with many panes at many levels."[26] Often graduates remembered these times as significant in their education because it helped them to develop deeper relationships with their peers and their teachers.

But there were other ways too that the Quaker influence was perpetuated in school. Frequently Quaker speakers were invited to the campus on Charles Street. In 1977, for example, Tom and Nan Brown, and John Nicholson, all of Westtown School, talked to faculty and students during the opening days of classes. At other times workshops were held with the administration, faculty, Trustees, and members of the Meeting to discuss Quaker methods and philosophy. They considered questions such as, what is the Friends' view of pupil discipline, and how does the school make its constituency aware of the values, spiritual and intellectual, for which it stands.[27] Quaker Day, a special day set aside for students in the high school, was another activity that reinforced the traditional values. A theme of one Quaker Day, "prison awareness," became a popular social concern of many high-school students who formed an organization to study and try to improve conditions in the state's prisons.[28] In reply to the concern expressed by a member of the Board of Trustees that Friends was losing its Quaker tradition, a student representative on the Board replied that "the annual Quaker Day has exposed all students to these values...they are an integral part of daily student life."[29] The discussion within the Quaker community would no doubt go on over whether the Friends School of the present was more or less "Quakerly" than that of the past, but the majority seemed to be convinced that the school was in safe hands.

It was inevitable perhaps that the identification between Friends School and Byron Forbush strengthened as the years passed. Although a study by the National Association of Independent Schools suggested that six years was the average length of time a headmaster ought to serve in one institution, at Friends the partnership between school and man remained strong well beyond that guideline.[30] The Board of Trustees discussed the question of how long a headmaster can continue to be effective, but they concluded firmly that there was a greater advantage of stability and continuity in supporting a successful administration. J.

Frederick Motz, on completing his term as chairman of the Board of Trustees in 1978, complimented Byron Forbush by saying that he "has been the school. The constant pressures he confronts he handles with wisdom, courage and understanding."[31] This view coincided with the conclusion of the Friends Council on Education conference on what an ideal headmaster should be like. He or she "should exercise leadership, be a person of recognized professional attainment, and should be able to select a faculty who will be willing and able to implement the policies of the school as a Friends School."[32]

What the Trustees and patrons expected of Headmaster Forbush, he in turn expected of his faculty. In welcoming his faculty back to school one September day in 1972, he reminded them of the concepts important to a Quaker education: "This school is a place where teachers risk the investment of their lives so that a student does not settle for a casual second-rate achievement. This school continues to search for unfolding truth." Ideally a headmaster would hope to find committed Quaker teachers to fulfill this goal. But given the small numbers within the Society of Friends, teachers had to be found elsewhere. Like his father who relied on personal contacts within Quaker organizations, Byron Forbush continued to use the "Old Boy" network for finding capable teachers. Nevertheless, it was representative of the differences between the two men that Byron also relied more heavily upon professional agencies, such as Independent Educational Services, to find new faculty.[33] From 1960 through 1982 Friends hired an average of 6.8 new instructors or administrative personnel each year. The fewest hired were 3 in 1962 and 1976, and the most was 16 in 1981. Gradually the staff hired by Bliss Forbush was replaced by new teachers, some of whom "sported" long hair and beards, but all of whom were ready to educate this new generation of babyboom children. Marian Millard expressed the feelings of some of the older stalwarts on her retirement from teaching in 1965: "After forty-one years of blowing the whistle and directing the athletic program, I want to put the whistle in moth balls or happily hand it over to someone peppy and qualified to uphold the best traditions of health and physical education for girls."[34] It would be hard to imagine a new group of teachers any more "peppy" than those retiring and certainly it would be a challenge to match their records of long service to Friends. When Lawrence Peacock retired in 1969, he was completing 43 years at the school. A few of the others retiring at this time who dedicated much of their careers to Friends were Ruth Dibert (38 years), Alice Shoff (37 years), M. Eleanor Starr (37 years),

Illus. 10-4   Fifth graders participate in an innovative economics program, introduced in 1981.

Eleanor Dilworth Mace (37 years), Eleanor High (35 years), Robert Richardson (29 years), Robert Nicolls (25 years), Marjorie Richardson (28 years), Claire Walker (28 years), Frank Shivers (25 years), and Martha C. Parsons (23 years).[35] Similarly there were other nonteaching staff members like Frank Wedeking, George Schubert, Dorothy Michel Mardos, and Katherine Gorsuch as well as numerous employees on the maintenance, kitchen, and custodial staff who were a part of Friends School for more than a quarter of a century.[36]

The new teachers who accepted Byron Forbush's challenge to "risk the investment of their lives" in helping their students search for truth were as highly qualified as their predecessors. By the 1980s there were three at Friends who held doctorates and forty who had finished master's degrees. Compared to those retiring, the new staff were more often graduates of public universities and had a broader range of experience in a diversity of schools. Even so, as the new instructors were gradually blended into the teaching staff there seemed to be little if any change in the atmosphere of Friends. Stanley B. Johnson, Principal of the Upper School, observed that the character of the faculty did not significantly change. They continued to be "solid citizens," he said, with similar values and a firm grasp of their subject matter.[37] The Middle

States Association evaluations, which were conducted every ten years, confirmed the impression that the quality of instruction remained high and the sense of camaraderie continued to be exceptional.

A good example of the unique character of Friends School and of the nature of Byron Forbush's leadership is the development of the Middle School. In 1970 Friends returned to a pattern similar to that of earlier years when it separated the sixth, seventh, and eighth graders into a distinct division. William Ellis, an exchange student from England in the 1950s, was hired as the director and given a broad latitude of authority within which to work. It was typical of Dr. Forbush to hire creative individuals and then to give them freedom to work out their ideas without unnecessary interference.

The Middle School was staffed with a blend of old and new teachers, all of whom understood that these were transition years for students just entering puberty, wrestling with new emotions and concepts of themselves and others. Ruth Dibert, a veteran English teacher, called them her "cherubs" but ripped their compositions to shreds. Doris Neumann, a compassionate social studies and geography teacher, gave them a new awareness of human rights and community service. Some of the male teachers taught the boys that it was acceptable to be an athlete and like poetry or good books as well. Often students were permitted to develop their own ideas, as in the case of "Kite Day" when they learned from and enjoyed the wonders of kites. The most successful experiment in the Middle School was the camping program. Overnight trips to Black Rock and Point Lookout became important teaching experiences not only in science and physical education but also in human relations and problem solving. The camping program did much to reduce the fractiousness and contention among these budding teenagers and was soon carried on into the Upper School and also developed in the lower grades.

Similar creativity and progressive methods of education were practiced by teachers in the Lower and Upper Schools. In 1981 the fifth grade won national television attention with an economics project in which the students set up a bank and established a form of currency. Fifth grade pupils earned chips or currency by wiping tables, collecting trash, cleaning blackboards, inspecting lockers, raking the lawns, or other similar jobs. This "income" could then be spent for special privileges such as using the fifth grade lounge, eating in an unsupervised lunchroom, reading to the pre-primary children, or caring for the animals in the science room. The value of the project, according to

Illus. 10-5   Many of the kitchen, custodial and maintenance employees, some of whom served as bus maids and bus drivers, had been employed at Friends since Park Avenue days when this photo was taken in 1950. They are: (first row) Stanley Smith, Louise Hudson, Mary Napper, Wilhelmina Weedon, Eva Blount, Alma Flournoy, Erdine Chandler, Bertha Payne; (second row) William Boston, Burke Smith, Anna Garrett, Eva Lassery, Dorothy Reed, Pearl Harris, Virginia Augins, William Smith; (third row) Samuel Garrett, Oscar Thompson, Rino Hall, Richard Poulson; (fourth row) Charles Gaskins, Garfield Hudson, Alexander Beard, William Mayo, Sampson Barnes.

Lower School Principal, David Peerless, was in helping students "learn the economic processes and at the same time realize reaping the rewards of being a productive and trusted member of the school community."[38]

On the whole the years between 1960 and the early 1980s were successful ones from the point of view of the Administration and the Board of Trustees. Both financially and structurally Friends adjusted well to the economic growth of these decades. The administrative team put together by Byron Forbush was more professional and complete than that of any of his predecessors. What is more impressive about Friends School during these years, however, is that it was able to retain its humaneness and its Quaker character. Time and again alumni, in looking back over their school years, commented that Friends was successful because each student was treated as an individual. The staff and the atmosphere they created helped each child to discover his or her strengths and weaknesses and to find those areas in which they could succeed. Not every graduate would look back with fondness at his or her years at Friends, but most felt a remarkable degree of satisfaction with the education gained there. This was an achievement of no small note, given the student unrest and social upheaval of the 1960s and 1970s.

Illus. 11-1   Lacrosse attackman Dan Kardash (no. 25) scores a goal against Boys' Latin in May 1966.

CHAPTER 11

Two Centuries Completed

The baby boom that brought prosperity to the private schools of Baltimore also brought a large generation of American students who were not content with the comfortable world of their middle- and upper-middle-class predecessors. Seldom have American schools been so shaken by a rebellion from within as they were in the late 1960s and early 1970s. The civil rights movement, anti-Vietnam War protests, women's rights movements, and concern for the environment all stirred the nation's youth in colleges and universities, and spilled over to their younger brothers and sisters in secondary schools. Since the older generation had failed so miserably to eliminate war, poverty, inequality, and injustice from society, the newcomers insisted on the right to try their own solutions. They demanded greater freedom from authority and the right to choose their own destiny, whether it be in the selection of elective courses that were "relevant" or in serving with the nation's armed forces.

The rebellious inclinations of this baby-boom generation that flooded the schools in the 1950s was at first masked by tremendous consumerism. Attention focused at first on the demands for diapers, dolls, baby powder, and paperback copies of Dr. Benjamin Spock's *The Common Sense Book of Baby and Child Care*. As young couples of the 1950s looked optimistically to a future of steady employment and rising wages, they not only decided to have an extra child or two, but they promised themselves that these offspring would have the best of everything that money could buy. They spent $100 million buying raccoon hats for their little "Davy Crocketts," and poured out millions more for Silly Putty, Slinkys, Hoola Hoops, skateboards, and Barbie Dolls. Later as this new generation reached adolescence they became mass consumers of records, radios, cameras, and lipstick. It was no small wonder that makers of music and fashions began to pitch their products to a younger audience. And of course their parents insisted on the best education money could buy.

The atmosphere that pervaded the Friends School campus in the 1950s is best described as cheerful and optimistic. Girls with names like Frannie, Twinkle, Mopsey, Kitty, Babs, Tucky, and Weedie, dressed alike in blue cotton uniforms with white cuffs and collars, dark blue sweaters, white socks, and the ever-popular black-and-white saddle shoes. Boys wore ties with coats or letter sweaters, crew socks, and kept their hair in crew cuts or short ivy-league styles. Their parents sent them to Friends for several reasons: because it had a good academic reputation in Baltimore, because it was coeducational, because of the diversified student body, because of the sound moral education that the Quaker affiliation promised, or simply because the public schools seemed to some parents to be so inadequate. If all went well, the large majority of those who graduated (90 percent or more) would go on to college, often to the same school one of their parents had attended.[1]

Until the mid-1960s the student attitudes at Friends continued to be optimistic and accepting. A collection of articles in the campus newspaper, Quaker Quill, entitled "What do you believe?," revealed that high school students in 1963 were aware of current problems. They mentioned fear of nuclear war, teenage drinking, violence, excessive materialism, and a lack of clearcut goals and values as the principal concerns of the day. But nearly every article went on to denounce the critics who were predicting the decline of American civilization. The Friends School students of 1963 still had confidence and hope in society and several of them urged readers to turn to religion and spiritual growth as the solution to these problems. Even in the aftermath of President Kennedy's assassination they continued to be optimistic.[2] One of the major issues in the campaign for student government that year was whether or not there should be a Coke machine in the cafeteria. A little over a year later, in 1965, when the school considered the first change in the dress code in thirty-five years, the students joined peacefully with faculty and parents on committees to work out the new regulations. They complained goodnaturedly about overcrowding in the locker rooms and chemistry labs and debated whether the Beatles were more meaningful than Elvis Presley, but generally they seemed happy with their situation.[3]

If any year marked the beginning of rebellious change at Friends, it was 1967. Earlier students had taken note of the trends toward nonconformity among their older brothers and sisters in the nation's colleges, but it was only in 1967 that they began to question the authority of the Quaker institution. The first complaints focused on examinations. Where their predecessors in the 1950s moaned humor-ously about the pressure of exam time and then urged their peers to buckle down and study hard, the student leaders of the 1960s called for the abolition of senior exams and a reduction of emphasis on grades.[4] In the same issue of the student newspaper a girl wrote about the excite-ment, bewilderment, and uneasiness she felt when her sister brought home college classmates on their way to a protest march in Wash-ington. And only a few weeks earlier the administration raised for the first time the question of a drug policy for the school. Pamphlets on drug abuse went out to all parents just before the Christmas holidays.[5]

By the spring of 1968 there was no longer any doubt that the spirit of protest and rebellion had reached down to touch the youth of the Quaker school on Charles Street. That was the year of the *Tet* Offens-ive, of the assassinations of Martin Luther King, Jr., and Robert F. Kennedy, and of the capture of the U.S.S. *Pueblo*. The hit of the year on Broadway was the revolutionary *Hair*, "Laugh-In" with its irreverent humor was one of the most popular TV shows, Tiny Tim was "tiptoeing through the tulips," Julie Nixon married David Eisenhower, and the Hong Kong flu was running rampant. Between January 1 and June 15 there were 221 major demonstrations in American cities.[6] It was no surprise that the students at Friends felt that youth should have a turn at running things. Student articles in the *Quaker Quill* became more outspoken in their demands for change. One girl complained that required courses and assignments left no time for her to pursue her true interests. Another wrote satirically about parents who objected to the film, *Bonnie and Clyde*, but who did not object to the violence in Vietnam. Others wrote about the war, pollution, manned space flight, and Hugh Hefner's philosophy. In frustration a female correspondent wrote, "The young aren't satisfied with inheriting the present 'adult' world. We want to peacefully improve the world and it won't listen."[7] But like many of her classmates she was unsure of where reform should lead. It was easy enough to complain about injustice and hypocrisy, but it was difficult to know what to do about it or to find alternatives. A few turned to specific organizations, like the Students for a Democratic Society, to help define goals; but more often they looked to their teachers for direction.

The most influential and controversial of all the teachers in the late 1960s and early 1970s was John Roemer. A vice chairman of The Congress of Racial Equality and a civil rights veteran of many protest marches and several arrests, he brought to his teaching at Friends a

Illus. 11-2   John C. Roemer III teaching an Upper School history class in 1968–69.

dramatic style and a firm belief that "schools should be a vehicle for social reconstruction."[8] It was John Roemer who led students to question the validity of grades and to doubt some of the traditional values they had taken for granted. In his social studies and American history classes he was a dynamic instructor. To command attention he leaped onto radiators, shouted to emphasize a significant point, or wore costumes to dramatize a historical event. Although he never proselytized, he demanded that students be questioning and he tried to teach a sense of values. Since he was a member of the Quaker meeting, many trusted him, but there were large numbers of parents and faculty who were alarmed by his methods and ideas. He claimed to be a conservative who stood for the protection of the first ten amendments to the Constitution, but his critics often labelled him a radical.[9] Whether friend or foe, most agree, in looking back at the turbulent years of the late sixties, that John Roemer sometimes stimulated students to follow the protest movements beyond their level of maturity. More than a few students were left confused and disoriented by the questioning of values that he encouraged.

Other faculty also taught students moral values and participated in anti-war or anti-pollution movements, but their methods and effects were less disturbing than Roemer's. Doris Neumann, for example, had a more gentle or low-keyed way of presenting students with the moral questions of the day. She went with students on civil rights marches or anti-war protests in Washington, and later taught them the value of silent vigils. Together with other teachers who felt the responsibility of fulfilling the promise of a moral education that the Quaker affiliation of the school implied, she helped students in the search for truth that Byron Forbush encouraged. In a letter to parents in February 1970 he said, "What this school is all about, I suppose, is helping to develop intelligent, useful persons who throughout life will continually examine and re-examine their lives, searching for ways to improve themselves and the lot all humans share—all bound together by a concern for others—based on knowledge and spiritual development. . . ."[10]

By the 1969–70 school year student unrest had spread through the high school and touched a variety of issues. The anti-war movement was the most dramatic and significant of these issues and Friends' students responded with intensity. When they approached Byron Forbush with a request that the school be closed on October 15, 1969 in support of a national "Moratorium Day," he instead suggested they organize a program to examine and discuss the Vietnam War. Led by student Roberta Scott, they worked tirelessly to organize an impressive day of activities. Eighteen speakers, including notables such as Dr. Jerome Frank of The Johns Hopkins University, two films on Vietnam, and a guerrilla theater presentation were the events of the day. While not all teachers and students agreed on the points of view presented or debated, it was a valuable experience for the Upper School. The following spring, students again took the initiative and organized on "Earth Day" in support of the movement to protect the environment.[11] And other issues of national concern were usually discussed in the classrooms. But often the most disruptive issues were those that concerned the school itself. The national student rebellions peaked in spring 1970 at Kent State and Jackson State after President Richard Nixon announced the invasion of Cambodia. At Friends School the climax came at the same time but the event was the "Great Tie Strike."

For several years students in the high school had been pushing for more power in the decision-making process of the school. In many cases

Illus. 11-3   An addition to the Auditorium (center) *was constructed in 1975 to create a Middle School facility. It is flanked by the Upper School* (left) *and the Lower School* (right).

the Forbush administration, which included Stanley Johnson, principal of the Upper School, responded by setting up committees of students and faculty. These joint bodies examined the work-study programs, the honor code, school dances, voluntary meeting for worship, senior seminars, and even who should inspect the lockers. Some demands, such as the plea that all classes be voluntary, were rejected outright as unrealistic. [12] Even though Byron Forbush insisted that the school was "a reasonably open" one, there were students who developed a distinctly anti–administration attitude, not unlike their older counterparts in the colleges and universities. The tension between the administration and the minority of disgruntled students broke into the open at an assembly in the auditorium when the president of the Student Senate denounced the dress code and dramatically removed his necktie. When he invited all the boys in the high school to throw their ties on the stage, about half responded to the symbolic defiance of authority.

In the past the administration had been tacitly flexible regarding dress regulations. Although students were occasionally "hassled" for violating the rules, no one was ever suspended. Now the administration had no choice but to declare any boy reporting to class without a tie to be "not in good standing." When they arrived without ties the next day they were called out of class and sent to the auditorium where their parents were requested to pick them up. Over the next few days, after meetings with parents and students, all of the rebels were counselled back into class and the dress code remained in force. Eventually after endless meetings and discussions some small compromises were made, such as letting boys wear turtleneck shirts instead of neckties.[13]

The student rebellions of the late 1960s and early 1970s never reached a majority of the students in the high school and did not touch the younger children. At most perhaps 25 percent of the student body was involved in one or another of the various protest issues, whether they dealt with national events or were purely local in nature. There was always a group who tended to be more individualistic and outspoken or rebellious, but they were a little louder and more numerous during this time of national unrest. For the most part Friends students continued to be basically conservative. They were after all children still living at home, and despite the inclination of teenagers to question the judgment and values of adults, they continued to be strongly influenced by their parents. The largest group within the school were concerned simply with "growing up." They were not vocal and were more interested in sports, social activities, and their classes than they were in the problems of the outside world.[14]

With the end of the great tie strike the period of rebellion began to fade, much to the relief of Byron Forbush. This had been the only time in all of his years at Friends that he had any regrets about being the headmaster of the Baltimore school.[15] Emotions continued to run high through the spring semester of 1970, but the rebellious spirit was losing momentum. Occasional editorials and articles in the *Quaker Quill* accused the administration of poor communication with the student body, but gradually the attention of the high school returned to the normal routines of social events, athletics, lunchroom conditions, and class trips. One positive result was that students were invited to meet with the Education Committee to voice their concerns. A Student Affairs Committee, which had been organized earlier, was also used as a vehicle for conveying ideas or complaints to the Education Committee. They were treated politely and students for the most part seemed to feel that their concerns were being listened to.[16] When Friends formed the Board of Trustees, students were guaranteed representation on it.[17]

The next time a crisis of confrontation arose, the focal point was not the student body and administration but the Board of Trustees, and the consequences threatened to be far more serious. The issue this time was not the war in Vietnam nor was it school dress codes—it was the question of boycotting lettuce in support of the United Farm Workers Union. In the fall of 1975 several students raised objections to the school's purchase of nonunion lettuce for the lunch program. When the Board of Trustees came together that October arguments were presented in favor of a boycott. Several student committees, including the Religious Life Committee chaired by Bryan Carpenter, The Political Awareness Committee headed by Fred Durr, The Community Service Committee led by Jo Ann Staton, and The Student Senate, supported the ban on lettuce. In December when the Board met for the purpose of approving the annual budget, they were greeted by a silent, candlelight prayer vigil. Students, teachers, and even a few Trustees stood or quietly walked outside in the schoolyard before the meeting began. The school community was strongly divided between those who demanded that the Quaker institution live up to its principles by supporting the farm workers, and those who insisted equally as strongly that the school should not take a stand on what they believed to be a political issue. The division was so great that the ability of the Board of Trustees to continue as a governing body was questioned. The budget, except for the lunch program, was eventually approved, but tensions remained strong throughout the school year. Headmaster Forbush suggested a temporary, neutral policy of serving only Romaine lettuce in the lunchroom, but only after the Board Chairman, J. Henry Dasenbrock, called for a cooling-off period, brought in a professional counselor from another Quaker meeting, and held countless individual discussions between Trustees, was a cooperative spirit restored. Seldom had the Quaker methods of resolving conflicts and disagreements been so severely tested as in the lettuce boycott controversy of 1975–76.[18]

The conflict of these years was not restricted to students and administration. Faculty, too, followed the national trend of voicing discontent and demanding to be heard. There were two local issues in particular that threatened to disrupt the unity and loyalty that faculty felt toward Friends School. In addition to national events such as the Vietnam War, the civil rights movement, lettuce-workers' boycotts, and the movement for equality for women, which divided faculty, administration, and trustees into different opinion groups, the more parochial issues of tenure and free tuition for faculty children nearly caused a serious loss of morale. The tenure system, created by Bliss Forbush in 1949 to give security to the teaching staff, came under

Illus. 11-4   Computer instruction, 1982.

criticism by the Education Committee in 1971 after a tenured faculty member was fired by the headmaster and appealed to the Committee.[19] The case was settled before it came to a public hearing, but the incident convinced the Education Committee that the tenure policy was too restricting on the school. In 1971 tenure was replaced by a system of guaranteed annual and multiple year contracts. A few years later, in 1974, the Board of Trustees withdrew the benefit of free tuition to faculty children enrolled at Friends.[20] Thereafter only those who could establish financial need would receive aid. The loss of these two privileges—tenure and free tuition—led faculty to question the support of the administration and Board of Trustees. As a result in 1974 disgruntled teachers formed a Faculty Association, later called the

Faculty Meeting for Business, to express their concerns and to create an organization that could bargain with the administration if need be. Although several faculty refused to attend the meetings of this new organization for fear that it would be too "radical," the majority of the fifteen or twenty teachers who attended its meetings were for the most part quite moderate. The protest over the loss of tenure and free tuition was never strong and gradually subsided as most instructors found that their jobs were secure as long as they continued to do a good job. By 1977 the concerns of the Faculty Meeting for Business had shifted to "(1) improving faculty interrelationships within the school divisions, (2) faculty growth in the evaluation process and (3) salary scale guidelines. . . ."[21] In part the relations between teachers and the administration were improved when Byron Forbush created the Faculty-Administration-Board Personnel Committee to serve as a forum for discussing important issues and for defusing tension. An important achievement of this committee was the publication for the first time of faculty salary guidelines.[22] Issues raised initially in the Faculty Meeting for Business could often move on to the Faculty-Administration-Board Personnel Committee for resolution.

Another issue that raised emotions and caused concern in the post-1960 period was the question of race. Since 1955 one new grade had been integrated each year until by 1963 all of the first eight grades included a small number of black students. By then, however, there was increasing pressure to complete the process by removing any racial restrictions in the admissions policy and accepting black applicants for all of the Upper School grades. The momentum for change built slowly after John F. Kennedy's inauguration and the growth of a stronger civil rights movement. In spring, 1962, the Education Committee, under a rising level of tension, discussed a change in policy. The chairman had to call for a cooling-off period because "Feeling ran extremely high, bitterness was evident, clashes of personalities and within families were evident."[23] When the Education Committee reported that it could not reach unity on the integration issue and therefore would retain the old policy of gradualism, many members of Stony Run Meeting who felt the need to uphold Quaker principles of equality, protested vehemently.

In both the committee and the Monthly Meeting, although a majority felt the time had come to strike race as a condition for admission, a strong minority still resisted. The opponents of change argued that the gradual procedure of admitting blacks to one new grade each year had worked well and should be continued. Moreover, they insisted, a promise had been made to parents and there should be no sudden reversal of policy now. Nevertheless pressure continued to mount until the fall of 1963 when Byron Forbush and W. Berkeley Mann, chairman of the Education Committee, laid out a plan for full integration. Through letters and a series of meetings with each group of constituents and staff, the administration and Education Committee won overwhelming support to open the entire school to all applicants, regardless of race, at the beginning of the 1964 school year. This was an important victory in principle, but would clearly bring no great change in reality since Friends ordinarily had space to admit only four or five new students to the Upper School each year. Nor was there likely to be a flood of black applicants for the few positions open. Since the initial group of blacks admitted in 1955, applicants had been hard to find. The reason was not a financial one but rather was the result of social conditions. Not many black parents were eager to enroll their child in a school where he or she would be in a small minority, especially when the private schools of Baltimore had a reputation in the black community of being elitist and mainly for whites. Moreover relatively few black Baltimoreans had any awareness of or familiarity with white suburban schools like Friends.

The difficulty of finding sufficient numbers of willing and qualified black students was also the root of a more serious problem—that of social adjustment after the pupils were enrolled. Since the proportion of black students never rose above 12 percent of the student body, they were faced with many problems as a small but visible minority.[24] How one explains those problems depends greatly upon the perspective from which one looks at the situation. The memories and viewpoints of white students and teachers are quite distinct from the perceptions of black students and teachers.

For white classmates, memory recalls that black students were not treated any differently from anyone else. If they were in those classes that had one or two black pupils from the first grade on, they seem to have given the question of racial differences little thought at all. Especially if by high school a black youth proved to be a good athlete, he seemed to have no trouble being accepted. He would have many friends in school, be chosen for important positions in school organizations, and generally be respected. The blacks who stayed at Friends through graduation from high school appeared to their white classmates to have no unusual difficulties. They were intelligent, dressed similarly to white students, and came from family backgrounds with similar values.

During the late sixties and early seventies the large majority of the student body, in the high school at least, were firm supporters of the civil rights movement and several spoke out often against segregation in the school newspaper.[25] From the perspective of the white student, the experiment in integration was a success.

The administration and the governing board were not as convinced, however, that all was well. By 1968 and 1969 when the first black students began to graduate from Friends, the school leaders had begun to notice recurring difficulties. The Education Committee became aware of a pattern in which the first year a black pupil arrived at Friends, he or she experienced apprehension about the new environment. Somewhat dazed by the new social activities, the black child fell behind in school work until he or she overcame the initial culture shock. Scholastic grades were seldom good the first year. The second year then became the crisis year in which the black student had to improve his or her grades if he or she expected to continue.[26]

What really began to make the administration, faculty, and Education Committee aware that they still had a long way to go in the process of racial integration at Friends School was when black students in the Upper School began to speak out and to reveal their true feelings. No doubt greatly moved by the death of Martin Luther King, Jr., and encouraged by the greater articulation of discontent by black leaders in 1968, one well-respected black student shocked the school community when she rose in Collection one day to criticize her treatment by classmates and teachers. Many on the staff and in the administration had assumed that Quaker philosophy and values, and their general goodwill toward minorities, were sufficient to carry Friends through the integration process. Instead they learned that these first black students who stayed on through high school at Friends felt isolated and were conscious of subtle racial prejudice.

The greatest source of difficulty for the black students was the lack of numbers. With only three or four in each class they were highly conscious of being a minority and they tended to overcompensate by trying to prove their intellectual equality or superiority. By 1979, of the fifty-two black graduates of Friends, 100 percent had gone on to college.[27] Nearly every black student who spoke out about his or her experiences reported a feeling of inferiority or insecurity. They felt they were not accepted at first and had to prove themselves. Because they were so few in number it was not truly a case of integration in which a cultural exchange occurred. Black students were expected to take on the values and behavior of the white majority, but there was little reciprocity. The white students were not learning from their black classmates because there were too few of them and consequently the pressures on the minority were increased.[28]

Black students also suffered from the fact that the Friends campus was located in the northern, white section of Baltimore. Since the city's tradition of racial segregation continued even after the 1960s, this meant that black students were forced to live in two worlds: the school environment and their home neighborhood, usually some distance apart. Even when strong friendships formed between black and white children at school, they were seldom continued when classes were over or during summer vacations. The problem became more difficult as students reached high school and began to date. It was at this point that black students sometimes withdrew from Friends to seek a school where they were not in the minority. On the other hand those black students who adjusted best to the Friends School environment were often those who did not enroll in the white school until they were ready for high school. By then they had already formed a strong self-image and were less affected by their minority status. Particularly if the child was gifted in athletics and intelligence he or she was quickly accepted into the student life of the school. It was not unusual for blacks to be elected as class officers or team captains, or to become editor of the school newspaper. At the same time, however, they often felt the need to overcome the stereotype that all blacks are good athletes.

For those students who voiced their discontent, their complaints were surprisingly moderate. While calling for an increase in minority enrollment, they acknowledged the delicacy of the situation. Too sudden or too large an increase might, some said, cause a decline in white applications and thereby defeat the objective of a well-balanced enrollment. Instead they pointed to other ways the school could improve life for the black minority at Friends. They called for more black speakers at special events, for more courses on black history or more information on blacks in existing courses, for better minority representation on the governing board, and for more black teachers and administrators.[29]

Even with these complaints the students often went on to voice a strong sense of pride in Friends School. As one black senior wrote: "The school is one of the best institutions that can be found in Baltimore; and all of the students are lucky to be a part of it."[30] Others agreed that although they were not satisfied with their social experience at Friends, it had prepared them exceptionally well academically and they had no difficulty competing with other students when they went on to schools like Harvard, Yale, Cornell, Princeton, Brown, Oberlin, and Swarthmore.[31]

The problems black students faced at Friends in the late sixties and early seventies were not of course unique. No independent or public school that took on the responsibility of educating a diversity of students escaped the difficulties that arose from trying to overcome the centuries of racial and cultural prejudice in American society. If Friends had any advantage at all it was again in its strong commitment to Quaker principles and methods. The administration and Board of Trustees listened to the criticisms of minority students and their parents and took genuine steps to improve the situation. They were not always successful in resolving the problems but there is evidence of positive change. For one thing they began to hire black faculty. In 1967 Mrs. Odaris Coleman was hired by Byron Forbush to teach science in the seventh grade and in the Upper School.[32] A graduate of Morgan State College, she previously had taught in the Friends summer program for inner-city children. She was the first of seven black faculty who were hired over the next fifteen years, in addition to several part-time instructors who taught only one or two courses. Like the black students she felt at first a need to prove herself. "I was ostracized at first; and maybe it was me; maybe it wasn't them; maybe I didn't assert myself enough, because I had taken the posture that I'm here and I'm going to do a good job. After a period of time, I know they began to accept me professionally by virtue of what I was doing."[33] Although she came to feel comfortable in the school environment, her initial concern about being accepted perhaps explains some of the difficulty that Friends and other independent schools have had in hiring new black faculty. William Ellis, Director of the Middle School, in interviewing black faculty for new positions, found that many were wary of private institutions and preferred the public school system where they believed their opportunities for advancement were better.[34] The fact that public school salaries were often better only increased the obstacles to recruiting black teachers.

The attempt of Friends School to attract minority students and teachers, while not as successful as some had hoped, was a sincere effort. The spirit of social reform and the commitment to create a diversified educational environment that Bliss Forbush pursued in the 1940s and

Illus. 11-5   Participants in the 1975 Summer Writing Opportunity Program, a six-week enrichment program established in 1965 for Baltimore City public school students.

1950s continued during his son's administration. In 1965 Friends established its Summer Writing Opportunity Program. They selected twenty-four ninth grade students, both black and white, from several Baltimore junior-high schools. These were children of ability and promise whose only shortcoming was limited financial resources. A year later Friends opened a Head Start program for younger children.[35]

The Summer Writing Opportunity Program over the next two decades became an important enrichment experience for city students preparing to enter high school. Gordon Stills, who directed the program for twelve years, often organized an academic and recreational program around a central theme, such as "Renaissance Thought." Students studied literature, history, science, and art, and took study trips to the Walters Art Gallery or other places of interest. Later in 1978, with the support of a grant from the Goldseker Foundation, Friends established the BOOST Program, which brought in ten students from Morgan State University and the Community College of Baltimore to work with students in physical education and the pre-primary department. Between 1977 and 1982 the BOOST Program,

211

supported by school funds and a Geraldine Dodge Foundation grant, brought fifty-six minority professionals to campus serving as interns, professional aides, and teachers' assistants. [36]

A few years earlier the Board of Trustees had established a Committee on Minority Involvement to seek ways to improve opportunities for minorities at Friends. This study group quickly learned that while the school had a strong scholarship program and a genuine concern for its minority constituents, its greatest handicap was lack of publicity. Particularly among Baltimore's black community, Friends was not well known. Black parents who were teachers or professionals were sometimes familiar with Friends and sought enrollment for their children there, but for large parts of Baltimore's black community who could well afford the costs of private education, Friends School remained an unfamiliar institution. By the 1980s the efforts of a newly created Public Relations Office and a new Admissions Office promised to improve minority recruitment.

Despite the difficulties of recruiting and retaining minority students and faculty, Friends' reputation steadily grew during these years as a place with a lively pluralistic atmosphere. In 1978 the evaluation committee of Middle States Association of Colleges and Schools commended Friends as a strong institution with "an abundantly rich climate for learning. . . ." The first of its several "outstanding characteristics" that the Committee pointed out was the fact that "the student body is certainly representative of the school's philosophy which states that 'coeducation, and religious, racial and ethnic diversity are important elements of the environment in which most young people mature.' "[37] Besides the racial minorities, which included a number of Oriental students, a broad mixture of religions was represented at Friends. By the beginning of the 1980s the largest groups were Jewish, Catholic, and Episcopalian, each with between 12 and 17 percent, followed by Quakers with 7 percent. [38]

Regardless of their background, all students at Friends hoped to leave with a good education. Academically the school's reputation continued to rise as its financial base strengthened, its facilities improved, and additional capable faculty were hired in the 1960s and 1970s. Gradually the curriculum changed and broadened under the leadership of Byron Forbush, who tried to keep Friends in the forefront of Baltimore's independent schools. Old courses like Latin were dropped as a requirement for eighth grade pupils, but English requirements were increased. [39] As the interests and abilities of the faculty

Illus. 11-6 Commencement, Homeland Campus, 1981.

changed, new courses were added to the curriculum such as Russian history, Asian studies, Latin American history, history of the Middle East, and a course on "Emerging Africa."[40]

Overall, Friends offered a balanced curriculum that prepared students for college work in either the humanities or sciences. In the Upper School there was perhaps greater emphasis on the humanities, a reflection of the interest of the families from which the students came.[41] Nor were the arts neglected. The administration added a full-time art teacher in 1976 and later renovated the top floors of both the Upper and Lower Schools to create space for teaching studios. The original plays and operettas written and directed by Isabel Woods were gone, but Frances Bartley and Jack Brumit carried on a strong tradition that would have pleased both Miss Woods and Roman Steiner. The Mixed Chorus became one of the school's most popular activities. And the Middle School added a new dimension by introducing instrumental music to the curriculum in the 1970s.

Parallel to the curriculum or sometimes even part of it were a number of activities that enriched the children's education. One example is the involvement of Friends School students in foreign exchange programs and international affairs clubs. Beginning with the strong Quaker concern for helping the European survivors of World War II, the school continued to encourage students to correspond with their peers in other countries, to study foreign languages and cultures, and better yet, to visit other nations. Each week there were events and activities designed to instruct and call attention to people abroad. Exchange students like William Ellis, who later became Director of the Middle School, gave talks to the student body about their homelands.[42] Visiting teachers from Europe who had corresponded with students and faculty at Friends often stopped to speak to classes and tour the school. The Affiliation Committee helped set up student exchanges with Godalming Grammar School in England, and each year high-school language and history classes visited the United Nations headquarters in New York. Younger children put on plays and musicals with foreign settings and themes. In 1964 Friends was the first secondary school in the United States to be visited by teachers from the Soviet Union.

This strong interest in foreign affairs continued through the 1960s partly because of the national interest in the cold war and partly because of the Quaker School Affiliation Programs to aid people abroad. But there was an additional stimulus that came from teachers, especially Claire Walker, who encouraged students to reach beyond their own culture and language. Her enthusiasm carried over to her students and attracted others interested in Russia to Friends School. In 1965 she organized a Russian Institute on the campus and opened it to students of Baltimore city and the surrounding counties. A Washington bookstore provided books; and there were Russian canned goods, stories, songs, filmstrips, and short skits about the Soviet Union.[43] In 1955–56 she helped students start an International Relations Club with about thirty members. Later she established at Friends a newsletter of the Russian Committee of the National Association of Independent Schools, was elected vice president of The American Association of Teachers of Slavic and Eastern European Languages, and by 1970 began to escort students on tours to Moscow.[44] Until her retirement in 1975, student interest in international relations and especially Russia remained high.

When interest in international affairs began to weaken as it did in many schools in the late 1970s, student attention shifted to other issues such as prison awareness. From World War II until the present, Friends students at all levels were involved in projects of social concern. Besides sending packages of clothes, toys, and food to war-torn Europe in the 1940s, they later worked in urban renewal projects, put on variety shows at nursing homes, sent Christmas presents to patients at Crownsville State Hospital, worked in a tutoring program at The Johns Hopkins University, and planned work camps at the McKim Community Center in downtown Baltimore.[45] The emphasis on social action came from the Quaker Meeting and was transferred to the school by Byron Forbush and the faculty. As Dr. Forbush said:

> We feel that we have a responsibility, and we must pass on our sense of responsibility to the students who come here. An independent school cannot exist in an ivory tower. Giving our students this concept of service to others also helps make them better people, we feel, and this in turn is compatible with the Quaker ideal of the perfectibility of the individual. We think a good education is social and spiritual as well as intellectual and physical.[46]

Student publications and student government were other popular activities at Friends that made up a part of this concept of a well-rounded education. The *Quaker Quill* was the campus newspaper, published about ten times a year and filled with school news about guest speakers, Lower School activities, plans for the annual Bazaar or social dances, results of the latest athletic contests, stories about alumni, movie reviews, poems and short stories, and editorials on current events in the nation or in the school. A more serious publication was *The Mock Turtle*, a literary magazine that published the creative writings of high-school scholars.

Other students, with more political than literary interests, were likely to become involved in the Upper School Senate or the Junior Council, both of which worked as advisory bodies concerning school policies and social activities as well as discipline. Although the nature of these student organizations changed from time to time and interest fluctuated between intense involvement and bored indifference, the students who worked on the various committees and councils developed closer relationships with the faculty and learned leadership skills. Especially those who helped plan the annual Bazaar learned to work with parents, teachers, and alumni, and were responsible for handling substantial sums of money.

Of all the extracurricular activities, however, the programs in athletics probably touched the most students. Although the requirements changed from time to time, students in the Upper School were usually expected to participate in at least two sports each year. Since Friends was small compared to many Baltimore schools, there were not large numbers on any single team, which gave more children a chance to learn and even to become star players. The attitude toward sports printed in a *Quaker Quill* editorial as early as 1938 expressed the philosophy that still prevailed nearly a half century later: "The goal of our athletic program is to educate the whole man. We are naturally very much interested in winning our athletic contests, but we are particularly interested in the type of game played and the spirit with which it is played."[47] Whether or not one agreed with this philosophy depended in part upon how good an athlete one was and how much emphasis one placed upon having a winning team. Even though some parents and alumni were frustrated that the administration did not recruit better athletes and hire better coaches, Friends still had championship teams from time to time. Every graduate could remember a few shining moments such as the playoff against St. Paul's in 1954 that gave Friends the state championship in lacrosse, or when the "Big Red" team beat City College 8 to 4 at Homewood Field in 1963 for the MSA Lacrosse Championship.[48] Football, which was the most important sport for boys in the 1940s when Byron Forbush quarterbacked the team to the IAC Championship, was gradually replaced in popularity among the students by soccer and lacrosse in the 1980s.[49] For the girls, field hockey continued to be popular, but several championship teams in lacrosse and basketball put those sports at the top of the athletic program.[50]

A unique aspect of the sports program at Friends is the long history of emphasis on girls' athletics. Long before the government required schools to give equal support to women's athletics, Friends encouraged girls to participate in a variety of teams. In the 1940s while the boys went off with Robert Nicolls and Arthur Gray for a ten-day football camp at the end of each summer, the girls were at hockey camp with Marian Millard and Eleanor High.[51] Both the boys' and girls' athletic associations were important social organizations within the school, and each gave awards to outstanding athletes. The coeducational environment that Friends had pioneered in Baltimore in the nineteenth century carried over to the playing fields in the twentieth century.

And finally, student life at Friends School would not have been complete without the regular schedule of social dances, parties, and dinners. Classes hired bands or played records, decorated the auditorium around romantic themes like "Evening in Paris," and served refreshments to the dancers much like their predecessors had done in decades past. Administrators and chaperones occasionally worried

Illus. 11-7   Aerial View, Homeland Campus, 1982.

about the teenagers who tried to smuggle beer into the parties or smoke marijuana behind the gym, but they were no worse than in any other suburban school. "Steady" dating was common in the 1950s, but students more often socialized in groups in the later decades. And for seniors, June Week became the last chance for partying and celebrating their graduation from Friends.

The institution they left behind as they received their diplomas at commencement exercises each spring was a far different place from the small school on Aisquith Street where Friends began in 1784. Two hundred years of change separated Joseph Townsend and his first Quaker pupils from the community of 850 scholars who studied and played at the spacious campus on North Charles Street in the 1980s. Although the concept of a "guarded education" for a few was no longer the aim of the school, Friends still held to the goal of "assisting each individual realize more fully his potentialities, developing a way of life based on good will, friendliness, and brotherly love."[52] Despite all the changes that have occurred during the two centuries, that principle and the Quaker belief that there is "that of God in every man," have provided a thread of continuity linking the past to the present, and insuring the future of Friends School.

Eli M. Lamb
(1864–1899)

John W. Gregg
(1899–1903)

Edward C. Wilson
(1903–1927)

Louisa P. Blackburn
(1889–1899)

William S. Pike
(1927–1935)

Bliss Forbush, Sr.
(1943–1960)

Edwin C. Zavitz
(1935–1943)

Principals of the School and Headmasters*

Eli M. Lamb. . . . . 1864–1899†
Louisa P. Blackburn. 1889–1899
John W. Gregg. 1899–1903
Edward C. Wilson 1903–1927
William S. Pike 1927–1935
Edwin C. Zavitz. 1935–1943
Bliss Forbush, Sr.. 1943–1960
W. Byron Forbush II 1960–

W. Byron Forbush II
(1960—)

* The terms "Principal" and "Headmaster" were not used before 1864.

† From 1889 to 1899 Lamb's school was separate from the Meeting's school.

Notes

Chapter 1

1. Several issues of the *Maryland Journal and Baltimore Advertiser* between January and March, 1784, contain references to the severity of the winter and the ice on the Bay. The harbor remained closed from January 2 to March 26.

2. For the best description and analysis of Baltimore's economic development during and after the Revolution see Gary L. Browne, *Baltimore in the Nation, 1789–1861* (Chapel Hill: University of North Carolina Press, 1980).

3. *Maryland Journal and Baltimore Advertiser,* 13 January 1784.

4. Minutes, Baltimore Preparative Meeting of Friends, 29 May 1788, Friends Historical Library, Swarthmore College.

5. *Maryland Journal and Baltimore Advertiser,* 27 January 1784.

6. *Votes and Proceedings of the Senate of the State of Maryland, 1783–84,* p. 71.

7. Advertisements for the sale of indentured servants and black slaves or for their recapture if escaped, made up a large part of every issue of the *Maryland Journal and Baltimore Advertiser* for 1784 and succeeding years.

8. John Thomas Scharf, *The Chronicles of Baltimore* (Baltimore: Turnbull Brothers, 1874), p. 55.

9. Bliss Forbush, *A History of Baltimore Yearly Meeting of Friends* (Sandy Spring, Md.: Baltimore Yearly Meeting of Friends, 1972), pp. 2–5.

10. William C. Braithwaite, *The Second Period of Quakerism,* 2nd ed. (Cambridge: Cambridge University Press, 1961), pp. 497–98.

11. Frederick B. Tolles, *Meeting House and Counting House: The Quaker Merchants of Colonial Philadelphia, 1682–1763* (New York: W. W. Norton and Company, Inc., 1963), p. 8.

12. Forbush, *Baltimore Yearly Meeting,* p. 49.

13. Minutes, Baltimore Preparative Meeting, 28 June 1787.

14. *Maryland Journal and Baltimore Advertiser,* 2 January 1784; and Kenneth Silverman, *A Cultural History of the American Revolution* (New York: Thomas Y. Crowell Co., 1976), p. 452.

15. *Maryland Journal and Baltimore Advertiser,* 3, 10, and 13 February 1784.

16. Ibid., 27 January 1784.

17. Diary of Richard H. Townsend, 1851–1879, 3 vols. Enoch Pratt Free Library, Baltimore, p. 24.

18. Minutes, Baltimore Preparative Meeting, 29 January 1784.

Chapter 2

1. Minutes, Baltimore Monthly Meeting of Friends, 31 March 1794, Friends Historical Library, Swarthmore College (hereafter cited as Minutes, BMM).

2. Thomas Woody, *Early Quaker Education in Pennsylvania* (New York: Columbia University Press, 1920), p. 62.

3. The best source of information on Townsend is the diary of his son, Richard. Joseph Townsend's name also appears frequently in the minutes of Baltimore Monthly Meeting and on the authorizations of payments to the school's teachers. See also Thomas W. Griffith, *Annals of Baltimore* (Baltimore: William Woody, 1824), pp. 128, 145.

4. Vernon Vavrina, "The History of Public Education in the City of Baltimore, 1829–1956" (Ph.D. dissertation, Catholic University, 1958), p. xviii.

5. *Maryland Journal and Baltimore Advertiser*, 25 May 1784.

6. Ibid., 6 January and 25 May 1784.

7. Ibid., 20 April 1784.

8. John Thomas Scharf, *History of Baltimore City and County* (Philadelphia: Lewis H. Everts, 1881), p. 224.

9. Griffith, *Annals*, p. 118; Scharf, *History of Baltimore*, p. 224; and Vavrina, "Public Education," p. xxiii.

10. Vavrina, "Public Education," pp. xx, xxi.

11. R. Freeman Butts and Lawrence A. Cremin, *A History of Education in American Culture* (New York: Henry Holt and Co., 1953), pp. 190–93.

12. Braithwaite, *Quakerism*, p. 533.

13. Woody, *Quaker Education in Pennsylvania*, pp. 29–30.

14. Rufus M. Jones, *The Later Periods of Quakerism*, 2 vols. (London: Macmillan and Co., Ltd., 1921) 2:666.

15. Howard H. Brinton, *Quaker Education in Theory and Practice*, 2nd rev. ed. (Wallingford, Pa.: Pendle Hill, 1958), p. 77.

16. William Penn, *Letters to Wife and Children: Tracts on Moral and Religious Subjects* (New York: Mahlon Day, 1823), p. 6.

17. Brinton, *Quaker Education*, p. 28; and Jones, *Quakerism*, p. 668.

18. Thomas Jones, "Educational Policies in the Philadelphia Yearly Meetings During the Nineteenth Century," *The Friend* (27 June 1940), pp. 483–84.

19. Lawrence A. Cremin, *American Education: The Colonial Experience, 1607–1783* (New York: Harper and Row, Publishers, 1970), p. 305.

20. Forbush, *Baltimore Yearly Meeting*, p. 54.

21. Brinton, *Quaker Education*, pp. 63–66; and Braithwaite, *Quakerism*, p. 536.

22. Townsend diary, p. 24.

23. See Report of the Baltimore Monthly Meeting, Eastern District to the Baltimore Quarterly Meeting, May 1814; and Minutes, BMM, 22 February 1793, 30 May 1794. Members of this committee included some of Baltimore's most prominent merchants,

such as John McKim, Elias Ellicott, Elisha Tyson, Gerard Hopkins, John Brown, and Joseph Townsend, now a dry goods merchant. See Minutes, BMM, 22 February 1793, 21 February 1794.

24. William Cook Dunlap, *Quaker Education in Baltimore and Virginia Yearly Meetings* (Philadelphia: William C. Dunlap, 1936), p. 30. See also Minutes, Baltimore Preparative Meeing for the Eastern District, 10 November 1807.

25. Forbush, *Baltimore Yearly Meeting*, p. 58; and Griffith, *Annals*, p. 181.

26. In January 1801, Baltimore Monthly Meeting rented a house for $240 per year on St. Paul's Lane and hired a teacher. This second school, however, disappeared before 1806. Minutes, BMM, 14 August 1800, 8 January 1801, and 9 January 1806. See also Education Committee, Report to BMM, 10 July 1880; and *Baltimore Town and Fell's Point Directory, 1796* (Baltimore: Pechin, 1796).

27. *Federal Gazette*, 8 October 1805. See also the Hayward File in the Maryland Historical Society.

28. *American*, 22 March 1808.

29. The merchants' plight is revealed in a letter from Elisha Tyson and Joseph James, two leading flour merchants, to Jefferson requesting an exception to the embargo, in order to ship 3,000 barrels of flour to New Orleans. A copy of the letter written in 1808, apparently made by the senders, is in the Friends School archives.

30. Richard Townsend's diary is an excellent source of information about Quaker life in Baltimore. For his comments on schools and education see pp. 43–58, and 64. Other students in the Old Town school in 1814 were Marcelious Balderston, Wilson and Isaiah Balderston, Joseph Matthews, Isaac Trimble, John Brown, Nathan Sheppard, and Eli West.

31. Woody, *Quaker Education in Pennsylvania*, p. 204.

32. See Brinton, *Quaker Education*, p. 54.

33. According to the Westtown catalogue, p. 352, Amos Bullock taught arithmetic there from March 1814 to June 1816. The original authorizations of payment, signed by Joseph Townsend, are in the Friends School archives. The name of the school varies slightly, being referred to in an 1816 voucher as the "Select School," and in an 1818 payment as the "Male School." See also Richard Townsend's diary, p. 79; and Dunlap, *Quaker Education*, p. 37.

34. Minutes, BMM for the Eastern Distict, 10 October 1816, 9 January 1817, and 6 March 1817. Members of the committee were John L. Peck, John Trimble, John Dukehart, William Proctor, Ely Balderston, and William Brown. See also the Eastern District Minutes for 4, 8, and 10 June 1818. Ellicott's enquiry was to Thomas Stewardson of Philadelphia. In his reply, in the Friends School archives, Stewardson reported that the four male teachers at Westtown received $500 each year and those with families were allowed to live in a large "infirmary." The five female teachers there received only half of what the men were paid.

35. The memo in the school archives is dated 16 September 1818.

36. Minutes, BMM for the Eastern Distict, 8 August 1815, and 10 October 1816. The committee included the same men who served on the committee for the boys' school as well as Esther Townsend, Phebe Lafetra, Ann Peck, Catherine Brown, Elizabeth Amos, and Elizabeth Trimble.

37.   Townsend diary, pp. 78, 89.

38.   Report of the Education Committee for the Girls' School, 4 November 1818; and Minutes, BMM for the Eastern District, 5 November 1818.

Chapter 3

1.   See Browne, *Baltimore*, pp. 91–94.

2.   Forbush, *Baltimore Yearly Meeting*, pp. 57–58, mentions a number of prominent Quaker merchants of this period.

3.   Ibid., pp. 51–52; and Townsend diary, pp. 65, 69.

4.   John McKim joined the Society of Friends as an adult in 1787. See the records of Baltimore Preparative Meeting, 22 February 1787.

5.   For a brief account of the Hicksite separation in Baltimore, see Forbush, *Baltimore Yearly Meeting*, pp. 64–70. Richard Townsend in his diary, p. 126, says the Orthodox members who withdrew from Baltimore Yearly Meeting at first held their meetings in Branch Tabernacle on St. Paul Street, which was "half school-house, half meeting-house."

6.   See Tina Hirsch Sheller, "The Origins of Public Education and the Evolution of an Urban Society: Baltimore City, 1790–1830" (M.A. thesis, University of Maryland, 1978).

7.   Both Brinton, *Quaker Education*, pp. 30–31 and Jones, *Quakerism*, 2:705 agree that the rise of public schools led directly to the decline in the number of Quaker schools, particularly at the elementary level.

8.   *Extracts from the minutes of Baltimore Yearly Meeting* (Baltimore: William Woody and Son, 1854), p. 14.

9.   Vavrina, "Public Education," pp. 1–3; and Percy Lewis Kaye, "Public Education in Baltimore," in *Baltimore: Its History and Its People*, ed. Clayton Coleman Hall, 2 vols. (New York: Lewis Historical Publishing Co., 1912), 1:560–62.

10.   Several of the reports of the School Committee to Baltimore Monthly Meeting and the minutes of the School Committee for 1846–48 show that they were ready to encourage the construction of three schools in different parts of Baltimore. Although the records are not entirely clear, apparently only the school at the Lombard Street Meeting House—the descendant of the original school in Old Town—enjoyed much success and survived. See also the School Committee Report of 10 January 1850, on the opening of the new classrooms by Jane S. Jewett.

11.   School Committee Report to BMM, 8 June 1854. By the 1850s the committee made regular reports on the enrollment and state of the school. See for example those for 4 March and 7 April 1853, 7 February 1856, 8 September 1859, 5 July 1860, 6 August 1863, and 7 July 1864.

12.   Ibid., 8 September 1859, and 5 July, 9 September 1860.

13.   Minutes, BMM, 9 October 1851; and Butts and Cremin, *History of Education*, p. 284.

14.   Tuition was set at $3 per quarter with the expectation of enrolling 60 to 70 pupils.

Non-Quaker families would be required to pay an additional $1 per quarter for books and stationery. Ibid., 5 November 1863.

15. Townsend diary, p. 56.

16. For a description of the Lancastrian method as it was used in Quaker schools, see Helen G. Hole, *Things Civil and Useful* (Richmond, Ind.: Friends United Press, 1978), pp. 11–12.

17. Townsend diary, p. 79. The common subjects taught in the Quaker schools of Pennsylvania seem to be about the same as those taught in the public schools. See Woody, *Quaker Education*, p. 192. An old, but excellent description of nineteenth-century schools is Clifton Johnson, *Old-Time Schools and School-Books* (1904; reprint ed., Gloucester, Mass.: Peter Smith, 1963).

18. Jones, *Quakerism*, p. 673; and Johnson, *Old-Time Schools*, pp. 364–67.

19. Quoted in Johnson, *Old-Time Schools*, p. 91.

20. Woody, *Quaker Education in Pennsylvania*, pp. 192–94.

21. Townsend diary, p. 79; and School Committee Report to BMM, 30 December 1847.

22. See *Extracts from Women's Meeting, Baltimore Yearly Meeting* (Baltimore: William Woody, 1848), p. 7.

23. Quoted in E. Douglas Branch, *The Sentimental Years, 1836–1860* (New York: Appleton-Century Company, Inc., 1934), pp. 295–96.

24. J. William Frost, *The Quaker Family in Colonial America* (New York: St. Martin's Press, 1973), p. 77.

25. Bliss Forbush, "Friends School's Unique Role, Past and Present: A Friends School Education," unpublished paper (Friends School archives, n.d.), p. 4.

26. David B. Tyack, *The One Best System: A History of American Urban Education* (Cambridge: Harvard Universiy Press, 1975), p. 190.

27. Branch, *Sentimental Years*, p. 296.

28. Thomas Stewardson to Thomas Ellicott, 14 March 1818, Friends School archives.

29. Frost, *Quaker Family*, pp. 81–83.

30. Townsend diary, p. 44.

31. Frost, *Quaker Family*, p. 82.

Chapter 4

1. Lamb apparently arrived several months earlier, but the first official record of his presence in Baltimore is a certificate of removal from Gunpowder Monthly Meeting which appears in the Minutes, BMM, 10 April 1862.

2. Minutes, BMM, 10 September 1863.

3. Interview with Felix Morley, 17 May 1979.

4. Minutes, BMM, 5 November 1863.

5. Ibid., 6 August 1863.

6. Education Committee Report, 5 July 1864.

7. Lamb's report to Education Committee, 6 July 1865.

8. Felix Morley, *For the Record* (South Bend, Ind.: Regnery/Gateway, Inc., 1979), pp. 34–35.

9. Minutes, BMM, 9 August 1866.

10. Education Committee Report, 6 July 1865.

11. Ibid., 8 March, 8 August 1866.

12. Minutes, BMM, 9 May 1867.

13. Ibid., 8, 14 August 1867.

14. Ibid., 5 September 1867.

15. Ibid, 5 March 1868.

16. Education Committee Report, 9 July 1868.

17. Lamb's report to Education Committee, June 1877.

18. *Extracts from Minutes of Yearly Meeting* (1876), p. 18.

19. Brinton, *Quaker Education*, pp. 41–42.

20. Jones, *Quakerism*, pp. 910–11.

21. Brinton, *Quaker Education*, p. 90. The same observation was made by Jones, *Quakerism*, p. 982.

22. Minutes, Education Committee, 13 September 1899.

23. Court of Appeals of Maryland, "Belle J. Erhardt and Joel B. Erhardt, her Husband, Helen J. Hunt and Thomas Hunt, her Husband vs. Baltimore Monthly Meeting of Friends, Park Avenue, et al. (March 29, 1901), p. 25. For comments on religion in the school, see the Education Committee Report, 9 June and 6 July 1870.

24. Enrollment figures for each school year are in the principal's annual report to the Education Committee, normally presented each July.

25. *Extracts from Proceedings of Baltimore Yearly Meeting* (Baltimore: J. B. Rose and Co., 1880), pp. 15–17. For an example of the discounts and financial statements of the school, see the Education Committee Report, 23 July 1884.

26. According to Lamb's annual report for 1878 only the teachers who taught German and French were not Quakers. The same patterns of change were found by Philip S. Benjamin, *The Philadelphia Quakers in the Industrial Age, 1865–1920* (Philadelphia: Temple University Press, 1976), p. 35.

27. Michael Katz, "The Origins of Public Education: A Reassessment," *The History of Education Quarterly* 16, no. 4 (Winter, 1976): 383. See also Tyack, *One Best System*, pp. 72–73; Lawrence Cremin, *The Tradition of American Education* (New York: Basic Books, Inc., 1977), pp. 93–94; and Joseph F. Kett, *Rites of Passage* (New York: Basic Books, Inc., 1977), pp. 168–69.

28. Education Committee Report to Baltimore Yearly Meeting, 29 October 1884.

29. Committee responsibilities remained largely unchanged between 1863 and 1899. See ibid., 8 August 1863; and Jonathan K. Taylor's testimony in "Erhardt vs. BMM," p. 62.

30. The Education Committee members are listed in the Minutes, BMM, 10 October 1877. Their occupations are noted in *Woods' Baltimore City Directory* (Baltimore: John W. Woods, 1877), pp. 96, 440, 509, 532.

31. *Circular and Catalogue of Students of Friends' Elementary and High School for Pupils of Both Sexes* (Baltimore: Friends School, 1872), p. 3.

32. Ibid., p. 16.

33. Ibid. (1877–78), p. 3.

34. Lamb's report to Education Committee, July 1877. By "junior classes," Lamb meant those classes below the final or senior year.

35. Minutes, Baltimore Yearly Meeting, 30 October 1876.

36. *Extracts from Baltimore Yearly Meeting* (1883), p. 32.

37. *Baltimore City Directory* (1877), pp. 957–58.

38. For a good example of the Friends' Elementary and High School curriculum, see the school catalogue for 1879–80, pp. 21–26.

39. Ibid.

40. Ibid. (1872), p. 5.

41. The "School Record" or report card of Rebecca J. Lupton for 1868–69 is in the Friends School archives.

42. School catalogue (1877–78), p. 8.

43. Ibid. (1871), p. 8.

44. Ibid., p. 10.

45. Ibid.; and Michael B. Katz, "The 'New Departure' in Quincy, 1873–81: The Nature of Nineteenth-Century Educational Reform," *The New England Quarterly* 40 (March, 1967): 15.

46. Lamb's report to Education Committee, 1879.

47. Ibid.

48. "Erhardt vs. BMM," p. 77.

49. Minutes, Education Committee, 23 July, 7 August 1884; and 7 May 1885.

50. Ibid., 31 July 1885.

51. Lamb's report to Education Committee, July 1886.

Chapter 5

1. See Frank R. Shivers, Jr., *Bolton Hill: Baltimore Classic* (Baltimore: Frank R. Shivers, Jr., 1978).

2. School catalogue (1883), p. 32.

3. School catalogues of the 1890s for the first time include photographs of the classrooms and describe the methods for teaching science. See for example the catalogue for 1897–98, pp. 27–28.

4. Addresses of Quaker families are sometimes listed in the monthly meeting records, and other addresses as well as occupations are listed in the annual city directories.

5. Each catalogue listed the fees. See for example 1877–78, pp. 18–20.

6. School catalogue (1875–76), p. 22. A brief biographical sketch of Gary is in Elinor Bruchey, *The Business Elite in Baltimore, 1880–1914* (New York: Arno Press, 1976).

7. School catalogue (1871), pp. 6–9.

8. Ibid. (1877–78), pp. 9–10.

9. Lamb's report to Education Committee (1872).

10. School catalogue (1883–84), p. 4.

11. For an example of Friends School salaries see the Minutes of the Education Committee, 15 June 1891, and 30 April 1898. For national trends see W. Randolph Burgess, *Trends of School Costs* (New York: Russell Sage Foundation, 1920), pp. 32–33.

12. In Eli Lamb's report of July 1884 he pointed out that thirteen of the sixteen teachers were Quakers and that one of the other three was interested in joining.

13. Vavrina, "Public Education," pp. 381, 384. See also Charles Hirschfield, *Baltimore: 1870–1900*, Johns Hopkins Studies in History and Political Science, series 59, no. 2 (Baltimore, 1941), pp. 89–92.

14. Hirschfield, *Baltimore*, p. 93.

15. See Cremin, *The Transformation of the School: Progressivism in American Education, 1876–1957* (New York: Knopf, 1961), pp. 24–27; and Hirschfield, *Baltimore*, pp. 115–117.

16. Minutes, BMM, 6 June, 4 December 1873; 10 February 1876; 2 July 1878; and Education Committee Report, November 1883.

17. See for example the Education Committee Report, 9 July 1879. That year the tuition for the "free scholars" was $291. Two hundred of that amount was paid by the Fair Hill Fund and the remainder came from the rent of the school building.

18. Minutes, BMM, 29 November 1886, 6 January 1887.

19. "Erhardt vs. BMM," p. 60. Edward Stabler, Jr., who was a member of the Special Committee which met with the Education Committee, testified that although Eli Lamb insisted that Baltimore Monthly Meeting pay the discounts, his committee recommended that only part of the bills be paid. In Stabler's words, the situation "was very unpleasant for the School Committee. . . ." Ibid., pp. 76–77.

20. Compare for example the catalogue for 1883–84, p. 11, with that of 1897–98, p. 17.

21. Dr. Morley was the father of Felix Morley, who attended Friends School from 1902 to 1911, and who was in turn taught by Mr. Harry. Morley interview.

22. The Committee was formed in November, 1888, only two months after the separation from Lamb. The sequence of events leading to the new school was explained by a member of the new committee, Jonathan K. Taylor in "Erhardt vs. BMM," pp. 60–61.

23. Minutes, Education Committee, 19 January, 4 April, 4, 27 May, and 7 December 1889.

24. Ibid., 19 January 1889.

25. "Erhardt vs. BMM," p. 60.

26. Minutes, Education Committee, 15 June 1891, 25 June 1893, and 24 March 1897.

27. Ibid., 27 November 1892, 11 November 1893, and 22 September, 21 October 1894.

28. Ibid., 26 October 1896.

29. Education Committee letter to Baltimore Yearly Meeting, 26 October 1898.

30. Minutes, Education Committee, 8 October 1898.

31. Ibid., 24 March 1899. For the following year Lamb was to receive 5 percent from the income of the same students.

32. Eli Lamb to Education Committee, 12 April 1899.

33. Minutes, Education Committee, 16 November 1898, and 9 March 1899.

34. John Dorsey and James D. Dilts, *A Guide to Baltimore Architecture* (Cambridge, Md.: Tidewater Publishers, 1973), pp. 15, 106.

35. "Erhardt vs. BMM," p. 63. Jewett had been one of the most persistent and enthusiastic supporters of a new school. The total cost of the building, land, and equipment was over $40,000. Education Committee Report to BMM, 4 November 1899. See also 21 April 1899.

36. School catalogue (1899–1900), pp. 10–11.

Chapter 6

1. Morley, *For the Record*, p. 34.

2. Baltimore *Sun*, 4 September 1899; Education Committee Report, 24 October 1900.

3. *Baltimore American* and *Sun*, 18 September 1899.

4. Ibid.

5. Minutes, Education Committee, 24 February 1899; and "Erhardt vs. BMM," p. 66.

6. "Erhardt vs. BMM," p. 52.

7. See, for example, Minutes, Education Committee, 27 September 1902.

8. "Erhardt vs. BMM," pp. 58–59; and the Friends School yearbook, *The Quaker* (1916), p. 40.

9. School catalogue (1899), p. 5; and "Erhardt vs. BMM," p. 49.

10. School catalogue (1899), pp. 7–8.

11. Minutes, Baltimore Yearly Meeting, p. 39.

12. Education Committee Report, 24 October 1900; and Minutes, Education Committee, 26 January, 24 November 1900.

13. Minutes, Education Committee, 23 January 1903.

14. Education Committee Report, 26 November 1914.

15. Minutes, Education Committee, 8 February 1903.

16. Bliss Forbush, "My Baltimore Book," 22 vols., unpublished private papers, Friends Historical Library, Swarthmore College, 7:15 contains an unidentified newspaper clipping dated 16 February 1927 at the time Wilson announced his retirement.

17. Wilson's "Statement of Growth" report to Education Committee, 21 January 1927.

18. Wilson's report to Education Committee, 24 November 1916.

19. Interviews with Morley; Selma Levy Oppenheimer, 5 March 1980; and Eleanor Dilworth Mace, 11 January 1980.

20. School catalogue (1899), p. 7; Education Committee Report, 30 October 1899; and *Program, Friends Elementary and High School, 1897–98,* pp. 4–5.

21. "Erhardt vs. BMM," p. 66.

22. Education Committee Report, 24 October 1900, and 24 October 1915.

23. Ibid., 14 November 1908.

24. Wilson's report to Education Committee, 7 October 1918.

25. Morley, interview; and Morley, *For the Record,* p. 33.

26. *The Quaker* (1917), p. 39.

27. Ibid.

28. Wilson's report to Education Committee, 10 October 1921.

29. *The Quaker* (1917), p. 38.

30. Interview with Hugo Dalsheimer, 10 February 1978.

31. Oppenheimer interview, 5 March 1980.

32. *The Quaker* (1921) p. 56.

33. Dalsheimer interview; and Morley interview.

34. Education Committee Report, 29 September 1924.

35. Wilson's report to Education Committee, 24 November 1916.

36. *The Quaker* (1918), p. 52.

37. Ibid.

38. Education Committee Report, 7 May 1917; and Wilson's report to Education Committee, 23 November 1917.

39. Wilson's report to Education Committee, 23 May 1921.

40. Mace interview; and Dalsheimer interview.

41. Wilson's report to Education Committee, 25 October 1917.

42. School catalogue (1917–18), p. 6.

43. See for example, ibid., pp. 10–12.

44. Wilson's report to Education Committee, 25 May 1914, and 25 April 1921.

45. Ibid., 10 February 1919; and Mace interview.

46. Cf. Butts and Cremin, *History of Education,* p. 454; and Tyack, *One Best System,* p. 62.

47. Minutes, Education Committee, 8 February 1905, 2 and 13 February 1906.

48. Education Committee Report, 23 February 1915, and 23 February 1920.

49. Tyack, *One Best System,* p. 60.

50. Education Committee Report, 3 March 1910.

51. Wilson's report to Education Committee, 8 October 1923.

52. Ibid., 21 October 1912.

53. Alan D. Anderson, *The Origin and Resolution of an Urban Crisis: Baltimore, 1890–1930* (Baltimore: The Johns Hopkins University Press, 1977), p. 42.

Chapter 7

1. Interview with Amy Federleicht Greif, 18 November 1980.

2. Wilson's report to Education Committee, 23 May, and 25 October 1921; and interviews with Esther Felter Mallonee, 4 April 1980, and Karl and Agnes Krieger Levy, 4 February 1980.

3. Charlotte Feast Hoffman, "Attending Friends School in the Days of World War I," *Sun Magazine* (22 June 1980), pp. 26–27.

4. Oppenheimer interview; and Greif interview.

5. Wilson's report to the Education Committee, 9 October 1922.

6. Education Committee Report, 9 April, and 5 October 1907.

7. Shivers, *Bolton Hill*, p. 3.

8. Morley interview.

9. Otto F. Kraushaar, *Schools in a Changing City: An Overview of Baltimore's Private Schools* (Baltimore: The Sheridan Foundation, 1976), p. 27.

10. Ibid., pp. 30–31.

11. School catalogue (1899–1900), p. 13.

12. Education Committee Report, 2 March 1915.

13. Wilson's report to Education Committee, 15 March 1926. The other schools were Roland Park, Boys Latin, Gilman, Marston's, Park, and Bryn Mawr.

14. Ibid., 27 February 1922, refers specifically to the size of debt at Bryn Mawr, Gilman, and Park.

15. In Edward Wilson's report of 9 May 1927 he remarked that Jewish enrollment was that high when he began in 1903. Felix Morley confirmed that when he attended Friends before 1912 the proportion of Jewish students was about one-fourth the total enrollment.

16. School catalogue (1877–78), p. 10.

17. Wilson's report to Education Committee, 25 April 1921.

18. Ibid.

19. The expansion of 1922 also included excavation of an area under the meeting house and the construction of a "large locker room, larger kitchen, pantry, and cold storage room." Education Committee Report, 9 October 1922.

20. Ibid., 4 April, 27 May, and 27 October 1911.

21. Helen Corse Barney letter to Friends School, 1 June 1977, in Friends School archives.

22. Minutes, Education Committee, 28 January 1905.

23. Education Committee Report, 25 January 1908. In 1906 electric lighting had been installed in the meeting house. See the committee report for 4 December 1906.

24. See school catalogue (1899), pp. 11, 12; Wilson's report to Education Committee, 25 October 1917; and Pike's report to Education Committee, 28 September 1931.

25. School catalogue (1899–1900), p. 15.

26. Ibid. (1904–05), p. 17.

27. Ibid. (1918–19), p. 81.

28. Ibid. (1927–28), pp. 74–75.

29. Ibid. (1899–1900), p. 24. Malcolm Hecht and Selma Kann Burgunder, students from 1905 to 1913, recalled that recitation was the usual method and that discussion was not common in the classroom. Interviews, 9 July 1980 and 30 January 1980.

30. School catalogue (1904–05), p. 27.

31. Interview with Lester Levy, 4 February 1980.

32. The High School Department approved the plan for the creation of the Taylor Literary Society on 7 November 1900. *Friends School Quarterly* (1901), p. 3.

33. Wilson's report to Education Committee, 26 April 1915.

34. Mallonee interview.

35. Wilson reported to the Education Committee on 24 November 1916, that the school had 1,000 stereographs and stereopticon slides, as well as a "moving picture machine."

36. Wilson's report to Education Committee, 15 December 1913; and school catalogue (1913–14), p. 34.

37. Education Committee Report, 24 May 1899.

38. Wilson's report to Education Committee, 13 December 1909.

39. Ibid.

40. See Sherry H. Olson, *Baltimore: The Building of an American City* (Baltimore: The Johns Hopkins University Press, 1980), p. 304.

41. Wilson's report to Education Committee, 7 October 1917, 29 April 1918, and 7 October 1918.

42. Edward A. Krug, *The Shaping of the American High School*, 2 vols. (Madison: University of Wisconsin Press, 1972), 2:55.

43. Wilson's report to Education Committee, 21 October 1912; and Minutes, Education Committee, 21 October 1912.

44. Terman's study, *The Measurement of Intelligence*, was published in 1916, and was adopted by Friends in 1918. See the school catalogue (1918–19), p. 23.

45. Wilson's report to Education Committee, 29 November 1920. The public schools began ability testing in 1922. See Vavrina, "Public Education," p. 453.

46. Wilson's report to Education Committee, 29 November 1926.

47. Pike's report to Education Committee, 1 December 1930.

48. Interview with Helen Corse Barney, 8 June 1977.

49. Hoffman, "Attending Friends School."

50. Wilson's report to Education Committee, 19 May 1924.

51. Ibid., 26 January 1925.

52. Ibid., 15 December 1913.

53. *Friends School Quarterly* (1901), p. 4.

54. See the Education Committee Report, 7 November 1934, for a list of student activities.

55. Wilson's report to Education Committee, 28 May 1923, and 26 January 1925.

56. Dalsheimer interview.

57. Mallonee interview; and Minutes, Education Committee, 20 March 1905.

58. Wilson's report to Education Committee, 29 January 1917, and 26 April 1926.

59. School catalogue (1914–15), p. 33.

60. Wilson's report to Education Committee, 15 December 1913, and 31 March 1914.

61. Education Committee Report, 23 May 1904.

62. Mace interview.

63. Forbush, "Baltimore Book," 16:56.

64. Wilson's report to Education Committee, 28 May and 8 October 1923.

65. *Friends School Quarterly* (1901), p. 3. The first game was played on the afternoon of 21 December 1900.

66. *Scarlet and Gray* (1908): 15; and Education Committee Report, 28 April 1909.

67. Ibid. 2(1910): 18–19.

68. Report from the Property Committee of Baltimore Preparative Meeting, 10 March 1908; Levy interviews; and interview with Bliss Forbush, Jr., 17 August 1981.

69. Education Committee Report, 16 May 1910.

70. Wilson's report to Education Committee, 10 February 1919.

71. School catalogue (1903–04), p. 9.

72. Education Committee Report, 4 December 1906; Minutes, Education Committee, 4 December 1912; and *Quaker* (1915), p. 41.

73. Wilson's report to Education Committee, 14 April 1924; and Baltimore *Sun*, 23 May 1928. The coach of the undefeated 1928 team was Milton McDonald, but he gave credit for the development of lacrosse to Oster (Kid) Norris, who was the school's first coach.

74. *Quaker* (1915), p. 48.

75. Pike's report to Education Committee, 4 April 1927.

Chapter 8

1. *Evening Sun* (Baltimore), 30 November 1936.

2. Olson, *Baltimore*, p. 256.

3. Wilson's report to Education Committee, 24 November 1924.

4. Ibid., 26 January 1925.

5. Isabel C. Roberts, Mary B. Hull, Anne W. Janney, and Thomas Burling Hull to Education Committee, n.d.

6. Wilson's statement to Board of Trustees, BMM, 20 May 1925.

7. Ibid.

8. Wilson's report to Education Committee, 26 January 1925; and William B. Marye, "Baltimore City Place Names, Part 4," *Maryland Historical Magazine* 59 (March 1964): 69.

9. Wilson's report to Education Committee, 4 May 1925.

10. Pike's report to Education Committee, 28 February 1927; and Minutes, Education Committee, 30 January 1928.

11. Wilson's "Statement of Growth to the Education Committee," 21 January 1927.

12. *Sun*, 22 May 1928.

13. *Evening Sun*, 5 May 1931. The cornerstone was reported to contain the 1931 yearbook, the *Scarlet and Gray* magazine, the *Roland Park Magazine*, the *Evening Sun*, the school catalogue, *Friends Intelligencer*, the *Directory* of BMM, a list of the building committee (Bliss Forbush was chairman), a list of the students at the time, and a set of coins for 1931.

14. Pike's reports to the Education Committee, 1 and 3 December 1930.

15. Education Committee Report to BMM, 5 February 1936.

16. *News-Post* (Baltimore), 13 December 1937; and Forbush, "Baltimore Book," 17:255.

17. Minutes, Education Committee, 13 May 1899. He was replaced as science teacher by John L. Etter when he became an administrator in 1926. Wilson's report to Education Committee, 25 January 1926; and Minutes, Education Committee, 14 February 1927.

18. Interviews with Harry S. Scott, Jr., 23 October 1980; and Margaret Tyson Bouchelle, 21 March 1980.

19. Pike's report to Education Committee, 3 October 1927.

20. Ibid., 1 October 1928.

21. Ibid., 28 November 1927.

22. Ibid., 27 February 1928.

23. Ibid., 4 March 1929.

24. Interview with Frances Homer, 3 June 1980.

25. Olson, *Baltimore*, p. 333.

26. Ibid.

27. Minutes, Education Committee, "Summary Report of Sessions of the Finance Committee," 25 June, and 13 September 1945.

28. Pike's report to Education Committee, 25 March 1929. Tuition ranged from $100 at the kindergarten level to $350 for the high school. Students also paid activity fees of $10 or less, bought their own books and supplies, could buy lunch for 50 cents, and ride the bus for $60 per year.

29. Ibid., 25 March 1929, and 31 March 1930.

30. Ibid., 31 October 1932, and 30 January 1933.

31. Margaret Tyson Bouchelle, a teacher, recalled that other than the children's remarks about President Hoover, whom their parents blamed for the Depression, there was little awareness among the younger pupils that a national depression existed.

32. Pike's report to Education Committee, 26 May 1930, and 25 May 1931.

33. Education Committee Report to BMM, 7 November 1934; and Minutes, Executive Committee of the Education Committee (not dated, but apparently in late December 1934).

34. Elizabeth Harry, Secretary of the Executive Committee, to William S. Pike, 28 January 1935.

35. *Sun*, 10 March 1935.

36. Minutes, Education Committee, 8 April 1935; and Education Committee Report to BMM, 30 December 1935.

37. Zavitz's report to Education Committee, no. 1, 1936 (Zavitz numbered his reports but he did not always give a specific date).

38. Friends School, "Announcement" (1937–38), p. 15.

39. Apparently Zavitz's reputation as a progressive was well known, for Jane P. Rushmore wrote to Bliss Forbush from Philadelphia that "Edwin Zavitz has no doubt engrafted enough progressive theory on the school to last for several years." The letter, in the Friends School archives, is not dated.

40. See Zavitz's report to Education Committee, 29 November 1937, January 1941, and February 1942.

41. Cremin, *Transformation*, p. 277.

42. Ibid., pp. 132, 140, 306–308.

43. Ruth Wrightson report to Education Committee, 24 April 1933.

44. Bouchelle interview.

45. Pike's report to Education Committee, 4 February 1929; and Education Committee Report to BMM, 3 November 1931.

46. Forbush, "Baltimore Book," 16:175.

47. Ibid., 20:25; and 21:242; and Zavitz's report to Education Committee, 26 October 1936.

48. Education Committee Report to BMM, October 1938.

49. *Quaker Quill*, 31 October 1941.

50. Ibid., 30 May 1941.

51. Zavitz's report to Education Committee, October 1938.

52. Scott interview.

53. Pike's report to Education Committee, 30 January 1928.

54. Ibid., 4 March 1929, and 25 May 1931; Education Committee Report to BMM, 3 November 1911; and Forbush, "Baltimore Book," 11:123.

55. Forbush, "Baltimore Book," 18:38, 52–53, 19:174, and 20:108–109.

56. Minutes, Education Committee, 14 June 1940. Actually Zavitz never went to France because of the German occupation. Instead he spent the entire year in Philadelphia working for the American Friends Service Committee, arranging to bring English children to the United States to escape bombings.

57. Ibid., 3 September 1942.

Chapter 9

1. *Contact*, 1 January 1940.

2. Zavitz's report to Education Committee, no. 4, December-January 1940; *Quaker*

Quill, 25 October 1940; Education Committee Report to BMM, 1 October 1943; and interview with Suzanne Davis Emory, 19 January 1981.

3. Bliss Forbush, "The Forbush Chronicle," 3 vols. (unpublished family history), 2:499.

4. Education Committee Report to BMM, 17 September 1945.

5. *Quaker Quill*, 23 January, 12, 27 February, 8 May, 2 October 1942, and 13 March 1944.

6. "Forbush Chronicle," 2:446–47.

7. Education Committee Report to BMM, 17 September 1945.

8. Bliss Forbush had actually begun as part-time headmaster on April 1, helping out when Zavitz was spending a portion of each week at Sidwell Friends in Washington.

9. "Forbush Chronicle," 2:475, 478.

10. Ibid., 2:478.

11. Zavitz's report to Education Committee, May 1943; and Minutes, Education Committee, 14 February 1944.

12. Ibid.

13. See chart in Minutes, Education Committee, 16 April 1946.

14. C. Newton Kidd headed the extensive campaign for the auditorium. Ground was broken in April, 1955; when completed, the building cost was $258,753.77, fully equipped. Progress Report of the Friends School Development Committee, 14 October 1957.

15. Business Manager's report to Education Committee, 14 October 1957.

16. Minutes, Education Committee, 20 June 1959.

17. Ibid., 20 December 1949.

18. In addition to the regularly scheduled evaluation in 1943, the Middle States Association returned to Friends in 1945 as part of an experiment to test new criteria for judging schools. Thereafter the decennial evaluations occurred in 1949, 1959, 1969, and 1979.

19. Education Committee Report to BMM, 17 September 1945, and September 1949; Report on Social Studies in the Lower School, 1 January 1946; and "Forbush Chronicle," 2:585–86.

20. Scharf, *History of Baltimore*, p. 224.

21. Griffith, *Annals*, pp. 127–28; Clarence Kenneth Gregory, "The Education of Blacks in Maryland: An Historical Survey" (Ed.D. dissertation, Columbia University Teachers College, 1976) p. 76.

22. Forbush, *Baltimore Yearly Meeting*, p. 55.

23. Townsend diary, pp. 82–83.

24. Forbush, *Baltimore Yearly Meeting*, p. 78; Vavrina, "Public Education," pp. 224–25; and Joel Acus Carrington, "The Struggle for Desegregation of Baltimore City Public Schools, 1952–1966" (Ed.D. dissertation, University of Maryland, 1970), p. 9.

25. Forbush, "Baltimore Book," 3:10.

26. Ibid., 3:xxi, 240.

27.   This statement is from an address he gave at Friends General Conference, Cape May. Printed in *Friends Intelligencer*, 97, 31 August 1940.

28.   *Afro-American* (Baltimore), 13 December 1941.

29.   Minutes, Education Committee, 26 April 1943.

30.   Ibid., 31 August, and 27 September 1943.

31.   See for example Education Committee Report to BMM, 1 October 1946; *Friends Intelligencer*, 27 April 1946; "Forbush Chronicle," 2:580–81, and 717; and Minutes, Education Committee, 16 December 1958.

32.   Notes of Human Relations Committee, 27 April 1949, filed with Education Committee Minutes.

33.   Martha C. Parsons, Report on Human Relations, January 1954.

34.   "Forbush Chronicle," 2:565; and memo in Human Relations file, 18 February 1946.

35.   "Forbush Chronicle," 2:565.

36.   5 December 1949.

37.   Minutes of the Meeting of Private School Association of Baltimore, 17 January 1951.

38.   Memorandum from Bliss Forbush, 20 February 1951.

39.   Carrington, "Desegregation of Baltimore," pp. 16–30; Julia Roberta O'Wesney, "Historical Study of the Progress of Racial Desegregation in the Public Schools of Baltimore, Maryland" (Ed.D dissertation, University of Maryland, 1970), pp. 61–62; and Vavrina, "Public Education," pp. 592–93.

40.   *Toward Equality: Baltimore's Progress Report* (Baltimore: The Sidney Hollander Foundation, Inc., 1960), p. 57.

41.   Minutes, Education Committee, March 1953.

42.   Ibid., 22 September 1953.

43.   Minutes, Education Committee, 16 June 1954.

44.   *New York Times*, 8 September 1954.

45.   "Forbush Chronicle," 2:731.

46.   Ibid., 2:733.

47.   Scott interview; and J. Austin Stone to Philip E. Lamb, no date.

48.   A report of the meeting is in the Minutes of the Education Committee, 27 September 1954. Dr. Robinson's speech was printed in pamphlet form and distributed widely to all patrons. See also "Forbush Chronicle," 2:733–34.

49.   Bliss Forbush, "The Treasure Chest: A Rosary of Interesting and Stimulating Thoughts," 20 vols. (unpublished papers in Friends Historical Library, Swarthmore College), vol. 11:n.p.

50.   Minutes, Education Committee, 16 November 1954.

51.   "Forbush Chronicle," 2:735.

52.   Alan Paton to Bliss Forbush, 2 February 1955, in "Treasure Chest," 8:n.p.

53.   Bliss Forbush's report to Education Committee, April 1955.

54. "Forbush Chronicle," 2:736; and rough notes in the files of the headmaster's office.

55. Informal notes in the files of the headmaster's office.

56. "Forbush Chronicle," 2:482, 489, 491.

57. Ibid. 2:664.

58. Ibid., 2:566. The tenure system is explained in a statement by the Education Committee, 20 December 1949.

59. Bliss Forbush's report to Executive Committee of Education Committee, 21 May 1946. Merrill Hiatt, who had been principal of the Upper School until that time, took the position of headmaster at Friends Academy, Locust Valley, Long Island, N.Y.

60. "Forbush Chronicle," 2:587.

61. Minutes, Education Committee, 19 May 1959; "Forbush Chronicle," 2:485; and Bliss Forbush, Jr., interview.

62. Interview with Bliss and LaVerne Forbush, 24 August 1981.

63. "Forbush Chronicle," 2:485; and Bliss Forbush, Jr., interview.

64. Forbush, "Treasure Chest,", vol. 11.

65. Ibid., vol. 9; Sun, 10 June 1952.

66. Susan Yardley, "Isabel Woods," unpublished paper in Friends School archives, July 1978.

67. Interviews with William A. Grant, 9 January 1981; Jon Oster and Stephen H. Sachs, 23 June 1981.

68. Interview with Robert Nicolls, 23 February 1981; and Minutes, Education Committee, 18 August 1938.

69. Quaker Quill, 17 May 1949; 14 May and 4 June 1954.

70. Ibid., 7 May 1969.

71. Interviews with J. Frederick Motz, 22 July 1981; Clarinda Harriss Lott and Thomas W. Murray, 4 March 1981.

72. Bliss Forbush's report to Education Committee, 14 March 1950.

73. Lott and Murray interview; and "Forbush Chronicle," 2:488.

74. "Forbush Chronicle," 2:490.

75. Minutes, Education Committee, 14 July 1950; Motz interview.

76. Lott and Murray interview; and interview with Anne Black Evans, 30 March 1981.

77. School catalogue (1955–56), p. 18.

78. Bliss Forbush, Jr., interview.

79. Minutes, Education Committee, 17 November 1953.

80. Bliss and LaVerne Forbush, interview.

81. Bliss Forbush's report to Education Committee, 29 January 1945; Sun, 16 June 1954.

82. Oster and Sachs interview.

83. Education Committee Report to BMM, 6–9 April 1959.

84. "Forbush Chronicle," 2:790.

85. Friends School *Alumni Bulletin,* 1 February 1960.

86. "Forbush Chronicle," 2:779.

87. Ibid., 2:737.

88. *Friends Intelligencer,* 21 July 1934.

Chapter 10

1. Byron Forbush's report to Education Committee, November 1966.

2. Minutes, Education Committee, 10 March and 13 October 1970.

3. Interview with John E. Carnell, 4 August 1982.

4. Charles Hutzler to Byron Forbush, 22 March 1973. Minutes, Education Committee, 15 February 1972; Bliss Forbush, Jr., interview; and interview with Byron Forbush, 17 June 1982.

5. Minutes, Education Committee, 17 April 1973.

6. Ibid., 15 February and 7 November 1972.

7. Bliss Forbush, Jr., interview.

8. Minutes, Board of Trustees, 20 September 1977.

9. Ibid., 20 December 1977.

10. Byron Forbush's report to Education Committee, March 1977.

11. Minutes, Board of Trustees, 20 November 1973.

12. At Friends Academy he was an instructor in history, assistant to the headmaster, principal of the Upper School, and acting headmaster. *Alumni Bulletin,* February 1960.

13. Bouchelle interview.

14. Forbush, "Treasure Chest," vol. 8.

15. Quoted from the Johns Hopkins *Newsletter,* October 1950. See Forbush, "Treasure Chest," vol. 10.

16. Byron Forbush to Bliss Forbush, 23 September 1959, in "Treasure Chest," vol. 13; and Byron Forbush interview.

17. Minutes, Education Committee, 20 October 1959.

18. Ibid., 17 January 1967.

19. Byron Forbush's report to Education Committee, May 1964, and June 1978; Minutes, Education Committee, 17 November 1970; and Minutes, Board of Trustees, 15 June 1978.

20. Minutes, Board of Trustees, 20 November 1973; and "Board of Trustees Handbook" (1982).

21. Minutes, Board of Trustees, 20 May 1980.

22. Ibid., 20 November 1973.

23. In 1962 Friends spent only 3.2 per cent of its funds for scholarships. Business Manager's report to Education Committee, 20 February 1962. See also Kraushaar, *Schools,* pp. 30–31.

24. Education Committee Report to BMM, October 1974.

25. W. Berkeley Mann to Bryon Forbush, 18 March 1964.

26.   6 October 1975.

27.   Byron Forbush memo to faculty, 28 August 1972; and Byron Forbush's report to Board of Trustees, September 1977.

28.   Byron Forbush interview.

29.   Minutes, Board of Trustees, 20 May 1980.

30.   Ibid., 21 February 1978.

31.   Ibid., 15 June 1978.

32.   "Friends Council on Education Conference to Discuss the Administration of Quaker Schools," n.d., n.p., in Friends School archives.

33.   Byron Forbush interview.

34.   *Quaker Quill,* 4 June 1965. Mrs. Millard continued at Friends as nurse and alumni secretary until 1967.

35.   Minutes, Education Committee, 19 May 1970; and personnel records in headmaster's office.

36.   Rino Hall, Dorothy Reed, Garfield and Louise Hudson, Bertha Payne, Doris Morris, Mary Napper Dughins, Erdine Chandler, John Byrd, Alexander Beard, William Boston, and Oscar Thompson.

37.   Interview with Stanley Johnson, 1 July 1982.

38.   David Peerless, "Principal's Overview of the Fifth Grade Economic Project" (unpublished paper in the headmaster's office).

Chapter 11

1.   Minutes, Education Committee, 20 February 1962.

2.   *Quaker Quill,* 20 December 1963.

3.   Ibid., 21 January, and 3 November 1965.

4.   Ibid., 1 June 1951, and 3 November 1967.

5.   Minutes, Education Committee, 17 October, and 19 December 1967.

6.   William Manchester, *The Glory and the Dream: A Narrative History of America, 1932–1972* (Boston: Little Brown and Company, 1973), p. 1122.

7.   *Quaker Quill,* 16 February, and 25, 30 October 1968.

8.   Ibid., 10 March 1967.

9.   He later became president of the Baltimore Chapter of the American Civil Liberties Union.

10.   Minutes, Education Committee, 17 February 1970.

11.   Roberta Scott-Macnow, "Moratorium Day" (unpublished paper), December, 1969.

12.   Minutes, Education Committee, 17 February 1970.

13.   Interviews with Carl Robbins, 1 March 1982; Jonathan and Mary Michelle Garman, 1 May 1982; Byron Forbush; and Stanley Johnson.

14.   Interviews with Steven Frenkil, 1 April 1982; Doris Neumann, 4 August 1982; Carl Robbins; and Byron Forbush.

15. Byron Forbush interview.

16. *Quaker Quill*, 13 February 1970; and Minutes, Education Committee, 6 June 1972.

17. Eventually the dress code was eliminated in 1979. When the charge of sex discrimination was raised because only girls were required to wear uniforms, both the faculty and the administration had had enough of the issue and the school abandoned a formal dress code in favor of standards for hair length and clothing styles.

18. Minutes, Board of Trustees, 21 October 1975, and 23 March 1976; *Quaker Quill*, 20 February 1976; and Byron Forbush and Neumann interviews.

19. Minutes, Education Committee, 13 December 1971.

20. Minutes, Board of Trustees, 24 June 1974.

21. Ibid., 17 May 1977.

22. Byron Forbush interview.

23. Special report on admission policy in headmaster's files, p. 7.

24. Minutes, Board of Trustees, 19 October 1976. A peak year was 1975–76 when black enrollment reached 11.7 percent.

25. Johnson interview.

26. Minutes, Education Committee, 16 December 1969.

27. Minutes, Board of Trustees, 27 March 1979.

28. Johnson interview; interviews with Theresa Redd, 24 July 1982; Frank Bond, 31 July 1982; Darryl Coleman, "Black Students and Faculty at Friends School" (unpublished paper in Friends School Archives, n.d.); and a statement by four black members of the senior class, Saundra Bond, Rufus Manning, Pamela Quarles, and Theresa Redd in Minutes, Education Committee, 18 April 1972.

29. Statement by Bond, Manning, Quarles, and Redd; and Coleman, "Black Students."

30. Coleman, "Black Students."

31. Redd interview.

32. Minutes, Education Committee, 20 June 1967.

33. Coleman, "Black Students."

34. Interview with William Ellis, 29 June 1982.

35. Minutes, Education Committee, 19 October 1965, and 18 October 1966. John Roemer was the first director of the Summer Writing Opportunity Program.

36. Minutes, Board of Trustees, 19 September 1978.

37. *Report of the Visiting Committee to Friends School,* 16, 17, 18 October 1978, reprinted in *Collection,* Winter 1979, pp. 3–4.

38. Byron Forbush's report to Education Committee, December 1980.

39. Ibid., April 1964.

40. Minutes, Board of Trustees, 20 January 1981.

41. Johnson interview.

42. *Quaker Quill*, 23 January 1959.

43. Ibid., 21 January 1965.

44. Ibid., 18 December 1959, and 31 January 1964; and interview with Claire Walker, 8 July 1982.

45. *Quaker Quill*, 18 February 1949, 22 February 1957, 9 October 1964, and 31 October 1969; Bliss Forbush, Jr., and Johnson interviews.

46. *Sun*, 7 November 1965.

47. *Quaker Quill*, 27 October 1938.

48. Ibid., 14 May 1954, and 31 May 1963.

49. Ibid., 14 December 1945.

50. Ibid., 12 November 1954; Byron Forbush's report to Education Committee, November 1962; and Johnson interview.

51. *Quaker Quill*, 1 October 1943.

52. Minutes, Board of Trustees, January 1975.

Interviews

Anna Hull Baker and Theodore E. Baker	March 14, 1978	by Dean Esslinger
Helen Corse Barney	June 8, 1977	by Carol C. Maus
Frank Bond	July 31, 1982	by Nicholas Fessenden
Margaret Tyson Bouchelle	March 2, 1980	by Marv Ellen Saterlie
Selma Kann Burgunder	January 30, 1980	by W. Byron Forbush II
John E. Carnell	August 4, 1982	by Dean Esslinger
Clyde M. Clapp	May 19, 1982	by Nicholas Fessenden
Trudi Feinberg Cohen	June 9, 1982	by Gail Katz
Melinda Burdette Curtis and Mark Curtis	January 27, 1982	by Barbara Mallonee
Gordon H. Dalsemer	March 19, 1980	by W. Byron Forbush II
Hugo Dalsheimer	February 10, 1978	by Carol C. Maus
Gretel Hanauer Derby	January 28, 1981	by Carol C. Maus
Ruth Celestia Dibert	March 2, 1981	by Dean Esslinger
Margaret Rawlings Eastwick	August 28, 1980	by Harry S. Scott, Jr.
William Ellis	June 29, 1982	by Dean Esslinger
Suzanne Davis Emory	January 19, 1981	by W. Byron Forbush II
Anne Black Evans	March 30, 1981	by Jack Matthews
Haines Ball Felter	January 25, 1980	by Nancy T. Grant
Bliss and LaVerne Forbush	June 6, 1978 and August 24, 1981	by Dean Esslinger
Bliss Forbush, Jr.	August 17, 1981	by Dean Esslinger
W. Byron Forbush II	June 17, 1982	by Dean Esslinger
Steven D. Frenkil	April 1, 1982	by J. Frederick Motz
Jonathan F. and Mary Michelle Garman	May 1, 1982	by Nicholas Fessenden
Cynthia Klein Goldberg and Harry R. Goldberg	April 14, 1982	by themselves
William A. Grant	January 9, 1981	by W. Byron Forbush II
Daniel S. Greenbaum	May 30, 1980	by Carol C. Maus
Amy Federleicht Greif	November 18, 1977	by Dorothy E. Michel Mardos
Ann Burgunder Greif	June 9, 1980	by Dorothy E. Michel Mardos
Barbara Kann Halle	March 18, 1981	by Nicholas Fessenden
Marion Silver Hayden	February 19, 1980	by W. Byron Forbush II
Frederick W. Hearn	July 23, 1981	by Nicholas Fessenden
Malcolm Hecht	July 9, 1980	by Nicholas Fessenden

Frances Homer	June 3, 1980	by Dorothy E. Michel Mardos
Stanley B. Johnson III	July 1, 1982	by Dean Esslinger
Eugene L. Jones	May 23, 1981	by Nancy T. Grant
Dorothy B. Krug	July 20, 1980	by Doris Neumann
James G. Kuller	May 8, 1980	by Nicholas Fessenden
Karl M. and Agnes Krieger Levy	February 12, 1980	by Nicholas Fessenden
Lester S. Levy	February 4, 1980	by Carol C. Maus
Clarinda Harriss Lott	March 4, 1981	by Carol C. Maus
Eleanor Dilworth Mace	January 11, 1980	by Dean Esslinger
D. Carlyle MacLea	January 29, 1980	by W. Byron Forbush II
Esther Felter Mallonee	April 4, 1980	by Nancy T. Grant
Bruce and Suzanne Bell Manger	May 3, 1982	by Linda Whiteford
Anne Homer Martin	April 22, 1980	by Gail Katz
Marian Bentley Millard	January 27, 1980	by Dorothy E. Michel Mardos
Felix Morley	May 17, 1979	by Dean Esslinger
Catherine Grauel Motz	July 7, 1982	by Dean Esslinger
J. Frederick Motz	July 22, 1981	by Nicholas Fessenden
Thomas W. Murray	March 4, 1981	by Carol C. Maus
Philip Myers	February 21, 1980	by Dean Esslinger
Doris M. Neumann	August 4, 1982	by Dean Esslinger
Ferdinand Neuberger	April 14, 1980	by Nicholas Fessenden
Robert A. Nicolls	February 23, 1981	by Dean Esslinger
Selma Levy Oppenheimer	March 5, 1980	by Carol C. Maus
Jon Oster	June 23, 1981	by Carol C. Maus
J. Daniel Peacock	February 4, 1981	by Gail Katz
Theresa Redd	July 24, 1982	by Nicholas Fessenden
Carl B. Robbins	March 1, 1982	by Stephen Balser
Cynthia Miller Rosenwald	January 30, 1981	by Nicholas Fessenden
Stephen H. Sachs	June 23, 1981	by Carol C. Maus
Carol Greif Sandler	March 31, 1982	by Linda Whiteford
Harry S. Scott, Jr.	October 23, 1980 and August 24, 1981	by Dean Esslinger
Claire Von Marees Stieff	April 17, 1980	by Dean Esslinger
Isaac L. Strouse	March 3, 1982	by Stephen Balser
Emma Belle Shafer Wagner	May 28, 1980	by Carol C. Maus
Claire Groben Walker	July 8, 1982	by Dean Esslinger
William B. Whiteford	January 28, 1981	by Carol C. Maus

Select Bibliography

Primary Sources

The principal repositories of information on Friends School are the Friends Historical Library at Swarthmore College, Swarthmore, Pennsylvania, and the archives and administrative offices of the school itself. The original records of Baltimore Monthly Meeting are at Swarthmore, as are the extensive personal papers of Bliss Forbush. School records, including minutes and reports of the Education Committee and Board of Trustees, the reports of the headmasters, financial records, information on alumni, students, and faculty, school catalogues, student newspapers and yearbooks, alumni bulletins, and miscellaneous materials are at Friends School in Baltimore. These records are too extensive to list separately here. References to specific sources of information are in the chapter notes.

Brown, Kirk. Scrapbook. Maryland Historical Society.

Bruno, Gordon A. "Baltimore Friends School, 1849-1928." Unpublished paper. Friends School archives, n.d.

Coleman, Darryl. "Black Students and Faculty at Friends School." Unpublished paper. Friends School archives, n.d.

Court of Appeals of Maryland. "Belle J. Erhardt and Joel B. Erhardt, her Husband, Helen J. Hunt and Thomas Hunt, her Husband, vs. The Baltimore Monthly Meeting of Friends, Park Avenue, et al." 29 March 1901.

Forbush, Bliss. "The Forbush Chronicle." 3 vols. Unpublished family history.

___. "Friends School's Unique Role, Past and Present: A Friends School Education." Unpublished paper. Friends School archives, n.d.

___. "My Baltimore Book." 22 vols. Friends Historical Library, 1921–43.

___. "Quaker Education in Maryland as Found in the Discipline." Unpublished paper. Friends School archives, n.d.

___. "The Treasure Chest." 20 vols. Friends Historical Library, 1915–73.

Scott-Macnow, Roberta. "Moratorium: Past, Present, and Future." Unpublished paper. 1969.

Townsend, Richard H. "The Diary of Richard H. Townsend, Compiled 1851–1879, Containing Historical, Biographical and Genealogical Information for 1688–1879 with an Index by John Shotwell Townsend." 3 vols. Baltimore: Transcribed by Works Progress Administration of Maryland, 1937.

Yardley, Susan. "Draft of a Paper on Isabel Woods." Unpublished paper. Friends School archives, 1978.

Secondary Sources

Adams, Herbert Baxter. *Public Education Work in Baltimore*. The Johns Hopkins University Studies in History and Political Science, vol. 17. Baltimore: The Johns Hopkins University Press, 1899.

Anderson, Alan D. *The Origin and Resolution of an Urban Crisis: Baltimore, 1890–1930.* Baltimore: The Johns Hopkins University Press, 1977.

Bard, Harry. "Observations on Desegregation in Baltimore: Three Years Later." *Teachers College Record* 59:268–81.

Beirne, Rosamond Randall. *Let's Pick the Daisies: The History of the Bryn Mawr School, 1885–1967.* Baltimore: The Bryn Mawr School, 1970.

Benjamin, Philip S. *The Philadelphia Quakers in the Industrial Age, 1865–1920.* Philadelphia: Temple University Press, 1976.

Braithwaite, William C. *The Second Period of Quakerism.* 2nd ed., Cambridge: Cambridge University Press, 1961.

Branch, E. Douglas. *The Sentimental Years, 1836–1880.* New York: D. Appleton-Century Co., 1934.

Brinton, Howard. *Friends for 300 Years.* New York: Harper and Brothers, Publishers, 1952.

——. *Quaker Education in Theory and Practice.* 2d. rev. ed. Pendle Hill Pamphlet, no. 9. Wallingford, Pa.: Pendle Hill, 1958.

Brooks, Neal A., and Rockel, Eric G. *A History of Baltimore County.* Towson, Md.: Friends of the Towson Library, 1979.

Browne, Gary L. *Baltimore in the Nation, 1789–1861.* Chapel Hill: University of North Carolina Press, 1980.

Bruchey, Elinor S. *The Business Elite in Baltimore, 1880–1914.* New York: Arno Press, 1976.

Burgess, W. Randolph. *Trends of School Costs.* New York: Russell Sage Foundation, 1920.

Butts, R. Freeman, and Cremin, Lawrence A. *A History of Education in American Culture.* New York: Henry Holt & Co., 1953.

Carrington, Joel Acus. "The Struggle for Desegregation of Baltimore City Public Schools, 1952–1966." Ed.D. dissertation, University of Maryland, 1970.

Church, Robert L., and Sedlack, Michael W. *Education in the United States: An Interpretive History.* New York: The Free Press, 1976.

Clark, Dennis. "Baltimore, 1729–1829: The Genesis of a Community." Ph.D. dissertation, Catholic University, 1976.

Cremin, Lawrence A. *American Education: The Colonial Experience, 1607–1783.* New York: Harper & Row, 1970.

—— *The Traditions of American Education.* New York: Basic Books, 1977.

——*The Transformation of the School: Progressivism in American Education, 1876–1957.* New York: Alfred Knopf, 1961.

Dorsey, John, and Dilts, James D. *A Guide to Baltimore Architecture.* Cambridge, Md.: Tidewater Publishers, 1973.

Dunlap, William Cook. *Quaker Education in Baltimore and Virginia Yearly Meetings.* Philadelphia: William C. Dunlap, 1936.

The Early Eighties: Sidelights on the Baltimore of Forty Years Ago. Baltimore: Mercantile Trust and Deposit Co., 1924.

Elson, Ruth Miller. *Guardians of Tradition: Schoolbooks of the Nineteenth Century.* Lincoln, Neb.: University of Nebraska Press, 1964.

Fleming, G. James "Desegregation in Maryland." *Journal of Negro Education* 25:273–84.

Flexner, Helen Thomas. *A Quaker Childhood.* New Haven: Yale University Press, 1940.

Forbush, Bliss. *A History of Baltimore Yearly Meeting of Friends.* Sandy Spring, Md.: Baltimore Yearly Meeting of Friends, 1972.

Frost, J. William. *The Quaker Family in Colonial America: A Portrait of the Society of Friends.* New York: St. Martin's Press, 1973.

Greene, Suzanne Ellery. *Baltimore: An Illustrated History.* Woodland Hills, Calif.: Windsor Publications, 1980.

Gregory, Clarence Kenneth. "The Education of Blacks in Maryland: An Historical Survey." Ed.D. dissertation, Columbia University Teachers College, 1976.

Griffith, Thomas W. *Annals of Baltimore.* Baltimore: William Woody, 1824.

Hall, Clayton Coleman, ed. *Baltimore: Its History and Its People.* 2 vols. New York: Lewis Historical Publishing Co., 1912.

Hirschfield, Charles. *Baltimore: 1870–1900.* The Johns Hopkins Studies in History and Political Science. Series 59, no. 2. Baltimore: The Johns Hopkins University Press, 1941.

Hole, Helen G. *Things Civil and Useful: A Personal View of Quaker Education.* Richmond, Ind.: Friends United Press, 1978.

Jacobs, Bradford McE. *Gilman Walls Will Echo: The Story of the Gilman Country School, 1897–1947.* Baltimore: Waverly Press, 1947.

Jacobsen, Phebe R. *Quaker Records in Maryland.* Annapolis: The Hall of Records Commission, 1966.

Janney, Bertha. "Baltimore Yearly Meeting." *Friends Intelligencer,* 26 December 1936, pp. 865–66.

Janvier, Meredith. *Baltimore in the Eighties and Nineties.* Baltimore: H. G. Roebuck & Son, 1933.

Johnson, Clifton. *Old-Time Schools and School Books.* 1904. Reprint. Gloucester, Mass.: Peter Smith, 1963.

Johnson, Gerald W. "Baltimore: A Very Great Lady Indeed." *The Century Magazine,* May 1928, pp. 76–82.

Jones, Rufus M. *The Later Periods of Quakerism.* 2 vols. London: Macmillan and Co., 1921.

Jones, Thomas E. "Education Policies in the Philadelphia Yearly Meetings During the Nineteenth Century." *The Friend,* 27 June 1940, pp. 483–85.

Katz, Michael B. "The 'New Departure' in Quincy, 1873–81: The Nature of Nineteenth-Century Educational Reform." *The New England Quarterly* 40:3–30.

— "The Origins of Public Education: A Reassessment." *History of Education Quarterly* 16:381–407.

Kraushaar, Otto F. *American Nonpublic Schools: Patterns of Diversity.* Baltimore: The Johns Hopkins University Press, 1972.

— *Schools in a Changing City: An Overview of Baltimore's Private Schools.* Baltimore: The Sheridan Foundation, 1976.

Morley, Felix. *For the Record.* South Bend, Ind.: Regnery/Gateway, 1979.

Olson, Sherry H. *Baltimore: The Building of an American City.* Baltimore: The Johns Hopkins University Press, 1980.

Owens, Hamilton. *Baltimore on the Chesapeake.* Garden City, N.Y.: Doubleday, Doran & Co., 1941.

O'Wesney, Julia Roberta. "Historical Study of the Progress of Racial Desegregation in the Public Schools of Baltimore, Maryland." Ed.D. dissertation, University of Maryland, 1970.

Paul, William George. "The Shadow of Equality: the Negro in Baltimore, 1864–1911" Ph.D. dissertation, University of Wisconsin, 1972.

Penn, William. *A Letter from William Penn, to his Wife and Children.* New York: Mahlon Day, 1823.

Scharf, John Thomas. *The Chronicles of Baltimore; Being a Complete History of "Baltimore Town" and Baltimore City from the Earliest Period to the Present Time.* Baltimore: Turnbull Brothers, 1874.

___. *History of Baltimore City and County from the Earliest Period to the Present Day: Including Biographical Sketches of Their Representative Men.* 2 vols. Philadelphia: Louis H. Everts, 1881.

Semmes, Raphael. *Baltimore as Seen by Visitors, 1783–1860.* Baltimore: Maryland Historical Society, 1953.

Sheller, Tina Hirsch. "The Origins of Public Education and the Education of an Urban Society: Baltimore City, 1790–1830." Master's thesis, University of Maryland, 1978.

Shivers, Frank R., Jr. *Bolton Hill: Baltimore Classic.* Baltimore: Equitable Trust Co., 1978.

Society of Friends, Baltimore Monthly Meeting. *A Sketch of "Old Town" Meeting House, Baltimore; and Some Account of Its Occupants, as Read on Its One Hundredth Anniversary.* Baltimore: J. W. Woods, 1881.

Stockbridge, Henry. "Baltimore in 1846." *Maryland Historical Magazine* 6:20–34.

Stockett, Letitia. *Baltimore: A Not Too Serious History.* Baltimore: The Norman, Remington Co., 1928.

Thomas, Anna Braithwaite. *The Story of Baltimore Yearly Meeting from 1627 to 1938.* Baltimore: The Weant Press, 1938.

Thornburg, Delmar Leon. "The Society of Friends in Maryland." *Maryland Historical Magazine* 29:101–15.

Tolles, Frederick B. *Meeting House and Counting House: The Quaker Merchants of Philadelphia 1682–1763.* 1948. Reprint. New York: W. W. Norton & Co., 1963.

Toward Equality: Baltimore's Progress Report. Baltimore: The Sidney Hollander Foundation, 1960.

Tyack, David B. *The One Best System: A History of American Urban Education.* Cambridge: Harvard University Press, 1975.

Valentine, Katherine T. "Trends in the Development of Public Secondary Education in Baltimore, 1839–1927." Master's thesis, The Johns Hopkins University, 1928.

Vavrina, Vernon Sebastian. "The History of Public Education in the City of Baltimore, 1829–1956." Ph.D. dissertation, Catholic University, 1958.

Woody, Thomas. *Early Quaker Education in Pennsylvania.* 1920. Reprint. New York: Arno Press, 1969.

___. *Quaker Education in the Colony and State of New Jersey.* Philadelphia: Thomas Woody, 1923.

FRIENDS FOR TWO HUNDRED YEARS

This book was composed in Goudy Old Style by Brushwood Graphics, from a design by Stephen Johnston. It was printed and bound by the J.D. Lucas Printing Company.

Index